Concise Legal Research

Concise
Legal Research

Sixth Edition

Robert Watt

Visiting Associate Professor,
Faculty of Law, University of Technology, Sydney

Francis Johns LLM (Syd)

Lecturer, Law Collection Consultant, Faculty of Law
University of Technology, Sydney

THE FEDERATION PRESS
2009

Published in Sydney by

The Federation Press
71 John St, Leichhardt, NSW, 2040
PO Box 45, Annandale, NSW, 2038
Ph: (02) 9552 2200 Fax: (02) 9552 1681
E-mail: info@federationpress.com.au
Website: www.federationpress.com.au

1st edition 1993
2nd edition 1995
3rd edition 1997
4th edition 2001
5th edition 2004
6th edition 2009
1st Indian reprint, Universal Law Publishing Co, Pvt, Ltd, Dehli, 2002

National Library of Australia
Cataloguing-in-Publication entry

Concise legal research
Robert Watt, Francis Johns

6th ed
Includes index
ISBN 978 186287 723 8

Legal research. Legal research – Australia. Law – Bibliography. Law – Sources.

340.072

Typeset by The Federation Press, Leichhardt, NSW.
Printed by McPherson's Printing Group, Maryborough, VIC.

Contents

Preface to 1st edition

The gestation period for the writing of this book has been many years. The School of Law at the University of Technology, Sydney, was one of the first of the Australian law schools to incorporate into its undergraduate program the formal teaching of legal research. The subject *Legal Research* has been taught as an introductory subject as part of the Skills program to the new law students since the law school was commenced in 1977. In the early 1980s, the Skills program was re-organised and a new subject – *Advanced Legal Research* – was added and aimed at those students who needed to be able to research Canadian and US law before undertaking their electives or theses. In more recent years, those subject areas have been supplemented by international trade, human rights and European Community law and materials. At the present time these subjects are also made available to students entering post-graduate studies in the Law School at UTS. During this period, as the teacher responsible for the materials and presentation, I have had ample time to reflect upon those areas that need detailed explanation or examples provided. Much of the material used in the resulting courses has found its way into this work. To the many students who took the interest to do more than was asked of them and to those who asked impossible questions and pushed me for answers, I thank them now. It is these students who make teaching worthwhile.

To my colleagues in the School and to those in the law libraries of Sydney, I also owe a special debt of gratitude. My professional origins are in law librarianship in Sydney and I have always felt pride in being associated with this discipline. This is due in no small measure to those colleagues who have given so much to, and consequently gained the respect of, the Australian legal community. The task of isolating the people who have been of particular assistance 20 years into one's professional life is to invite trouble, but I would take this risk and especially thank Lynn Pollack of the Law Courts Library, Sydney and Rob Brian, until recently the law librarian at the University of New South Wales. Their professionalism is such that law librarianship throughout Australia has benefited. For the same reasons, I would also like to thank Beverley Caska, Sandra Barrkman, Margaret McAleese, John Rodwell and Colin Fong. They too are leaders in this field and have over the years provided support and guidance. The staff at Osgoode Hall Law School, York University, Toronto, and Mr HC Jain of the Library of the Indian Law Institute, New Delhi, also deserve specific thanks. The time spent on study leave in these two institutions and the assistance I received from them proved invaluable. I acclaim Roger Shaw and those who work with him in the law collection of the UTS Library with gratitude for accepting the demands that I have made upon them and for the way they consistently provide the answers.

Finally I need to acknowledge my wife, Helen Lucas, for the patience and assistance she has provided in bringing this project to fruition. If there is any clarity in the writing of this work, it is practically in spite of the author and due to the work of Helen, and Kathryn Fitzhenry of Federation Press. My gratitude and thanks to both.

Preface to the 6th edition

With the 6th edition, and the introduction of Francis Johns as a co-author, comes the acknowledgment of the fundamental and centrality of the electronic methods of legal research. For many legal researchers who started their working lives before electronic storage and retrieval of legal information was even available, this day has been a long time coming. Yet with the general availability of much case law and statutes that can be accessed using Boolean methodology comes the need to ensure that the modern researcher is aware of the pitfalls that can trap him or her if care is not exercised in ensuring that what is located is relevant. All too often – particularly with case law – the keyword searching of a judgment data base will throw up ostensible diamonds only to find that, unless the context is also carefully examined, one is looking at a minority view and those diamonds are replaced by mere coal.

The reader will find that the URL is now no longer merely located in a separate section at the end of the work (which it still is for acknowledged ease when needed) but scattered throughout the whole text. Thus it is that the Internet now impacts on the researcher's task.

To all colleagues who have inspired me, and to students I have taught who continued to make it worthwhile, my most sincere thanks.

Robert Watt
January 2009

It is a privilege for Rob to have asked me to assist in the new edition of this text. I have taught with Rob over a number of years and have enormous respect for the depth of his experience and knowledge.

In the preface to the last edition Rob referred to the dramatic changes in legal research with the advent of the Internet and Google. While the medium has changed dramatically, the essence of legal research has not. This text reminds us that legal research resources are hierarchical and highly structured. The researcher needs keep in mind provenance, authority and currency. Online access to legal information tends to disguise the structure. It is now too easy for students to rely on serendipitous outcomes from a scattergun approach. This will only work some of the time. The discipline of legal research is still wedded to its hard copy origins. However, media neutral citations, the flexibility in court rules in relation to print-outs of online judgments, and the inevitable according of official publication status to government legislation sites means that hard copy will not have a monopoly on authority. We hope the value of this new edition lies in its continued thorough coverage of the discipline of legal research while integrating online resources within that discipline.

Francis Johns
January 2009

Acknowledgments

We acknowledge with thanks permission from the following institutions to reproduce material as set out below.

Lawbook Co: *Commonwealth Law Reports* vol 171; "Alphabetical Table of Acts Passed, Amended, Repealed or Proclaimed to Commence", *Australian Legal Monthly Digest*, July, 2003.

Lawyers Cooperative Publishing, a division of Thompson Legal Publishing Inc, *American Jurisprudence*, 2nd, Vol 8 "Bail and Recognizance".

LexisNexis, *Halsbury's Laws of Australia* "Mortgages"; "Cumulative Table of Amended Acts", *Australian Current Law*, February, 2004; *The Digest*, vol 14(2) "Criminal Law"; *The Digest*, "Cumulative Supplement", 2004; *Australian Current Law: Reporter*, "Cumulative Halsbury's Updating Table".

The Honourable Justice Olsson, Judges' Chambers, Supreme Court, Adelaide, *Guide to Uniform Production of Judgments*, 2nd edn, Annexure C.

HW Wilson Company: *Index to Legal Periodicals*, vol 85, no 2, November 1991. Copyright © 1991 by the HW Wilson Company. Material reproduced with permission of the publisher.

NSW Attorney General's Department: ss 1, 2 *Freedom of Information Act 1989*; part of *Commission for Children and Young People Act 1998*; example from part of page of *NSW Legislation in Force*, 2004.

Shepard's/McGraw-Hill Inc, p 3 of Shepard's Citations to the Federal Reporter.

West Publishing Company, page from *US Code Congressional and Administrative News*, PL100-386; *United States Code Annotated*, General Index, "Popular Names Index"; *Corpus Juris Secundum*, vol 8, "Bail". Reprinted with permission. Copyright © by West Publishing Company.

Introduction

What is Concise Legal Research?

King George III is reputed to have said that a lawyer is not a person who knows the law but one who knows *where to find it*. It could be added that a good and successful lawyer is one who can find the law quickly, and with the available materials. This is what is meant by **concise legal research.**

Until recently, the teaching of the skill of legal research had not been part of the teaching of law and this has resulted in many legal practitioners wasting much time, and consequently money, in searching for the law using basically non-effective or haphazard methods. From a qualitative study[1] conducted for the Law Foundation of NSW, it has been shown that many practitioners, when confronted with legal problems outside their area of immediate knowledge, rely heavily on the looseleaf service, or they consult their colleagues. This leads one to suspect that they may have trouble with even basic legal research and, without the necessary skills, they are much more likely to "do it by the seat of their pants". Without the knowledge, and the resulting confidence that such knowledge brings, there will always be the need to seek assistance, either formally by requesting a barrister for an opinion ("briefing counsel"), or more informally through colleagues.

It is now recognised that there are many aspects of legal research that can be taught. By fully understanding the function of many different types of publications generally available, the person who needs to find the latest case, or an Act or regulation that incorporates all amendments, can do so with confidence and thus save a great deal of time. Research need not be such a mystery that one feels that it is an accident, or at least serendipity, if the law is actually found. The emphasis in research must be on *confidence* – to be able to reach that point in researching a legal problem of getting up from the desk knowing that one has done all that is to be done, or can be done with available resources.

While reading this book ,one further aspect of efficient legal researching will become apparent: usually there is not just *one* method of finding a particular aspect of the law. In most instances there is a number of ways that research can be undertaken and the one used will depend both upon the book and computer resources readily available and the level of

---

1 *Legal Research and Information Needs of Legal Practitioners*, a discussion paper prepared for the Law Foundation of New South Wales by MSJ Keys Young, July 1992, pp 6-7.

knowledge already known about the subject matter being researched. Thus, when confronted with a legal problem, the initial aim must be to establish a *search pattern* to find the relevant law. This can only be done by carefully thinking through the problem and establishing what it is being looked for; evaluating the starting point from information already acquired; and then selecting and using that material which will allow the relevant law to be found; all without wasting time. By determining the most efficient research pattern initially, you will be able to end that search confidently, before widening your search to include other jurisdictions or re-evaluating your search pattern. When you have developed that confidence, *you* have become an efficient and effective researcher.

To that end, the materials examined in this book are not special or unique. They will be found in any of the larger law libraries. Most will also be found in the libraries of the medium and larger legal and accounting firms and in the libraries of many government departments.

One of the most vexed questions is to know when a researching task is finished. The confidence to put down the pen and close the books (or turn off the computer) only comes with experience. But for researchers just beginning, there is a temptation to continue searching for a case "on all fours" with the facts they are working with. The result is usually less than satisfactory. Rather than constructing a logical (legal) argument, undue reliance is usually placed upon the case which, in normally circumstances, merely adds to an argument rather than establishing it.

Finally, the researcher should never forget that the way that the research is presented is critical to success. Whether it be a brief, a case note or legal opinion, the researcher should strive to perfect the appropriate written style. Examples should be found and studied in an endeavour to determine the key elements.

Chapter 1

CITATION

Outline

1 Primary and Secondary Legal Materials
2 What is a Citation?
3 Standardisation of Citation Rules
4 Case Citation
   (a) The Parties
   (b) The Date of the Decision
   (c) The Reports
   (d) Additional Conventions Associated with Case Citations
   (e) CCH Citation Style
5 Legislative Citations
   (a) The Section
   (b) The Act
   (c) General Guidelines for the Citation of Legislation
   (d) Acts without Short Titles
6 Referencing Secondary Materials

1. Primary and secondary legal materials

The legal materials found in a library or accessed via the computer can be reasonably placed into one of two groups. The first group we shall call primary legal materials and in this group can be isolated all our legal sources. All of the *other* materials in the library or found on the computer are used basically to assist the researcher in understanding the law, and this group we call secondary materials.

Primary

The primary sources of law are those authoritative records of law made by law-making bodies. In our common law environment these records are:

(a) the legislation made by Parliament,

(b) the rules, regulations, orders and by-laws of those bodies to whom Parliament has delegated authority, and;

(c) the authoritative reports of the decisions of the courts.

More will said about these individual items below.

Additionally, there is probably a fourth source of law for Australia. In *Mabo v Queensland (No 2)* (1992) 175 CLR 1, the High Court recognised the existence of communal native title as part of customary law. Its relevance is limited and tightly circumscribed by the type of, and continued, relationship to that land of Indigenous peoples. It, thus, has no application outside this specific field and not thought of as a general source of law.

However, it must be appreciated that when making any statement that might be construed as a statement of law (for example, the fine for exceeding the speed limit, the fee that is legally required for a nurse to be registered or the various elements that constitute the crime of murder), it is essential that the statement of law be followed by the legal authority. That allows it to be seen as a statement of *law*, while also allowing for checking and verification.

Secondary

The secondary sources of law are those publications which refer and relate to the law while not being themselves primary sources. Traditionally they were the legal commentaries, the most famous of which is probably Blackstone's *Commentaries on the Laws of England* (1765). They have since developed to include all legal textbooks, encyclopedias, dictionaries, digests, journals, and the like. A court will not feel bound by secondary source material if cited in support of a proposition of law, although certain material such as the writing of learned and highly esteemed authors may well be of significant persuasive value in selecting between conflicting authorities.

In most cases the end goal for the researcher is to *find the law* and that will mean that a case, Act or regulation, or a mixture of all three, must be found and cited. Seldom will it be satisfactory to end the research with reference merely to a secondary source. They are of great assistance in finding and understanding the law but will seldom replace the legal authority itself.

2. What is a citation?

Because it is necessary to reference any statement of law that is made by attributing the legal (primary) authority or authorities, the starting point for legal research is to know how that law, contained in the report of a case, section of an Act or in a clause of a regulation, is referred to by the legal profession. This is known as the *citation* of cases, Acts and regulations. Thus we say that a case is *cited* in court by counsel to provide the legal authority for the proposition that is being put forward.

When setting down rules on how this should be done, we are looking at a mixture of conventions and legal rules. Most of the rules associated with cases are merely conventions although reinforced by the practice of the courts which require certain uniformity in documents submitted to them. The citation of Acts and regulations, however, tends to be governed by the *short title* authority contained within the Act itself and supplemented by the jurisdiction's *Interpretations Act*. For the purposes of the modern researcher, it is becoming even more essential than before that correct and standardised rules are observed. This is because of the present and growing use of the computer to find case and legislative references from material stored in electronic form.

3. Standardisation of citation rules

Recently under the auspices of the Australian Institute of Judicial Administration Incorporated, a *Guide*[1] was issued by a Working Party chaired by Justice LT Olsson of the Supreme Court of South Australia. The principal aim of the Working Party was to establish a standard format for the production of judgments, including cover sheets and the writing of catchwords for them. The use of such a format should promote uniformity, and thus facilitate far greater efficiency in the retrieval of judgments stored electronically. While the greater bulk of the *AIJA Guide* is given over to the format of the judgment and detailing the key and first level of sub-titles needed for uniformity of catchwords used to identify the subject matter of the case, a number of important rules with respect to citation of both case and legislation are included. These, it is hoped, will become standard throughout Australia. Because the writing of judgments is now, with the advent of word processing facilities, the first stage in

1 The Honourable Justice LT Olsson, Supreme Court of South Australia, Convener, AIJA Working Party, *Guide to Uniform Production of Judgments*, AIJA, Melbourne, 1999, 2nd ed, "AIJA Guide". See <*www.aija.org.au/online/judguide.htm*>.

electronic storage and retrieval, it is essential that the judges adopt the standardised approach.

There are various parts of the *AIJA Guide* which are most helpful to researchers. Of particular interest are the rules and various guides set out for the use of key-wording. Annexure 2 contains the key titles and first sub-titles that should be used. However, for our purposes it is Annexure C "General Style Guide" that is of most importance:

GENERAL STYLE GUIDE

1. DATES AND NUMBERS

Dates should appear as follows: 19 July 1984
Spell out numbers from one to nine
Percentages should be expressed as: 10 per cent
Times should be shown as: 7.30 am
Monetary amounts should be shown as: $1000 $4 $32.65
Fractions should be shown as: 1/2

2. ABBREVIATIONS

section	s 3	s 3 and s 4	s 3, s 4 and s 5
paragraph	par (a) and par (b)	par (a), par (b) and par (c)	
subsection	s 3(2)	s 3(2), s 3(3) and s 3(4)	
regulation	reg 4	reg 4 and reg 6	reg 4, reg 5 and reg 6
Order	O 3		
Rule	r 2 and r 3	r 2, r 3 and r 4	
Clause	cl 5	cl 6 and cl 7	cl 15, cl 16 and cl 17
Chapter	ch 1		
Proprietary Limited	Pty Ltd		
Limited	Ltd		
Part	Pt I	Pt I and Pt II	Pt I, Pt II and Pt III
Division	Div		
Schedule	Sch		
Mr			
Mrs			
Dr			
Regina, Reg etc	all – R		

3. BOOKS AND JOURNALS

Smith, G *Administrative Law* 2nd ed Oxford University Press, London, 1970.

Mason A, "Future Directions in Australian Law" (1987) 13 MULR 149

Rogers, B "The Pitfalls in Occupational Health and Safety Law" Journal of Occupational Health and Safety Vol 15 No 4 1998 at 13.

4. LEGISLATION

Prisons Act 1903 (SA)
Crimes Act 1900 (no comma before date)
Contracts Review Act 1980, s 7(1) (Section references after Act)
Supreme Court Rules 1970, Pt 24, r 12.

5. COURTS

The reference to a court is always lower case except when referring to the Court in which the judgment is produced.

6. CASE CITATION

References to decided authorities in the text of a judgment may be dealt with in a number of ways:

(a) References in text of the judgement may be set out in full throughout the judgment or in full when first occurring and as "supra" or "ibid" thereafter as currently adopted by FCR, FLR, LGRA, ALJR:

Collins v Repatriation Commission (1980) 48 FLR 198 at 211 – 212 (when first appears)
Collins v Repatriation Commission (supra) at 213 (when next occurs), or
Collins v Repatriation Commission at 213.

One advantage of always setting out a citation in full is that it is then possible to search by citation and retrieve all references. If judgments are not cited in full each time they are referred to this may well have a deleterious effect on the performance of search engines and the automated inclusion of hypertext links.

(b) When a case list is provided (as in NSWLR) references may be cited in the text:

R v Smith (1978) 151 CLR 551 (Full reference when first appears).
Coleman v Buckingham's Ltd [1963] SR NSW 171; 80 WN (NSW) 593.
R v Smith at 556 (when appears thereafter – without supra).
Coleman v Buckingham's Ltd (or *Coleman* but not *Buckingham's*) at 773; 593.

(c) References in the text of the judgment may be confined to the name of the case followed by a numerical reference in brackets, eg, *R v Smith* (2). The actual citation is then shown at the foot of the page adjacent to the corresponding numeral, as currently adopted in the CLR reports series:

(2) (1978) 151 CLR 551 (full reference when first appears)
(2) (1978) 151 CLR at 57 (when appears thereafter)

NOTES:

(1) The method to be adopted may well depend on:
established practices;
styling of authorised reports and ease of reference.

(2) The method most compatible with computerised retrieval for on-line use is (a), because of the difficulties in relation to hypertext links caused by the other methods (see discussion in the Guide, paragraph 5.8).

(3) As court designated citations are adopted these also ought to be shown.

7. PINPOINTING PAGE AND PARAGRAPH: 'HYBRID' OR 'COMBINED' PINPOINT CITATIONS

(1) In conventional print citations, a citation can be more specific than a page number, referring to a section based on margin letters, eg *Person v Company* (1998) 152 ALR 34 at 52E.

A print judgment will now have both page and paragraph numbering. It is recommended that, in future, pinpoint citations refer to both page and paragraph numbers.

The conventional print citation will take a reader to the first page of the judgment; it is then necessary to take the reader to both the page and paragraph within the judgment.

To pinpoint only to the paragraph when the reader is using a print copy of the judgment referred to would require a reader to turn through the judgment so as to locate the paragraph, where use of the page number would have taken them directly to the page. Further, pinpointing only to the paragraph is not helpful when a paragraph spans more than one page.

To pinpoint only to the page when the reader is using a print copy of the judgment referred to will take the reader to a page on which there may be many paragraphs, in which case use of the existing paragraph number emulates the current practice of pinpointing with added margin letters
A-G.

To pinpoint only to the page when the reader is using an online copy of the judgment referred to a print version should be to the page and paragraph number:

EXAMPLE:

Person v Company (1998) 152 ALR 34 at 52 [27]

(This pinpoints paragraph 27 on page 52 of the judgment.)

8. PARALLEL CITATIONS IN PRINT

(1) A judgment with a medium neutral citation may be published in a report and given a print citation. Thus:

Person v Company [1998] HCA 25

is later reported as

Person v Company (1998) 152 ALR 34

(2) The medium neutral citation is effectively part of the title of the judgment, having been allocated by the court at the time of delivering the judgment, and appearing at the head of the print reported judgment.

(3) It is recommended that future citations of the judgment should be to both the medium neutral citation and the print citation. the medium neutral citation is placed first, but not necessarily in italics with the case name and is separated from the print citation by a semicolon.

(4) To refer only to the print citation means a user with only online access is unable to locate the judgment. Equally, to refer only to medium neutral

citation means a user with only print access is unable to locate the judgment.

(5) Failure to parallel cite the medium neutral citation and the print citation will severely limit a person's ability to conduct an online database search: if the search is for the medium neutral citation, the case will not be found unless it has been recorded with parallel citations.

(6) Thus parallel citations should be in the following form:

Person v Company [1998] HCA 25; (1998) 152 ALR 34

(7) For a parallel pinpoint citation, the recommended form is:

Person v Company [1998] HCA 25 at [27]; (1998) 152 ALR 34 at 52

9. PAGE REFERENCES

R v Smith (1978) 151 CLR 556
at 566 – 567 (if quote runs on)
at 566, 559 (if separate quotes)

10. QUOTATIONS

Anything over five lines is usually indented within double quotation marks. Stops to be deleted from quotes to accord with overall style.

11. RELEVANT STATUTORY/DOCUMENTARY TEXT PROVISIONS

It is recommended that consideration be given, where appropriate, to preceding the actual text of the judgment with a preliminary statement – setting out the text of the relevant statutory or documentary provisions.

12. UNDERLINING

Anything to be emphasised should be printed in italics or a different type font and not underlined. Documents with underlining converted to html create a false hypertext link for what is underlined. This can be very confusing.

NOTES:

- *Do* leave spaces between two page references (eg 556 – 557), otherwise the computer will read the figures as a single continuous string.
- Above all else BE CONSISTENT, or the computer may not find all relevant references.

House styles

These guidelines should be noted by researchers and where appropriate should be followed. However, this is a field where over the years there have been many attempts to unify and bring order to an area noted for disorder. Many of the larger publishers have established "House Style" guidelines already in place. These rules might be based upon the *Style Manual for authors, editors and printers* (6th ed, John Wiley and Co, 2002) to which the publishers supplement with further rules for legal materials. Thus some remove all stops in abbreviations (as this book does) notwithstanding mode of citation authority or the like. To some publishers, the production of legal works will be governed by a mixture of rules, conventions and aesthetics. In Australia, like Canada, there will be one day a style guide generally accepted. Until that day, the *AIJA Guide* should be considered as most appropriate. Because of some of the reasons listed above, there is an element of *Do as I say rather than do as I do* in this work. Let the researcher understand that and never become dogmatic about style. While there is no absolute right and wrong in citation, merely generally accepted preferred methods, the aim should always be for consistency and audience comprehension.

Having made in this chapter a number of general observations about citation, any failure to follow the normally accepted rules may indicate to others ignorance, or at least a lack of understanding, on the part of the writer. Thus a little time should be spent on getting them right. For sake of completeness, there are some important aspects of citation that need further explanation. What follows, in both case and legislation citations, is an examination of some areas that give the most trouble to researchers in their early days.

Electronic citation

Read the material in the *AIJA Guide* (2nd ed) and you will see that care has been taken by the author to provide ways of referencing case material taken from online sources. The need for medium-neutral citations (meaning citations that did not depend upon the publication in print form) became apparent in 1997 when a meeting was held in Sydney of court representatives, legal publishers and staff of the Australasian Legal Information Institute (AustLII) and a medium-neutral citation format was adopted. The High Court of Australia took the lead in January 1998 when its judgments included a medium-neutral citation. While it was hoped that this medium-neutral citation would be able to be used alone from that time on, soon afterwards the High Court indicated that it was permissible to use it alone, BUT ONLY until the authorised citation in the Commonwealth Law Reports (CLRs) became available. Then, the only citation acceptable to the Court would be either the CLR citation alone or used in parallel with the medium neutral citation.

The *AIJA Guide* (2nd ed) recommends (para 6.10) that, because the court designated medium-neutral citation is effectively part of the title of the judgment (having been allocated by the court at the time of delivering the judgment), it should be retained as a parallel citation whenever the judgment is cited. Thus, the recommendation of the *AIJA Guide*, embodied in their general style guide, is to always include both.

Reference

An excellent guide when a researcher needs to cite (or source) material that may not be covered by the *AIJA Guide* is A Stuhmcke, *Butterworths Guide: legal referencing*, 3rd ed, LexisNexis Butterworths, 2005.

4. Case citation

Set out below are two pages from the *Commonwealth Law Reports*. These will be used as examples of the various rules governing citations as they are raised. Those who are not familiar with the reporting of cases might observe the *catchwords*, the *headnote*, *outline of the facts*, the *arguments of counsel*, all before the judgment commences. While ownership of copyright of the judgment is not clear, there is no doubt that the publishers own the copyright in all these aspects of the reported judgment. Extreme care must be taken never to infringe that copyright.

What is included in a case citation?

As noted previously, the word *citation* is used in legal writings to refer to the way the legal profession specifically refer to the law in their legal writings and applies to either a reference to a case, to an Act or to a regulation. At a later stage legislative citations will be looked at but now, when referring to *case citations*, be aware that the citation contains:

- the name of the parties in the case;
- the date that the decision of the court was delivered (*handed down*);
- the volume number of the law report series where it has been printed (*reported*);
- the abbreviation of that report series; and
- the first page of the report.

The citation will contain all that information and *in that order*. However, because there are special rules or conventions that apply generally to case citation and specifically in the choice of parties' names, the date and report abbreviation, these will be examined in some detail.

(a) The parties

Abbreviations: there is a number of common abbreviations used for words often found in the names of the parties. Some of these are set out in the *AIJA Guide* above, but other common examples include:

Attorney General	AG
Board	Bd
Commissioner	Commr
Commonwealth	Cth
Company	Co
Department	Dept
Director of Public Prosecutions	DPP
Federal Commissioner of Taxation	FCT
Motor Vessel	MV
Steamship	SS

It will not always be appropriate to abbreviate these words and there will be many others that you can. If having noted the various guides set out here you are still in doubt, err on the side of caution and *do not* abbreviate.

Some examples of common problems associated with parties' names

Ships

Where a ship is concerned, notwithstanding that the party's name beginning the case will be shown in the traditional manner, there is also the name of the ship separately set out beneath the parties. This then becomes the normal way of citing that particular case. See example below.

Example of ship name in citation

Monte Ulia (Owners) v Banco and Others (Owners) The Banco	*The Banco* [1971] P 137

Re and Ex Parte

Note that there need not necessarily be two parties in a case that is reported. In many instances the court plays an advisory or guardianship role and one party may appear before the court seeking assistance. For example an executor may seek assistance as to the interpretation of a clause in a will, or a young couple may seek the permission of the court to marry pursuant to s 12 of the *Marriage Act 1961* (Cth). In these instances accept what is at the top of the page in the report and merely modify it in terms of abbreviation already discussed. On these occasions you will often find *Re* or *In re* (in the matter of) and *Ex parte* (on one side). They are placed at the beginning of the citation, ie, before the parties names, except if they are to appear in an alphabetical listing. Then it is the principal's name that takes priority and *Re* is relegated in that list only to a position at the end where it will not interfere with that listing.

Multiple Party Names

In many instances there is more than one party to an action or there has been an amalgamation of cases and a single report is given which enables those cases to be dealt with. In that case the usual practice is to merely use the first case that appears in the report. In much the same way a report will identify a party as "and another". This adds nothing to a citation and is usually left out.

Common Case Names

It is common practice in the study or discussion generally of the law, ie, outside the areas where the strict rules of citation are observed, for legal students, teachers and the profession to shorten the names of cases where unduly long party names are involved, or else give more descriptive names to cases where the parties names have not always sufficiently identified the case. Thus there are numerous *Victoria v Commonwealth* cases reported in the *Commonwealth Law Reports*. To assist in identifying a particular one, common names are given and extensively used in legal literature. If in that literature citations are not given, or incorrectly given, great difficulty can be encountered in finding the case. The practice of common names has almost reached semi-official status with the occasional inclusion in the reports of High Court decisions in the *Commonwealth Law Reports* of common names following the identification of the parties. Placed in square brackets in the report series, the editor of the CLR has provided the common names:

Tasmanian Dam Case (1983) 158 CLR 1
First Fringe Benefits Tax Case (1987) 162 CLR 74
Second Fringe Benefits Tax Case (1987) 163 CLR 329
Incorporation Case (1990) 169 CLR 482
War Crimes Act Case (1991) 172 CLR 501
Marion's Case (1991) 175 CLR 21

Where these cases have been referred to in later volumes of the CLR, the common name has been used. This could well lead to confusion between those instances where a common name, duly given in the reports, needs to be distinguished from informal common names acquired by general usage. The former may well be cited as such in any legal document while the latter should only be cited after the full and formal citation has at least been initially given. A sensible rule would be to capitalise the word "Case" where the common name has been given in the report, and to leave the word in lower case in other instances.

Example from Commonwealth Law Reports

592 HIGH COURT [1990-1991.

GIANNARELLI AND OTHERS . . . APPELLANTS;

AND

WRAITH AND OTHERS . . . . RESPONDENTS.

[No. 2]

H. C. of A. 1990-1991. SYDNEY, 1990, Dec. 13. 1991, Feb. 20. McHugh J.

High Court — Practice — Costs — Taxation — Taxing officer — Powers — Legal professional privilege — Effect of refusal to tender privileged documents — Whether other party entitled to see tendered privileged documents — High Court Rules, O. 71, r. 70.

Order 71, r. 70 of the High Court Rules provided: "The taxing officer may, for the purposes of taxation of costs — (a) summon and examine witnesses either orally or upon affidavit; (b) administer oaths; (c) direct or require the production of books, papers and documents; (d) issue subpoenas; (e) make separate or interim certificates or allocaturs; (f) require a party to be represented by a separate solicitor; and (g) do such other acts and direct or take all such other steps as are directed by these Rules or by the Court or a Justice."

Held, (1) that if the taxing officer was of the opinion that there is a genuine factual issue between the parties, he could exercise the powers under O. 71, r. 70.

Per curiam. So long as the taxing officer exercises his powers "for the purpose of taxation of costs" and not capriciously or unreasonably, he need not have any evidence before him.

Pamplin v. Express Newspapers Ltd., [1985] 1 W.L.R. 689, at p. 697; [1985] 2 All E.R. 185, at p. 191, applied.

(2) That a party applying for taxation could refuse to produce documents on the ground that they were subject to legal professional privilege.

Baker v. Campbell (1983), 153 C.L.R. 52, at pp. 115-116, applied.

(3) That the taxing officer was not entitled to refuse to tax a bill on the ground that the party seeking taxation had refused to produce privileged documents.

Pamplin v. Express Newspapers Ltd., [1985] 1 W.L.R. 689; [1985] 2 All E.R. 185, and *Goldman v. Hesper*, [1988] 1 W.L.R. 1238; [1988] 3 All E.R. 97, considered.

(4) That a party who produced documents, whether privileged or not, could not object to the taxing officer's showing them to another party.

Pamplin v. Express Newspapers Ltd., [1985] 1 W.L.R. 689; [1985] 2 All E.R. 185, applied.

QUESTIONS referred pursuant to O. 71, r. 19(3) of the High Court Rules.

On 13 October 1988 the High Court dismissed an appeal by

Emilio Giannarelli and others against a decision of the Supreme Court of Victoria and ordered that they pay the respondents, Daryl Wraith and others, their costs of the appeal. The respondents submitted a bill of costs totalling $44,159.23 for taxation. One of the appellants' objections to the bill was that the respondents were not entitled to recover the costs of the appeal because they were never at risk in respect of costs, since the costs were to be fully paid by the [illegible]dents' insurer. On [illegible] 1990 th[illegible] [illegible]ficer wrote to [illegible]

[illegible]

ta[illegible] [illegible] respo[illegible] until produ[illegible] of the documents or such of them as he is empowered to require the respondents to produce? 4. Upon production of the documents, if any, is the taxing officer entitled or obliged to make copies of the documents available to the appellants or their legal advisers notwithstanding objection from the respondents to such being done?"

J. F. Walsh, for the appellants, referred to *Pamplin v. Express Newspapers Ltd.* (1); *Goldman v. Hesper* (2); and *Neville v. London "Express" Newspaper Ltd.* (3).

R. L. Berglund, for the respondents, referred to *Gundry v. Sainsbury* (4); *R. v. Archbishop of Canterbury* (5); *Inglis v. Moore [No. 2]* (6); *Reg. v. Miller* (7); *O'Donnell v. Reichard* (8); and *Adams v. London Improved Motor Coach Builders Ltd.* (9).

Cur. adv. vult.

1991, Feb. 20.

McHUGH J. delivered the following written judgment:—

The Registrar, sitting as a taxing officer, has referred to me four questions arising in a taxation of costs in the Court. The reference was made pursuant to O. 71, r. 19(3) of the High Court Rules ("the Rules"). The first question concerns the power of the taxing officer to require the respondents to produce documents for the purpose of

(1) [1985] 1 W.L.R. 689; [1985] 2 All E.R. 185.
(2) [1988] 1 W.L.R. 1238; [1988] 3 All E.R. 97.
(3) [1919] A.C. 368.
(4) [1910] 1 K.B. 645.
(5) [1903] 1 K.B. 289.
(6) (1979) 25 A.L.R. 453.
(7) [1983] 1 W.L.R. 1056; [1983] 3 All E.R. 186.
(8) [1975] V.R. 916.
(9) [1921] 1 K.B. 495.

Common names, given by text writers, lecturers and others, can often leave students confused. There are lists, including an Appendix in previous editions of this work. However, CaseBase has a *common names* field that can be used to find a full citation from the shorter reference. This is now the best place to start.

General Rule: Use the side-note or table of contents

If in doubt as to the possibility of abbreviation or shortening by leaving out extraneous material that might appear in the report, the easiest way of resolving that doubt is to examine the *Table of Contents* at the front of the volume and take your lead from the publication itself. In most instances it follows the common practice. However, if you do use this table as a guide you must also understand that in order to place cases in alphabetical order, it will sometimes relegate to a secondary place, ie, after the parties proper name, any commonly occurring phrase such as *Ex parte* or *Re*.

In the example from the *Commonwealth Law Reports*, the sidenote on the second page has left out *and others* but indicates the importance of *[No. 2]* by including it in the citation. This is always done to identify this particular case from another involving the same parties.

(b) The date of the decision

The date that appears in a citation serves the basic purpose of allowing the researcher to know when the case was decided, that is, when it was handed down. However, this basic purpose is somewhat confused by the fact that some law reports use the date to identify the various volumes of the law reports. If the *All England Law Reports* are examined, it can be seen that each year there are three or four volumes, identified as [1985] 1 All ER; [1985] 2 All ER; etc. The *Commonwealth Law Reports* are numbered sequentially: 162 CLR, 163 CLR etc. It will be apparent that in the former case, the date of the volume provides the (approximate) date of the decision, while in the later there is virtually no assistance to determine the date of the decision. The date will have to be added. But in many instances the date cannot be taken from the spine of the law report because it merely indicates that in that volume there are cases decided in the years indicated.

This can be seen more clearly from the CLR example. Observe in the sidenote that counsel argued the case in the High Court while it sat in Sydney on 13 December 1990, but the decision was handed down on 20 FEBRUARY 1991. The date that will appear in the citation will thus be "1991", even though at the top of the page the notation *[1990-1991 171*

CLR] appears and those same two dates also appear on the spine of the volume 171. The date at the top of the page merely indicates to the researcher that this case extended beyond one year, while the spine indicates that in volume 171 there are cases handed down in 1990 and 1991. A rule of thumb is always to remember that a case can never be handed down on two occasions, so there can never be a double year reference when the date is only for information, that is, when it appears in round brackets.

Examples of Case Citations

H v H (MINOR) (CHILD ABUSE: EVIDENCE) K v K (MINOR) (CHILD ABUSE: EVIDENCE)	*H v H (Minor) (Child Abuse: Evidence)*
Hinch v The Attorney-General of the State of Victoria; Macquarie Broadcasting Holdings Ltd v The Attorney-General of the State of Victoria	*Hinch v Attorney-General (Vic)*
In re Parliamentary Election for Bristol South East	*In re Parliamentary Election for Bristol South East*
HC Sleigh Ltd v State of South Australia	*HC Sleigh Ltd v South Australia*
Worth v Clasholm and Another	*Worth v Clasholm*
Abdul Rahmen Al Baker v Robert Edmund Alford and Another	*Al Baker v Alford*
D (JR) v D (JM)	*D (JR) v D (JM)*

Example

Pamplin v Express Newspapers Ltd [1985] 1 WLR 689
Baker v Campbell (1983) 153 CLR 52

On occasions if there is a delay in the publication of a case in a report series where the square bracket is used in citations, it may be necessary to add the date in round brackets in order not to mislead the researcher. However, the difference would need to be more than just one or two years to make this double-dating valid unless there are extenuating circumstances.

Example

Central London Property Trust Ltd v High Trees House Ltd (1946) [1956] 1 All ER 256n

---

The *Square and Round bracket Rule* can thus be summarised: where the year is essential because it is an integral element of the citation, then the year is in square brackets. If the year is not essential (for example, where there is a sequential volume number), it is still included but put in round brackets to indicate the date of the case.

(c) The Reports

You will have observed in the preceding section that the name of the report series is included in a citation. One of the purposes of citing a case, apart from identifying the parties, is to allow interested persons to locate and read the complete decision of the case. In order to obviate the need to give a complete and full reference to the name of the report series, standard abbreviations for the various law reports have been developed. There is no choice in the matter, but one can find in the early pages of most report series the abbreviation that is to be used. Always couched in much the same way, examples from widely used report series include:

Examples

These reports are cited thus:
[2000] 2 All ER

The mode of citation of this volume of the COMMONWEALTH LAW REPORTS will be as follows:
197 CLR

The mode of citation of the Volumes of the Law Reports commencing 1 January 1991, will be as follows

[1991] Ch.	[1991] Fam.
[1991] 1 Q.B.	[1991] 1 A.C.
[1991] 2 Q.B.	[1991] 2 A.C.

It can be seen from the last example that there are four different series of the *Law Reports* which are the authorised reports of the English courts, and when citing from a particular series of the *Law Reports* the appropriate abbreviation is used.

Example of finding a report series

Let us assume you wish to read the decision in *Fremlin v Fremlin* (1913) 16 CLR 212.

Your first task is to ascertain the report series represented by the abbreviation "CLR".

To do this you must got the lists of abbreviations.

Osborn: *Common Law Reports* (1853-1855)
Commonwealth Law Reports (1903 to date)

Prince & Bitner:
Cyprus Law Reports (1883 to date)
Canada Law Reports
Columbian Law Reports
Common Law Reports

Fong & Edwards: *Commonwealth Law Reports*

It thus follows that the *context* of the citation will help you. If the citation comes from the *Australian Digest*, it will necessarily be an Australian case and you can eliminate the Cyprus, Columbia and Canada Law Reports.

You have the year of the case and in Osborn's list you have the dates of the reports. It is obvious that it cannot be the Common Law Reports for they were only published between 1853-55.

However, it may be necessary to arrive at a conclusion by a *process of elimination*. In this example the "CLR" reference in the citation is the Commonwealth Law Reports.

Where to find report citation lists

From what has been written above, it will be appreciated that care must be taken to use the correct mode of citation, in order to allow those searching for the report series to reverse the process and to obtain from a list of abbreviations the full name of the reports. Although there is not a completely standardised and universal list, the following publications contain lists of commonly used abbreviations:

- Colin Fong *Australian Legal Citation: a guide*, Prospect, 1998
- *CaseBase – Abbreviations* (LexisNexis)

- *Osborn's Concise Law Dictionary*, 10th ed by M Woodley, Sweet & Maxwell, 2005
- Donald Raistrick *Index to Legal Citations and Abbreviations*, 2nd ed, London, Bowker-Saur, 1992
- *Bieber's dictionary of legal abbreviations*, 4th ed by Mary M Prince, Buffalo NY, WS Hein, 1993
- Monash University Law Library's Abbreviations of Legal Publications <*www.lib.monash.edu.au/legal-abbreviations*>
- Cardiff University's *Index to Legal Abbreviations* <*www.legalabbrevs.cardiff.ac.uk*>. The Cardiff Index was conceived by Dr Peter Clinch and produced by the staff of the Information Service, Cardiff University. Of special interest is the page "About the Cardiff Index to Legal Abbreviations". Here can be found an extensive bibliography relating to legal abbreviations covering many jurisdictions and over a long time span. Dr Clinch received the prestigious British and Irish Association of Law Librarians Wallace Bream Memorial Award 2004 for the work.

Citation guides

There has been a number of good guides published recently to assist the researcher in citing legal materials, including the vexed question of **electronic citations**. In those listed below there is also a comprehensive lists of abbreviations:

- Anita Stuhmcke, *Legal Referencing*, 3rd ed, LexisNexis Butterworths, 2005
- Pearl Rozenberg, *Australian Guide to Uniform Legal Citation*, 2nd ed, Thompson, 2003
- *Australian Guide to Legal Citation*, 2nd ed, Melbourne University Law Review Association, 2002 and electronically available at <*http://muir.law.unimelb.edu.au/PDFs/aglc_dl.pdf*>

There are others – particularly from the United States. For an excellent summary of the US rules, see Peter W Martin, *Introduction to Basic Legal Citation* (LII 2003 ed) available at <*www.law.cornell.edu/citation*>.

(d) Additional conventions associated with case citations

Italics or Underlining: When citing a case, place the names of the parties in the italic script. The reason for this is conventional only but is one that is widespread. This now also includes the "v". Italic effect is achieved in manuscript or handwritten form by underlining the words. Endeavour to avoid underlining in material that will be stored electronically.

Example

Carbine v Powell (1925) 36 CLR 88 **OR**
Carbine v Powell (1925) 36 CLR 88.

Never say versus: In Australia and England, unlike the United States, the legal profession never render in speech the "v" between the parties as "vee" or "versus". It is rendered as "and" if the case is a civil action, and as "against" if the action is criminal. Thus, in the example above, in speech it would be referred to as "Carbine and Powell", whereas in a criminal case written as, eg, *R v Smith*, it would be spoken of as "the Queen (or Crown) against Smith".

Criminal cases on appeal: As noted both above and below, criminal actions are brought in the name of the Crown: thus *R v Smith*. However, if Smith is convicted and takes the case on appeal, the situation is more complex. At the first level of appeal (eg, to the Court of Criminal Appeal or to the Full Court of the Supreme Court), the convention in most States is to use the same style, ie "*R v Smith*", even though it is Smith who is the appellant. When the case is further taken on appeal (ie to the Federal Court or the High Court), the convention is the same as any other case and the party instigating the proceedings is named first. Where it is the accused who appeals in this situation, then the convention is not to use "R" but the term "The Queen": thus "*Smith v The Queen*".

R in speech: In that last example you see that "R" is rendered in speech as "the Queen" (or "the King" as appropriate to the period although if in doubt keep to "the Queen") or "the Crown" (still the most common in court). The use of State names or the Commonwealth as a party is not an invitation to alter what appears in the report to "R" however.

(e) CCH citation style

To conclude this section on case citation, mention will be made of one particular area of citation that creates some concern. This is in the area of the citation of CCH materials, particularly case reports in their looseleaf services. The principal problem arises from the use of two sets of numbers throughout the various services. The number at the top of the page is a page numbering system and has been placed there for the use of persons filing new material. The number at the bottom of the page relates to the material within the service and refers to the paragraph numbering system.

Example

At p V of vol 6 of *Australian & New Zealand Insurance Cases* (CCH) is the following statement: "Cases reported in this volume should be cited by reference to the paragraph number (¶) which appears at the bottom of each page as follows (year of report) 6 *ANZ Insurance Cases* ¶-."

In that volume is the case *Lumley General Insurance Ltd v Vintix Pty Ltd.* It is at paragraph 61-087 and reported between pages 77,330-77,336. This might appear confusing but it should be noted that this report series is derived from the looseleaf service *Australian and New Zealand Insurance Reporter.* The cases occupy paragraph 60-000+ of that service. As they fill the looseleaf volume they are periodically removed and bound. They keep the original paragraph and page number.

Some publishers when citing CCH material use the page number instead. With a book this seems reasonable but it can cause confusion, particularly if an author is not consistent. When faced with a CCH citation and in doubt, a rule of thumb is to check the break between tab and paragraph: a paragraph citation has a *dash,* the page citation has a *comma.*

There is one further problem with CCH reports. The convention of ( ) and [ ] (ie round and square bracketing), used to indicate if the date is for information or essential in locating the volume, is not always followed. An example is the *Australian Torts Reports* (CCH). The mode of citation recommended for this report series is "(1999) Aust Torts Reports ¶". Thus, the citation for the case that begins the 1999 volume is *Gray v Motor Accident Commission* [1998] HCA 70; (1999) Aust Torts Reports ¶81-494. This decision was handed down on 17 November 1998.

5. Legislative citation

(a) The section

The law in an Act is contained within a section or sections of that Act and it is not usual that reference is made solely to the Act itself as a legislative authority. The normal methods of citing such a section reference is as follows:

section 20, or
sec20, or
s20, or
s 20

There is a degree of choice here; even though references within legislation itself tend to favour *sec*, the *AIJA Guide* favours s followed by a space.

There is another area of choice. Assume that the law is contained within a section, maybe in a sub-section, or paragraph, sub-paragraph or sub-sub-paragraph. How then to cite the authority? The choice is between:

s 20(1)(a)(i)(A) or sec 20
sub-sec 20(1)
para 20(1)(a)
sub-para 20(1)(a)(i)
sub-sub-para 20(1)(a)(i)(A)

The second way is known as "*advanced forward referencing*" and is the way that legislation tends to make reference to itself. It is extensively used in Commonwealth Government departments. It is not popular, however, because of the cumbersome nature of the citation in some instances. The modern movement towards Plain English drafting will mean that in the future, in new principal Acts, the draftees will seldom go past the paragraph strata. Even now the sub-sub-paragraph is rarely used.

Example of Citing from an Act

The following extract is from the *Crimes Act 1900* (NSW):

Power of arrest in cases of certain offences committed outside the State

352A. (1) This section applies to an offence:

(a) that is an offence against the law of a State (other than New South Wales) or a Territory of the Commonwealth; and

(b) that consists of an act or omission which, if it occurred in New South Wales, would constitute;

(i) an indictable offence; or

(ii) an offence punishable by imprisonment for 2 years or more.

(2) A member of the police force may, at any hour of the day or night and without any warrant other than this Act, apprehend any person whom he has reasonable cause to suspect of having committed an offence to which this section applies.

(3) A person apprehended under this section shall be brought as soon as practicable before a court and the court:

(a) may discharge the person; or

(b) may:

(i) commit him to custody; or

(ii) admit him to bail,

pending the execution under a law of the Commonwealth of a warrant or provisional warrant for his apprehension or his earlier release from bail, or discharge from custody, under subsection (7).

Various questions that demonstrate the use of legal authority arise when citing the law from this section if the Act. Thus: do the NSW police have the authority to apprehend a person who has committed an indictable offence in Victoria? Yes, pursuant to s 352A(2) of the *Crimes Act 1900*. Is there a legal obligation for the police to bring that person quickly before the court? Yes, pursuant to s 352A(3) of that Act. Is there authority for such a person to be able to seek bail? Yes, pursuant to s 352A(3)(b)(ii) of the Act.

Amendments to sections

In most jurisdictions, when a new section is being inserted, the new section number includes a capitalised letter to indicate it is an amendment.

Example

Section 15AB of the *Acts Interpretation Act 1901* (Cth)

This is a good example because if the *Acts Interpretation Act* is examined, it is clear that the letters used do not really follow a preordained scheme. The present order in the Act is: ss 15, 15A, 15AA, 15AB, 15AC, 15AD, 15B and 15C. The draftees have endeavoured to place an amendment within the most logical place in the Act. Some Acts, eg, the *Income Tax Assessment Act 1936*, are notorious for the amendment numbering system. Personal favourites include ss 159GZZZBE, 160APYBAB and 221YHZDAA. Attempts in 1997 and 1998 to introduce plain language into the tax law by enactment of a new Act in 1997 appear to have been quietly shelved.

(b) The Act

The *official citation* of an Act of Parliament in most Australian jurisdictions is by the number of the Act and the year it received Assent.

Example

Act No 38, 1976

In Victoria before 1 January 1986, there was a sequential number:

Example

No 10214

Since the amendment of *Interpretation of Legislation Act 1984* s 9, Victoria now is in line with the other States and Commonwealth, although in semi-official settings the citation quite often appears as: No 7/1991.

Short title

If, however, the Act has a *short title* it is acceptable and usual to cite that Act by the short title. The authority to use this method of citation comes from the Act itself although it is always an option only. Section 10 of the *Interpretation of Legislation Act 1984* No 10096 (Vic)[2] provides accordingly for that jurisdiction.

Example of Short Title of Act

Section 1 Freedom of Information Act 1989 No 5

Part 1 Preliminary

Part 1 Preliminary

1 Name of Act

This Act may be cited as the *Freedom of Information Act 1989*.

2 Commencement

This Act commences on a day or days to be appointed by proclamation.

(c) General guidelines for the citation of legislation from the various Australian jurisdictions

One of the less notable, but nonetheless welcome, features in recent years of co-operation between the various Australian States and the Commonwealth has been in the area of the standardisation of the citation

2 Section 10 of the *Interpretation of Legislation Act 1984* (Vic), amended to come into effect on 1 January 1986, allows for the short title shown within the Act or, if not provided, the title above the enacting words or preamble.

of legislation. To most legal researchers the provision of written material with the correct citation of the legislation of the various Australian jurisdictions was a nightmare. There had to be constant checking to see if the legislation should be in italics, whether there was to be the inclusion of the date of the last amendment in the citation of the original act, whether the jurisdiction included a comma between the short title and the date and other idiosyncratic features of citation. In this area, the provision of "correct" citations seldom depended upon common usage but nearly always had the sanction of legislation, either through the mode of citation provision in the act itself or, in other areas, the *Interpretation Act* enacted by the legislature which provided general rules in some instances.

During the 1980s, however, there was a welcome trend towards uniformity and since most citation rules are common to all Australian jurisdictions. With the exception of Victoria, the short title authority tends to come from the Act. Yet while there are some older Acts not yet amended, particularly in New South Wales, the convention is to place the full short title, including the year, in italics. Indeed it would be fair to lay down a general rule that all Acts, regulations, case and publication names are fully italicised.

(d) Acts without short titles and no legislative provision

In England the practice of giving short titles within the Act is also followed but it has not always been so. The practice commenced in the early 16th century and developed slowly. By the mid-19th century most legislation carried a short title. When such an Act is being referred to which does *not* have a short title, it is necessary to cite that legislation by the official title, ie, by the number of the Act in the year it was passed, or in England, by the regnal year and chapter number (referred to as the "regnal citation"). This form of citation is not always convenient, since a short title does give some general indication of the subject matter of an Act. Consequently in 1896 the British Parliament collected all legislation that was in force at that time and for which there was no short title, and by the *Short Titles Act 1896* gave to all those Acts a short title. This Act now contains the necessary authorisation for using the given short title of any one of the early Acts.

Example of continued use of Regnal Citation

The importance of this can be seen in the study of Australian legal history. The Imperial Act establishing the Supreme Court of NSW in 1823 was 4 Geo IV, c 96. It was only intended to be a temporary measure and was replaced in 1828 by 9 Geo IV c 83. Neither of these acts had short titles when enacted by Parliament. However, by 1896 only the latter was still on the statute books and was given the short title *The Australian Courts Act 1828*. The former, without the benefit of the 1896 Act, is still referred to by the regnal citation.

---

6. Referencing secondary sources

There are times when writing legal essays and the like, that reference needs to be made to material other than primary law sources. Many examples of this material are set out in Chapter 5. These include encyclopedias, textbooks and journal articles. What are the rules with regard to the referencing of this material? (Note that while we tend to *cite* primary legal materials, we merely *refer* to secondary materials.)

Many journals, faculties and publishing houses have their own rules for citation and referencing. When writing for these publications or faculties, the researcher should approach them and seek a copy of those rules. Journals usually set out how copies can be obtained on those occasions when they are soliciting material from authors. However, if such rules are not made available, the researcher should endeavour to find a set of rules that is reasonable for the task and to comply with them.

One such set which provides a broad cross-section of rules associated with secondary source referencing can be found in the *Style Manual for authors, editors and printers* (6th ed) John Wiley & Co).

However, the cardinal rule is that whichever set is used, the researcher should ensure consistency of style. Nothing detracts from a piece of written work more, legal or otherwise, than such inconsistency. It might be in the style of citations or references, or even standardised spelling, but in any case a reader (or examiner) may suspect that if the presentation is so inconsistent, so might well be the logic of argument of the contents.

Chapter 2

Primary Source Material

Commonwealth, NSW, Selected Australian Jurisdictions and UK

Outline

1 The Australian Legal Environment
2 Legislation as a Source of Law
3 Principal Acts and Amending Acts Distinguished
4 Finding Legislation
   (a) Where to Begin
   (b) The Comparative Method of Subject Searching
5 The Date of Commencement of New Legislation
6 Current Awareness Services and Legislation
7 The Legislation of the Commonwealth of Australia
8 The Legislation of the States
9 The Legislation of the Territories
10 The Legislation of the United Kingdom
11 Interpretation of Legislation – Use of Extrinsic Aids
12 Legislative Histories

1. The Australian legal environment

Australia is a federation and, while the political concept is not difficult to understand, it makes a great difference when researching the law in Australia. There is the initial problem of always having to be conscious of two jurisdictions that can affect the outcome of any legal problem. A sound knowledge of constitutional law is needed if the researcher is to feel confident in going straight to the State or federal statutes. The existence of two legal systems and the interaction between them will be another problem. While it is easy enough to comprehend State courts exercising State jurisdiction, when we have State courts exercising federal jurisdiction it becomes more complicated. And there is always the role of the High Court of Australia which, under the constitution, has both an original and an appellate jurisdiction. Also, there is the problem of the evolving Australian legislative relationship with Britain. This is bound up with our gradual evolution as an independent nation. The Australian States were originally colonies. How did federation affect that status and are there any residual effects in law-making? And finally, and coupled with all this, is the effect of the common law upon any legal problem. It is no easy task for a legal novice to understand the relationship between the common law and legislation. Certainly the ground rule that the common law must always give way to a legislative enactment can be seen to operate in cases of clear collision, but there is room for a great deal of manoeuvring. And here too, it takes a long time in law to know, or at least with confidence guess, whether a matter is governed by legislation or is possibly subject to legislative constraint.

Federation

The federation of the six Australian colonies occurred on 1 January 1901. For the last decade of the 1800s representatives of the various colonies had laboured upon and finally had approved by the colonialists, the draft which went to the Imperial Parliament at Westminster. After minor changes[1] it was accepted and embodied in the British enactment *Commonwealth of Australia Constitution Act 1900* s 9.

The function of the Constitution was to create the entity to be known as the Commonwealth of Australia, a federation composed of the six original colonies, now to be known as States. It created the machinery of government, both legislative and executive, and imposed upon the new entity as well as the whole federation, a court system. The new Commonwealth was not given unlimited power, for it was never to replace the law-making function of the States. Those powers which were seen as appropriate to a central government were selected with much thought by the draftees and, after extensive debate,[2] included. There were two

1 For a detailed history of the drafting of the Constitution and problems associated with its acceptance in London, see JA La Nauze, *The Making of the Australian Constitution*, Melbourne UP, 1972.

2 The debates of the various Australasian conferences were originally printed but were rare until reprinted in 1986 by Legal Books, Sydney. In five volumes with a sixth volume containing commentary, indices and guide, they are now widely available in most law collections. The debates of the Grand Convention of 1787 which drafted the US Constitution are set out in M Farrand, *The Records of the Federal Convention of 1787*, reprinted by Yale UP, 1966, while Madison's Journal of the debates is contained in J Elliot, *The Debates of the several State Conventions on the adoption of the Federal Constitution in 1787*, 2nd ed, reprinted by Franklin, 1965.

models we could utilise: the United States Constitution drafted in Philadelphia in 1787, and the Canadian Constitution, an Act of the Imperial Parliament then known as the *British North America Act 1867*.

The Canadian Constitution had been drafted at a time when there was some fear of the future intentions of the United States. To many there was a real fear of invasion. The way that the various powers were shared between the new Dominion Parliament and the provinces reflect this fact. All power went to the central government, with only those specific areas relevant to day-to-day living, being granted to the provinces. In the Constitution of the United States, the situation was reversed. Specific powers were allocated to the central government while the States kept the residual powers. In this respect the American model was chosen as more appropriate by the Australian colonial leaders who were conscious of the continued existence of the States after federation, but they were reluctant to abandon the existing form of executive government in the various colonies for the American presidential system. Therefore, following the lead of Canada, they retained the form known as cabinet or the Westminster system. While the Australian Constitution thus bears a remarkable resemblance to the US model in structure[3] and legislative division, the actual way the Parliament functions is much closer to the Canadian model.

Hence for the power of the Australian Government to enact a law, there must be, in s 51 of the Constitution, the specific power given. These are sometimes called the heads of (legislative) power. Always be aware that there is the possibility of confusion in terminology. Power is shared between the Commonwealth and the States – this is called the division of power. The Commonwealth has three specific types of power: legislative power, executive power and judicial power. There are some constraints to make sure that these are kept separate – this is called the separation of powers. The terms mean quite different things in constitutional law.

Returning to the heads of power, once a legislative power can be found to support Commonwealth legislative power, the Commonwealth can make laws with respect to that head of power. Once it does so, such laws will be superior to State law if there is any inconsistency between the two laws. This is because the Commonwealth has not been given

3 This has been a very important fact for the High Court in interpreting the Australian Constitution. Because of the way the three arms of government have been isolated following the US Constitution, so the High Court has implied into Australian constitutional law a number of American constitutional concepts, the most important being the strict separation of the judicial power from the executive and legislative powers. This has had a profound effect upon the way the Commonwealth can legislate, particularly in important areas like arbitration and conciliation.

exclusive power under s 51 to make laws upon these subjects, merely concurrent power with the States. Until the Commonwealth makes a law any State law is perfectly valid. There is, in s 52 of the Constitution, a number of areas where the Commonwealth has been given exclusive power, just as there are some provisions scattered throughout the Constitution where the States and both Commonwealth and States have been denied the right to make certain laws. The examination and understanding of these provisions is done in the study of constitutional law, but at least an elementary grasp is needed to understand why a researcher may need to go to both Commonwealth and State law to solve a legal problem.

The effect of federation on Australia as a colony

In 1901, as has been noted, the six colonies were federated into a new Commonwealth of Australia. Was the new entity a colony? Although the question is not totally free from doubt, the answer does seem to be clear that it was. In the drafting of the Constitution, the Australians representing the various colonies were not drafting a document of independence. There is nothing in their debates that indicates they were considering severing the colonial links with Britain. Nor was Britain giving independence. There is nothing in the debates in Parliament at the time of enactment which indicates this. In fact the changes made indicate a desire to strengthen Imperial ties. Notwithstanding the argument that by giving certain powers, for example, external affairs within s 51, the new entity was effectively being allowed by the Imperial Parliament to exercise a role which is inconsistent with that of dominion status, there was no attempt at all by the Australian authorities until the late 1930s to exercise such a power. And that was long after recognition by Britain, in the *Statute of Westminster 1931*, that the Empire was effectively at an end, particularly for the principal entities of Canada, Australia and New Zealand.

The *Statute of Westminster 1931* applied only to the "Dominions", which, as defined, excluded the Australian States. This limitation of the Statute was to cause later problems for the States in severing their legislative ties with Britain and in it providing sovereign law-making power for them. This problem was finally overcome in 1985 and 1986 when the Commonwealth and States passed a number of Acts which allowed two things to happen. First, with all the States requesting, the Commonwealth was allowed under s 51(xxxviii) of the Australian Constitution to enact legislation which would have the effect of severing the final colonial links with Britain. Secondly, and to ensure this was finally and legally correct, Australia also requested Britain to enact legislation in the exact terms. There was no trouble here, for Britain had for many years made it known that it was willing to do anything that we in Australia wanted in order to tidy up loose constitutional ends. It could do nothing, however, until we *requested* and *consented* to such legislation under the terms of the *Statute of Westminster*. With all these pieces of legislation in place, and all political sensibilities satisfied, in March of 1986 the two principal Acts came into force and the final colonial links with Britain were severed.

Thus, in considering what is the constitution of Australia, it is quite clear that the document known as the Australian Constitution is the focal point, but the *Statute of Westminster 1931* and the *Australia Acts 1986* (Cth) and (UK) are also relevant.

Court structure

The Australian court structure has, since federation, undergone quite extensive change. Initially the States inherited the legal system that had previously existed in each of the colonies. Thus in NSW the Supreme Court, created in 1823, was to continue at federation with no change at all to jurisdiction or structure. Appeals lay to the Privy Council, as they did from all colonial superior courts under Imperial legislation. All that resulted was that there was an additional right of appeal to the High Court of Australia. The same applied in the other States.

There was little need for a federal court structure immediately. Provision was made in the Constitution for a federal court, and in 1903 the High Court of Australia was established to exercise the power granted in its original jurisdiction. But in most other federal matters the Commonwealth took advantage of the Constitutional power which provided for the vesting of federal jurisdiction in the established State courts. There would be an appeal, in both federal matters as well as State matters, to the High Court in its appellate jurisdiction.

Originally there could also be a further appeal from the High Court in federal matters, but not *inter se* matters, as well as State matters from either the High Court or State supreme courts, to the Privy Council. These were abolished by Commonwealth legislation in 1968[4] in matters of federal and Territorial jurisdiction, in 1975[5] with respect to appeals from the High Court from State courts, and finally in 1986[6] with matters directly on appeal from State Supreme Courts.

In 1976, with an increasing case list in federal matters and in order to unify a disparate federal legal structure, the Federal Court of Australia

---

4 *Privy Council (Limitation of Appeals) Act 1968.*

5 *Privy Council (Appeals from the High Court) Act 1975.*

6 *Australia Act 1986,* necessarily in both Commonwealth and Britain.

was created. Many of the original jurisdictional matters previously vested in the High Court were transferred to it as well as other specialised matters in the areas of administrative law, industrial relations, trade practices and the like. Not included was the Family Court of Australia. In the *Family Law Act 1975*, this was separated and provided with a Full Court as the appellate court with a final right of appeal to the High Court in most States.

The State courts are different in each of the States although there is a degree of similarity. The structure of each of the court hierarchies is set out in Appendix 1 in C Cook and others, *Laying Down the Law*, 7th ed, LexisNexis Butterworths, 2008.

The common law and the question of reception of law

Part of the intellectual baggage of the original colonial settlers was the common law. This was a rule of the common law itself.[7] Problems arose in Australia because at the time of the initial establishment in NSW it was effectively a penal colony, and its status changed to that of "ordinary" colony only gradually. Part of this process included the establishment of more appropriate colonial court and law-making arrangements. To this end 4 Geo IV c96 was enacted in 1823 after the British Government received the Bigge Report.[8] By this Act, the Supreme Court of NSW was established together with the Legislative Council. Two years later, by letters patent, an Executive Council was also created. But the problem of the reception of the law of England was to continue to plague the colonial judges.

Finally, by 9 Geo IV c83, later to be given the short title of the *Australian Courts Act 1828*, the date of the coming into force of the Act, 25 July 1828, was to be taken as the date when English law, that is the common law and English legislation that was applicable to the conditions of the colony as at that time, was declared to be the law of the colony. The Act merely declared the date. The authority for the reception of the law was the common law itself.

This Act applied to NSW and the colony of Van Diemen's Land (later Tasmania) which were both then in existence. The colonies of Victoria

7 In *Mabo v Queensland (No 2)* (1992) 175 CLR 1, important aspects of this area of law have been re-examined by the High Court. The literature on the effect of the *Mabo* decision is now beginning to flow through.

8 The early documentation relating to the creation of NSW and the other Australian colonies is widely scattered. The relevant sources, and where they can be conveniently researched now in Australia, has been set out in Watt, "Sources and literature of Australian law – Pt II" [1985] *Lawasia* 1

and Queensland were then part of NSW and so their law also dates from this time. The other colonies came into existence in a more orthodox manner and the date is the date of their foundation. This has been regularised in both Western Australia by *Interpretation Act 1984* s 73, wherein the date is 1 June 1829 and in South Australia by *Acts Interpretation Act 1915* s 48, wherein the date is 28 December 1836.

There were always two problems associated with the reception of law. The first was associated with the determination of whether English legislation was applicable to the colony at that time. The second problem concerned rigidity of that legislation that was specifically to apply to the colonies *because they were* colonies of Britain.

Applicable English Legislation

Under the terms of declaring the laws and statutes of the realm that were to be applied to the colony, s 24 of the 1828 Act set out that the only law which should be applicable to the colony would be that which was suitable for the conditions of the colony *at that date*. Over time general rules were established by both the Privy Council and the High Court on the way this should be done. Because of the many cases that have examined the question,[9] books have been published that list the legislation which either the courts or authors have decided did apply to the various colonies.[10] As early as 1922, Sir Leo Cussen in Victoria examined those books and put forward a list which should be adopted in Victoria. His recommendations are embodied in the *Imperial Acts Application Act 1922*.

In NSW it was not until the government was forced to act with the public outcry over the decision of *Garrett v Overy*[11] that a report of the NSW Law Reform Commission was acted upon. Its report, LRC 4, has a detailed historic introduction and the text of the bill which was subsequently enacted as the *Imperial Acts Application Act 1969*. By that enactment, the English legislation which we inherited is either specifically set out as applying to New South Wales in its original form or,

9 The principal cases were set out by the Full Supreme Court of NSW in *Garrett v Overy* (1968) 69 SR (NSW) 281.

10 Three of the most important are A Oliver, *The Statutes Index*, 1874, containing a "Chronological table of statutes of the Imperial legislature (not specifically adopted by local Acts) which relate to the Colony of NSW, or affect the Colony ... also of those judicially decided or presumed to be in force in NSW", TP Webb, *Compendium of Imperial Laws and Statutes in force in Victoria*, Sweet & Maxwell, 1892 and HB Bignold, *Imperial Statutes in force in NSW*, LBC, 1913.

11 (1968) 69 SR (NSW) 281.

alternately, is incorporated into local Acts. A third list itemises that English legislation that is repealed. A residuary clause has the effect of repealing any other English Act not previously mentioned in the *Imperial Acts Application Act.*

See *Laying down the Law,* 7th ed, pp 397-398 for a list applicable to other Australian jurisdictions.

Paramount legislation

This legislation was to be treated differently from the legislation which generally applied in England at the reception date. The reasons for this lie in the terms of the *Colonial Laws Validity Act 1865*. Before this time it was commonly accepted that the local legislatures could amend that legislation that had become applicable to them by 9 Geo IV c 96. However, doubts were raised and after problems in South Australia the *Colonial Laws Validity Act 1865* was enacted. This Act provided for general amending of the applicable legislation, and validated such legislation. But s 2 of the 1865 Act did not validate, indeed made void, any local statute which was repugnant to a British statute which applied to the colony *by express words or necessary intendment*. The 1865 Act created the distinction between English general statutes and Imperial statutes. The former could be amended or repealed but the latter could not as it would be a local law repugnant to the Imperial will.

It was this 1865 Act that was at the centre of the concessions made by the British Parliament in the *Statute of Westminster 1931* for the Commonwealth and the *Australia Acts 1986* for the States.

Note: Many of the early problems associated with reception are discussed generally in A Castles, *An Australian Legal History*, LBC, 1982.

2. Legislation as a source of law

One of the outstanding features of modern life is that legislation, in its many forms, is there to restrict and control. Thus legislation, be it the Acts or the statutory rules made under the authority of those Acts, is of prime importance in legal researching. Whether we adopt the quantitative approach and examine any and every jurisdiction and note the expansion in the size of the new legislation and delegated legislation that is being produced every year, or the less visible and quantifiable governmental intervention in all aspects of our life, or the apparent reluctance on the part of the judiciary to settle new problems caused by technology and the like, the material that can be found in the statute books is increasingly important and its place must be understood. There are two problems that should be emphasised: the first is the place of the *Interpretation Acts* that set out rules associated with the interpretation of legislation. The second, is the types of problems that are going to be solved by legislation.

Act Interpretation Acts in each Australian Jurisdiction

Each Australian jurisdiction has an *Interpretation* (or *Legislation*) *Act* that facilitates the interpretation of the legislation in that jurisdiction.[12] While many Acts will contain interpretation sections that allow words and concepts frequently used in any particular Act to be defined for the use of the reader (these are usually grouped together in the early sections of the Act) there are many words that will always need to be interpreted in all acts in the same way or rules that will always apply in the interpretation of legislation. Rather than setting them all out in every Act, they have been gathered in one interpretation Act for that jurisdiction. This Act will always apply in the interpretation of legislation, unless specifically rejected in an Act.

Examples of use of Interpretation Acts

When does an Act come into force? The answer maybe in the Act. Thus, when the NSW Parliament enacted the legislation that changed the NSW Institute of Technology into the University of Technology, Sydney, s 2 of that Act stated: "This Act shall commence on 26 January 1988." The Act did not stipulate at what time of the day but the *Interpretation Act 1987* (NSW) s 24 states it to be at the commencement of that day. So, unless there was something to the contrary in some Act, that rule applies to all NSW legislation. There are similar provisions in other Australian Interpretation Acts.

Similarly, if the Act had not provided on which day the Act should come into force, there is a provision in all Australian Interpretation Acts which sets a time. In the Commonwealth, NSW, Victoria and Western Australia, it is 28 days after assent. In Tasmania, it is 14 days after assent and, in Queensland, South Australia and Northern Territory, it is on the day of assent. In the ACT, because assent is not necessary, it is when notified in the Territory *Gazette*.

In NSW, there has been an interesting shift away from the use of the *Interpretation Act*. Until recently, it was to the *Interpretation Act 1987* s 56 that

---

12 *Acts Interpretation Act 1901* (Cth); *Interpretation Act 1987* (NSW); *Interpretation of Legislation Act 1984* (Vic); *Acts Interpretation Act 1915* (SA); *Acts Interpretation Act 1954* (Qld); *Interpretation Act 1984* (WA); *Acts Interpretation Act 1931* (Tas); *Legislation Act 2001* (ACT) and *Interpretation Act 1978* (NT).

a researcher went to determine the amount of a penalty unit – a term which appears regularly in a great deal of NSW legislation. However, penalty unit is now defined in the *Crimes (Sentencing Procedure) Act 1999* s 17.

Legislation as the sole source of law

There are many areas of legal research that rely almost exclusively on legislation for their determination. There is no interaction with the common law and little recourse to the cases for guidance. These will mostly involve fines, penalties, procedures and general regulatory matters.

At another level of research, there is the codification of law. At the heart of the civil law, with its origins in the Roman law codification of Justinian, it has been found in modern times to be a useful way of unifying regional variations. Thus, in France at the beginning of the 1800s, and Germany at the end, we can find codification of their law. In the common law context there tends to be a basic rejection of such developments in favour of piecemeal and empirical development – although in Australia this is not completely the case. In the jurisdictions of Queensland, Western Australia, Northern Territory and Tasmania there has been codification of aspects of their criminal law. This does mean that the interpretation of that part of the law may vary, as the court determines whether to look at material in existence before the code was drafted. The Commonwealth *Criminal Code*, progressively applied to Commonwealth offences since 1997, was completed and finally applied to all Commonwealth offences from 15 December 2001.

Normally it will be a mixture of legislation and the common law that will determine a matter. In some problems the interaction will be slight. Thus, in the area of taxation there will be little room for substantive common law principles. But still, in the application of that law, there may well be interaction. This will be the case where it comes into contact with public law generally and administrative law specifically. In other areas, like contract and tort law, these are traditionally common law areas and the researcher will have to be very careful to ensure that the common law underpinnings of the subjects are understood, and also that legislative changes to these doctrines are located and the extent of their operation understood. In some areas, and one example that quickly comes to mind is contempt of court, a common law area has little legislative intervention and in order that researchers understand the concept, and the way it operates in practice, they will spend practically all their time reading the cases.

Such knowledge about these matters will only be acquired as researchers become more proficient in their knowledge of the law. But such knowledge alone does not necessarily make researching easier. For research to be effective and concise, legal knowledge must be combined with a sound knowledge of the researching tools available. This should always be kept in mind.

3. Principal Acts and amending Acts distinguished

When an Act is initially enacted by the Parliament it is a complete entity: it has a beginning, a middle and an end. It can stand alone and a reader will be able to observe the complete provision. It may well be part of a series of Acts which are needed, for constitutional purposes, to achieve a particular result, particularly in the area of taxation, but otherwise it is complete. This can be thought of as the "principal" Act[13] although at this stage it will not contain that reference within itself. Later, if a provision within that Act is to be altered there are theoretically two ways it can be done. The first method is for Parliament to enact another Act and make a new provision which conflicts with the original provision, either with or without reference to it. Even if no reference is made to the earlier Act, under the rules of statutory interpretation the later provision prevails. The second method is done the way that amendments are usually carried out in Australia. This is by specifically altering the initial Act. Usually with the word "amendment" somewhere in the title of the later Act, a later Act will identify the original Act as the "principal" Act and will proceed to identify the part that needs to be changed. It will usually then remove the section or part of it and substitute the new provisions. Recent changes in drafting practice have seen transitional arrangements also included in the principal Act which will be removed at a later stage when obsolete.

Time has been spent on this aspect for the simple reason that in searching for a legislative authority for an amended provision, many researchers confuse the effect of the amending Act and seek to attribute to it the authority for a particular provision. An example will make this clearer.

---

13 This is not a term of art but more a description. The NSW Parliamentary Counsel's Office describes them as "Acts of significance which have a lasting application and are considered for reprinting" *New South Wales Legislation in Force,* 1 January 1992, p 1. In more recent editions, this has been modified to those "Acts which would normally be expected to be accessed in an up-to-date form and which are regularly reprinted".

Example

The question arises as to the amount that the Governor-General is paid and the authority for that salary. Looking in the subject index a reference is found to the *Governor-General Act 1974*. If one goes to the annual volume of legislation for 1974, the salary provision is found in s 3:

3. The annual sum payable out of the Consolidated Revenue Fund for the salary of the Governor General shall be $30,000.

The salary was increased to $37,000 by the *Governor-General Amendment Act 1977*; to $70,000 by the *Governor-General Amendment Act 1982*; to $95,000 by the *Governor-General Amendment Act 1988*; reduced to $58,000 by the *Governor-General Amendment Act 1995*, increased to $310,000 by the *Governor-General Legislation Amendment Act 2001* and to $394,000 by the *Governor-General Amendment (Salary and Superannuation) Act 2008*. In each of these Acts, the authority for the payment is contained within the Schedule of the amending Act.

Thus looking at the latest Act, s 3 instructs that each "Act that is specified in a Schedule to this Act is amended or repealed as set out in the applicable items in the Schedule concerned". That Schedule then provides that in s 3 of the *Governor-General Act 1974* "Omit '$365,000', substitute '$394,000'".

Consequently – and because of the way the legislation is drafted – s 3 of the 2008 Act is the authority for the change to take place and s 3 of the 1974 Act is the authority for the Governor-General being paid this amount. When there is to be another change to salary in the future, s 3 of the 1974 Act will need to be altered again.

---

4. Finding legislation

(a) Where to begin: subject index or key word text searching?

The usual starting point for the finding of legislation is with a particular subject. The researcher would like to find all the legislation that pertains to that subject. From here, the traditional approach is to utilise one of the subject indexes that are available in many jurisdictions. The availability of the legislation in electronic form has changed much. And this is one area where even the experienced researcher must now rethink traditional research strategies. Can the researching task be simply solved by going to an appropriate database and seeking the location in it for a particular word? For example: what is the penalty for stowing away on a vessel? While "stowing away" failed to elicit the required answer, by searching "stowaway", there were three effective hits, and one to s 104 of the

Navigation Act 1912. However, if you wanted to know what was the monetary amount of a "penalty unit" found in practically all NSW Acts, it would be pointless searching merely on the words "penalty unit" because of the frequency that the words appear. Always remember that the subject index has been compiled by an expert and will provide many aids, for example *see* and *see also* references to facilitate searching. The subject index and key word text searching are not natural alternate approaches but rather their use will depend upon the type of researching task and the legal expertise of the researcher.

Available Subject Indexes

Electronic Subject Index for All Australian Jurisdictions: Lawlex

Lawlex is an electronic service which allows the searching of all Australian jurisdictions using designated subject headings. Consequently as all new principal legislation is received, it is indexed under those terms.

Note particularly how the service defines "principal legislation": "Principal legislation includes all new Bills, Regulations, Plans and By-laws that do not simply amend another statute, but themselves create legal rights or obligations."

(i) Commonwealth

For the Commonwealth, there is only one general index: *Wicks Subject Index to Commonwealth Legislation*. Unfortunately this publication is not comprehensive although this is by design: the compiler expects those using it to do so in conjunction with the index at the end of each reprint. In order to produce the index annually at a cheaper price, only broad subject headings are used to get a person to the relevant Act. Using general headings will get the researcher to the relevant Act in most cases but, because there is no index at the end of Commonwealth reprints, the researcher must use the *Table of Contents* at the beginning of each Act in order to find specific provisions quickly.

For very recent legislation one must use the legislative indexes which appear in each of the current awareness publications: the "Legislative Index" in the *Australian Legal Monthly Digest* (ALMD) and *Australian Current Law: Legislation*.

(ii) New South Wales

There are two indexes available for searching NSW legislation: Wicks Subject Index to the Acts and Regulations of New South Wales, located in

New South Wales Statutes Annotations and References (Lawbook Co), and the index found in *New South Wales Statutes Annotations* (Butterworths).

These are supplemented by the subject indexes of legislation for the current year in ALMD and *Australian Current Law: Legislation*.

The volumes 13, 14 and 15 of the now defunct *Red Statutes* (1824-1957) have retained some use. That index was remarkably comprehensive and still provides valuable information. If a library has that set, it should not discard those three volumes at least.

(iii) Victoria

Index to Subject Matter of Victorian Legislation is now produced annually by the Office of Chief Parliamentary Counsel. For recent legislation, the current awareness services can be used.

(iv) South Australia

A *Subject Index to South Australian Legislation* has been now produced online by the Australian Law Librarians' Association [ALLA] (South Australian Division) Inc. It can be found at: <*www.slsa.sa.gov.au/legislation_index*>. For recent legislation, the current awareness services can be used.

(v) Queensland

A broad subject index is included at the end of *Queensland Statutes Annotations* (Butterworths). For recent legislation, the current awareness services can be used.

(vi) Western Australia

Table 1 entitled "Index of Statutes" in volume 3 ("Index" of the *Statutes of Western Australia* (annual)) provides a starting point to find legislation in that jurisdiction by subject. For recent legislation, the current awareness services can be used.

(vii) Tasmania

There is a subject index in "Part 2: Subject Index to Tasmanian Statutes" in *Indexes to the Legislation of Tasmania* compiled in the Office of Parliamentary Counsel. For recent legislation, the current awareness services can be used.

(viii) Australian Capital Territory

While there is no general index to ACT legislation, the Australian Capital Territory Parliamentary Counsel's Office has available to be downloaded at least a subject index to the information found in *one* of the longer and more complex Acts: the *Legislation Act*. See *<www.pco.act.gov.au/pages/draftpubstand/la_index.htm>*. For recent legislation, the current awareness services can be used.

(ix) Northern Territory

There is no subject index for the Northern Territory. For recent legislation, the current awareness services can be used.

Example from *Halsbury's Laws of Australia*

[295-8265] Discharge registered by mistake In general, registration of the discharge of a mortgage[1] as a result of an error by the mortgagee has the effect of extinguishing the security.[2] Where the registration of a discharge of mortgage occurs as a result of an error by the Registrar-General, the register may be corrected pursuant to the Registrar-General's statutory power to amend the register.[3]

Notes

1. See [295-8250].
2. *State Bank of New South Wales v Berowra Waters Holdings Pty Ltd* (1986) 4 NSWLR 398; *Scallan v Registrar-General* (1988) 12 NSWLR 514. Compare *Elder's Trustee and Executor Co Ltd v Bagot's Executor and Trustee Co Ltd* [1964] SASR 306. In relation to the effect of the discharge on the personal covenant of the mortgagor see [295-8380]-[295-8400].
3. (ACT) Land Titles Act 1925 s 160
   (NT) Real Property Act 1886 (SA) s 220
   (NSW) Real Property Act 1900 s 12
   (QLD) Land Title Act 1994 s 15
   (SA) Real Property Act 1886 s 220
   (TAS) Land Titles Act 1980 s 163
   (VIC) Transfer of Land Act 1958 s 103
   (WA) Transfer of Land Act 1893 ss 180, 188(ii).
   See also *FNCB Waltons Finance Ltd v Crest Realty Pty Ltd* [1977] NSWLR 621.

(b) The comparative method of subject searching

Many practitioners with extensive and expensive collections of legal material which provide an Australian-wide view of legal topics fail to exploit that material adequately in their search for interstate material, while many will appreciate that the simple textbook on the subject will in many cases provide comprehensive footnotes to the specific legislative provisions. Thus, DE Fisher, *Water Law* (Lawbook, 2000) provides an excellent source of the many and varied aspects of water law from *all*

Australian jurisdictions. But there are other publications less used which can provide an even better service. There is always the current awareness services, as well as the legal encyclopaedia and encyclopaedias of forms and precedents.

5. The date of commencement of new legislation

The date of commencement of an Act is fundamental to the researching of all legislation. Even though an Act has been passed by the two chambers of Parliament[14] and has received assent, the legislation is not necessarily in force. It may state that it comes into force on the date of assent or at a date to be proclaimed or a date that depends upon another event, eg another Act coming into force, or there may be nothing indicated at all.

"Date of assent": This is a not uncommon practice and this phrase will be specifically mentioned in the legislation in those jurisdictions where legislation will bring the legislation into force at a different time, usually 28 days after the date of assent.

"At a date to be proclaimed": This is perhaps the most common practice and it allows the executive arm of government to prepare themselves for the new Act. This might entail, for example, getting personnel trained and accommodation allocated and stationery printed, so that on the day the Act comes into force all is in readiness. This could not have been done before enactment for no one would have been sure of the final form of the legislation.

> [The proclamation is made by the Governor or Governor-General and will be published in the *Government Gazette* of the relevant State or, if a Commonwealth Act, in the *Australian Government Gazette*.
>
> **Note**: until the substantive provisions of the Act have been so proclaimed, the Act has no force and is not law.]

If there is no such indication in the Act: In the Commonwealth, NSW, Victoria and Western Australia, by the operation of legislation[15] the Act comes into force 28 days after the date of assent. In Tasmania[16] it is 14 days after the assent, while in Queensland, South Australia and the Northern

---

14 Except in Queensland where there is only one chamber.

15 Cth: *Acts Interpretation Act 1901* s 5A; NSW: *Interpretation Act 1987* s 23(1); Victoria: *Interpretation of Legislation Act 1984* s 11; WA: *Interpretation Act 1984* s 20(2).

16 Tas: *Acts Interpretation Act 1931* s 9.

Territory[17] it is at the date of assent. In the ACT, with no assent, it is on the date of notification in the *Government Gazette*.[18]

6. Current awareness services

References to the current awareness services abound in any book about legal research. They provide the latest information in practically all areas. This is the case whether it be finding cases, articles, words and phrases, or, as in this section, the latest Act. In Australia we are particularly well served by the legal publishers. There are two commercially produced publications which provide information on recent developments in legislation, cases decided pursuant to legislation, and bills introduced into the chambers, for the Commonwealth and all the States and Territories.

The ***Australian Legal Monthly Digest*** (ALMD) (Lawbook Co) is issued monthly and forms part of the Australian Digest Service. While each monthly issue contains brief numbered paragraphs dealing with new cases, legislation and books on each of the subject topics, a second issue is provided containing a series of cumulating tables. This includes lists of new Acts, recent cases and subject indexes and makes the ALMD easy to use and a valuable tool in updating the law. In updating legislation, see the "Alphabetical Table of Acts Passed, Amended, Repealed, or Proclaimed to Commence". This table sets out legislation that has been amended, repealed or proclaimed during that particular year and further identifies, section by section, the legislation so affected in that year. A companion service is the *ALMD Advance*, a fortnightly service which provides a precis of major cases and legislative development.

Electronic: Online access to the *Australian Legal Monthly Digest* is part of Lawbook Co's *FirstPoint*.

The references are to sections in the body of the ALMD which provide a digest of the particular changes.

Australian Current Law (LexisNexis Butterworths) from 1991 has been published in 2 parts: the *Reporter*, published fortnightly and dealing with superior court decisions of Australian federal and State courts, and *Legislation*, providing details of federal, State and Territory legislation, and published monthly. It is issued in booklet form and filed in a

17 Qld: *Acts Interpretation Act 1954* s 15A; SA: *Acts Interpretation Act 1915* s 7; NT: *Interpretations Act* s 6(1).

18 ACT: *Australian Capital Territory (Self-Government) Act 1988* (Cth) s 25(2).

An example from the Australian Legal Monthly Digest

ALPHABETICAL TABLE OF ACTS PASSED, AMENDED, REPEALED OR PROCLAIMED TO COMMENCE

The **Alphabetical Table of Acts Passed, Amended, Repealed or Proclaimed to Commence** enables you to locate, in the current year's ALMD, Acts of the Commonwealth, State and Territory Parliaments which have been passed, amended, repealed or proclaimed to commence. Reference is given to the paragraph numbers where the Acts have been summarised (Supply, Appropriation and Private Acts are not summarised).

For Acts noted in a previous year's ALMD, refer to the **Alphabetical Table of Acts Passed, Amended, Repealed or Proclaimed to Commence**, contained in the January-December Cumulative Tables booklet for that year.

Step 1: Select the appropriate jurisdiction and search for the Act alphabetically. Entries in *italics* refer to Acts first noted in the current year's ALMD.

Step 2: Note the paragraph number(s) listed next to the Act name. Refer to this paragraph number(s) in the relevant Digest of Law booklet(s). Where no paragraph number is listed, the Act is yet to be summarised in the ALMD.

Australian Capital Territory

ACTEW/AGL Partnership Facilitation Act 2000 am by Act No 56/2003 §**2347**

Administration & Probate Act 1929 am by Act No 1/2004 §**2169**, Act No 2/2004 §**2126**

Administration (Interstate Agmnts) Act 1997 am by Act No 56/2003 §**2347**, Act No 58/2003 §**2099**

Adoption Act 1993 am by Act No 1/2004 §**2169**

Annual Reports (Govt Agencies) Act 1995 am by Act No 5/2004 §**2016**

Annual Reports (Govt Agencies) Act 2004 (No 8)

Annual Reports Legn Amdt 2004 (No 9)

Artificial Conception Act 1985 am by Act No 56/2003 §**2347**; rep by Act No 1/2004 §**2169**

Australian Capital Territory — *cont*

Children & Young People Act 1999 am by Act No 56/2003 §**2347**

Commercial Arbitrn Act 1986 am by Act No 48/2003 §**2162**

Confiscation of Criminal Assets Act 2003 am by Act No 48/2003 §**2162**, Act No 56/2003 §**2347**

Construction Occupations Legn Amdt Act 2004 (No 13)

Construction Occupations (Licensing) Act 2004 (No 12)

Cooperatives Act 2002 am by Act No 47/2003 §**2345**

Coroners Act 1997 am by Act No 48/2003 §**2162**

Court Security Act 2001 am by Act No 48/2003

ring-binder. The various cumulative indexes and tables are replaced each month. These tables are then republished annually. A companion service is LexisNexis AU Legal Express, a daily electronic update of legal news including case law and legislation.

The "Cumulative Table of Acts Passed" and the "Cumulative Table of Amended Acts" in *Australian Current Law: Legislation* provides a table of legislation passed, and amended, by the Commonwealth, State and Territorial legislatures during that year. Additional Tables show reprinted

An example from the Australian Current Law: Legislation

Cumulative Table of Amended Acts

This table includes Acts amended since 5 December 2003

	Iss	*Subj*
Commonwealth		
A New Tax System (Family Assistance) Act 1999	JAN —	405
A New Tax System (Family Assistance) (Administration) Act 1999	JAN —	405
A New Tax System (Family Assistance) (Administration) Act 1999	FEB —	405
A New Tax System (Wine Equalisation Tax) Act 1999	JAN —	405
Aboriginal and Torres Strait Islander Commission Act 1989	JAN —	5
Aboriginal Land Grant (Jervis Bay Territory) Act 1986	JAN —	5
Acts Interpretation Act 1901	JAN —	385
Air Force Act 1923	JAN —	150
Air Navigation Act 1920	JAN —	35
Air Services Act 1995	JAN —	35
Airports Act 1996	JAN —	35
Amendments Incorporation Act 1905		
Commonwealth Electoral Act 1918	JAN —	345
Commonwealth Services Delivery Agency Act 1997	JAN —	345
Comprehensive Nuclear Test-Ban Treaty Act 1998	JAN —	215
Copyright Act 1968	JAN —	240
Corporations Act 2001	JAN —	120
Corporations (Repeals, Consequentials and Transitionals) Act 2001	JAN —	120
Criminal Code Act 1995	JAN —	130
Customs Act 1901	JAN —	405
Customs Legislation Amendment Act (No 1) 2002	JAN —	405
Customs Legislation Amendment and Repeal (International Trade Modernisation) Act 2001	JAN —	405
Defence Act 1903	JAN —	150
Defence Force Discipline Act 1982	JAN —	150
Defence Force (Home Loans Assistance) Act 1990	JAN —	150

Acts, Regulations made, reprinted and amended, miscellaneous Orders and Notices and parliamentary bills for the same jurisdictions.

Australian Current Law is also available online.

7. The legislation of the Commonwealth of Australia

Until relatively recently the legislation of the Commonwealth of Australia developed as most other jurisdictions. It was produced as principal Acts which, in turn, were amended by Acts enacted by the Parliament for that specific purpose. To keep track of relevant and current legislation, these principal Acts were periodically incorporated into major sets – arranged alphabetically. This was done most recently in 1973. The *Acts of the Commonwealth Parliament 1901-1973* were published in 12 volumes.

Reprints

Because this was a messy way of keeping legislation up to date – there always being a need for supplementary volumes – in the 1970s and 1980s most Australian jurisdictions began to keep their legislation in what is known as *reprint* form. Accepting that some Acts were amended more than others, as amendments were made to these so they were formally incorporated into the principal Act and reprinted for sale and distribution to libraries.

But even these Acts would get out of date and so, in the case of Commonwealth Acts, the major legal publishers in their annual – *Commonwealth Statutes Annotated* (Lawbook Co) and *Federal Statutes Annotated* (LexisNexis Butterworths) – provided amendments since the last reprint. And when used in conjunction with the current awareness publications – ALMD and *Australian Current Law* – a researcher could keep track of Commonwealth legislation.

However, while still the principal way of finding legislation in paper, it is an extremely cumbersome method with the advent of the personal computer and the internet. Now there is no question that in finding the very latest legislation on any topic, there can be no reason for bypassing the electronic copy of Acts which are freely available on the internet for all Australian jurisdictions.

ComLaw

The Attorney-General's Department ComLaw *<www.comlaw.gov.au>* site comprises Commonwealth Acts and the Federal Register of Legislative Instruments (FRLI). The FRLI includes regulations and other instruments. While the Acts published on the ComLaw site are not regarded as the official publication the online FRLI is the official publication of that legislation (see "Proposal for Authorised Electronic Versions of Commonwealth Acts" Attorney General's Department, Civil Justice Division, December 2005 for discussion).

ComLaw provides point in time consolidations of Acts and Regulations from 1 January 2005 downloadable in a variety of formats including HTML, PDF, RTF and Word 97-2003. Prior to 2005 consolidations are available, however, they are downloadable only in text format and are sourced from the original ScalePlus service. There are no point in time consolidations prior to 1973 and not all consolidations between 1973 and 2005 are available. In ComLaw, legislation is displayed with tabs that link to supporting material such as explanatory memoranda, explanatory instruments, amended acts or enabling legislation where relevant.

ComLaw's significance lies in it being a source for official publication of FRLIs. It has been proposed that ComLaw Acts also be authoritative *<www.ag.gov.au/www/agd/.../Authorised_electronic_versions_of_Acts_public_consultation_paper_December_2006final.doc>*. The Evidence Amendment Bill 2008 includes provisions to effect this change (see Sch 3 Pt 3 cl 5(1)).

8. The legislation of the States

(a) New South Wales

The Legislative Council was established in New South Wales in 1824, and a bicameral Parliament in 1856. The legislation of New South Wales from 1824 has been published in a number of different series. Since 1920 the annual volumes of the *Statutes of New South Wales* have been published by the Government Printer.

Several incorporations of New South Wales legislation have been published. These save time in finding an Act and tracing any later amendments to it. An incorporation contains the legislation passed up to the cut-off date, with all amendments affecting that legislation incorporated into the original legislation. The two best known are the "Green Statutes, 1824-1937" and the "Red Statutes, 1824-1957". The current method, informally adopted in the late 1970s, uses the reprint method.

Reprints

Under the *Acts Reprinting Act 1972*, when an Act is reprinted it incorporates all amendments that have been made to it. Since the late 1970s, there has been an active reprinting programme which means that now most of the principal Acts, which are still in force, have been reprinted. The more recent principal Acts will not be reprinted until required by demand or until sufficient amendments make it viable.

Although they can be arranged by date, it is more usual to find a full set of reprints arranged alphabetically by the short title of the Act. The date of its reprinting is well publicised on the front of the Act and it is from this date that the Act needs to be updated.

Up-Dating the Reprint

(a) *The reprints are kept up to date by periodically reprinting*. The specific date will be governed by such factors as the demand by the public and quantity of amendments that need to be included. Little used Acts can go for years before being reprinted.

(b) The next step is to consult *New South Wales Legislation in Force,* compiled by the Parliamentary Counsel's Office and issued quarterly. In the first part is an alphabetical list of NSW Public Acts currently in force. Those that are "principal" Acts are shown in bold, together with the date of the last update sheet and any subsequent amendments. The other Acts listed here are "amending" Acts which, having served their purpose, are awaiting repeal to get them out of such a list of current legislation. This is available in paper or can be downloaded free of charge from <*www.legislation.nsw.gov.au*>.

Example of a reprinted Act

Reprinted as at 16 December 2003

New South Wales

Commission for Children and Young People Act 1998 No 146

Contents

(c) Also available from the Parliamentary Counsel's Office are monthly and weekly tables about Acts and delegated legislation which provide a variety of information relating to the making, amending, repealing and reprinting of Acts, regulations and the publication of associated proclamations. These are available in paper or can be downloaded free of charge from <*www.legislation.nsw.gov.au*>.

(d) The final step is the current awareness services: either the *Australian Legal Monthly Digest* or *Australian Current Law: Legislation.*

NSW Legislation in Force (compiled by the NSW Parliamentary Counsel's Office, quarterly)

While important in keeping reprints up to date, its other contents make it indispensable to the researcher. As the successor to *Alphabetical and Chronological Tables of the New South Wales Statutes 1824-1969*, and supplements (1970-1981, 1982-1985), its Public Acts and Acts repealed tables allow past Acts to be located and tracked to see current status.

It also identifies laws of other jurisdictions (usually Commonwealth) that are treated as NSW laws and those NSW Acts (or parts of Acts) not as yet proclaimed to commence.

Example from *NSW Legislation in Force*

Public Acts

Act | **Reprint**

Anti-Discrimination 1977 No 48◊ — 20.3.2001
Attorney General, Premier (Pt 9A)
Uncommenced ams included in current reprint (see Uncommenced amendments on p 158: 1997 No 77 (Sch 2.1 [3] and so much of Sch 2.1[5] as omits secs 97, 98. 100, 101A 109 and 112); 1998 No 11 (Sch 6.1 [1]).
Am 2001 Nos 34, 121; 2002 No 6; 2003 No 17

Antiochian Orthodox Church Property Trust 1993 No 20◊ — —
Attorney General
Anzac Memorial (Building) 1923 No 27◊
Premier
Am 1934 No 32; 1959 No 32; 1984 No 113; 1987 No 48; 1991 No 94; 1999 Nos 31, 44; 200 No 93; 2001 No 121; 2003 No 40

Apiaries 1985 No 16◊ — 16.9.1991
Minister for Agriculture and Fisheries
Am 1992 No 112; 1997 No 77; 1998 No 116; GG No 4, 8.1.1999, p 32 (10); 2001 No 121; GG No 93, 19.7.2002, p 5475 (561)
Am 1998 No 169; 1999 Nos 31, 85

Application of Laws (Coastal Sea) 1980 No 146◊ — 29.5.2001
Attorney General

Apprenticeship and Traineeship 2001 No 80◊ — 2.3.2004
Minister for Education and Training
Uncommenced ams included in current reprint (see Uncommenced amendments on p 65): 2002 No 103 (Sch 4.3).

Appropriation 2003 No 31◊
Appropriation (Budget Variations) 2003 No 2◊
Appropriation (Health Super-Fund Growth) 2003 No 75◊
Treasurer
Appropriation (Parliament) 2003 No 32◊
Appropriation (Special Offices) 2003 No 33◊

Electronic form

Online: There are two sites for NSW legislation online. The first source is the official *Government of New South Wales Legislation* homepage at <*www.legislation.nsw.gov.au*>. Maintained by the Parliamentary Counsel's Office since June 2002, this site does include consolidated legislation – both Acts and statutory instruments, but also historic versions of legislation and an archival collection of NSW (sessional) legislation as made since 1990. This also has good searching and browsing facilities. The second site is AustLII where, with the SINO search engine, searching is relatively easy. While consolidations are provided alphabetically, unfortunately there are no numbered (sessional) collections here. Care must be taken that the electronic source being accessed is current.

Commercially, NSW legislation is available on LexisNexis AU and TimeBase, the latter also including historic details of amendments and commencement dates. It is updated weekly.

(b) Victoria

Form of Legislation: In 1958, all Victorian legislation was brought together and consolidated. This is the only true consolidation that has been carried out covering all the law of an Australian jurisdiction. Mostly the name "consolidation" is given to the reprinting of all legislation at a particular time. While such a set does incorporate all the amendments, there is no parliamentary input at this time. Currently Victorian legislation is published in pamphlet form and annual volumes and is periodically reprinted. Pursuant to s 9 of the *Interpretation of Legislation Act 1984*, as amended in 1985 and effective from 1 January 1986, Victorian Acts are now numbered sequentially according to the year they were enacted.

Tables of Acts: A *Cumulative Acts Tables* (annual) provides various tables:

- alphabetical table of Acts,
- unrepealed principal public Acts, and
- chronological table of Acts.

This is supplemented by Monthly Acts Tables and Unrepealed Principal Public Acts Table (twice a year).

Electronic form

Online: There are two sites for Victorian legislation online. The first is *Victorian Legislation and Parliamentary Documents* homepage <*www.dms.dpc.vic.gov.au*>. This site contains the *Victorian Statute Book* with sessional Acts since 1996, *Victorian Law Today* with consolidated Acts and *Parliamentary Documents*, with current Bills. The second site is AustLII, where, with the SINO search engine, searching is relatively easy. Again, consolidations since 1996 are set out alphabetically but with no sessional Acts provided. Care must be taken that the electronic source being accessed is current.

(c) South Australia

Form of Legislation: There has been a recent reprint of South Australian legislation: *South Australian Statutes 1837-1975*, in 13 volumes. Volumes 12 and 13 are subject index volumes. Otherwise, South Australian Acts are printed in pamphlet form and annual volumes and are periodically reprinted.

Table of Acts: After a number of years when the annual volume of South Australian legislation contained a *Table of Acts*, recently the Attorney-General's Department published a separate index volume: *Index of South Australian Legislation*.

In one alphabetical sequence, this index contains all South Australian Acts that are in force as at 31 December 20XX, or have been repealed or have expired since 31 December 1975. (For information before that date see the 1975 consolidation of *South Australian Statutes*.) Also included are the dates the Acts came into force; amendment information since 1975; regulations made under the Acts and relevant case annotations.

Update: Use *South Australian Legislation Update*, a fortnightly, cumulative publication.

Electronic form

Online: The legislation of South Australia is available at <*www.legislation.sa.gov.au*>, being a site maintained by the State's Parliamentary Counsel. The site includes Acts, Regulations and Bills.

Of special interest is the Acts list, because not only is set out alphabetically all of the principal Acts, but included also are recent *point-in-time* copies of these Act. Thus, with the *Adoption Act 1988*, one can find the current Act incorporating the amendments to the Act made by the *Justice of the Peace Act 2005*, while also available separately is the principal Act prior to those amendments but including the amendments inserted by the *Adoption (Miscellaneous) Amendments Act 1996*. The original Act as enacted in 1988 is not available.

AustLII also maintains an alphabetical list of consolidated Acts and session Acts back to 2003.

(d) Queensland

After the extensive legislative alterations in 1992, the publication of Queensland legislation is not greatly altered. The Acts are initially published in pamphlet form and later in annual volumes. Also published annually are the *Explanatory Notes* associated with those Acts.

Update: After the extensive review of Queensland legislation in 1992, a number of new publications made an appearance.

- *Queensland Legislation Annotations*, from 1996 in 2 vols:
  "Current Legislation" (published every 6 months)
  "Repealed Legislation" (published annually)
- *Queensland Legislation Update*
  Pt 1: "Update to Queensland Legislation Annotations; Tables of Bills Introduced and Acts Assented To"
  Pt 2: "Table of Queensland Legislation Reprints"
  Pt 3: *Queensland Legislation Annotations* Weekly Updates
- *Queensland Legislation Reprints*

The Office of Parliamentary Counsel has prepared a *Queensland Legislative Guide* for distribution to show how they are most effectively used.

Annotations: Queensland Legislation Case Annotations, 1996 (1 vol) plus updates (Butterworths).

Electronic form

Online: Queensland legislation is electronically available on the internet from the Office of the Queensland Parliamentary Counsel at <*www.legislation.qld.gov.au*> in both reprinted (consolidated) and annual form.

While it also appears to be on the AustLII site. Care must be taken that the electronic source being accessed is current.

(e) Western Australia

***Form of* Legislation**: The legislation of Western Australia is produced in pamphlet form, later in bound volumes. In the 1960s, *The Reprinted Acts of the Parliament of Western Australia, 1939-1962* was published, in 22 volumes, but now the reprints appear periodically.

Tables of Acts: Vol 3 "Index" of the Statutes of Western Australia contains:

Table 1:	Acts in Force,
Table 2:	Acts of the Imperial Parliament adopted but unrepealed,
Table 3:	Repealed Acts, and
Table 4:	Subsidiary Legislation.

Electronic form

Online: Western Australian legislation is available electronically from the State Law Publisher. See <*www.slp.wa.gov.au/legislation/statutes.nsf/default.html*>. It is also available on AustLII. It is also on the commercial service TimeBase.

(f) Tasmania

Form of Legislation: Tasmanian legislation has been reprinted: *Tasmanian Statutes 1826-1959 (Reprints)*. As in other States, Tasmanian Acts are printed in pamphlet form and later (sometimes much later) in bound annual volumes. There are also reprints. Tasmanian reprints can be found in any one of three places: in consolidation, as appendices to the annual volumes or as part of the continuing Reprints of Statutes programme that commenced in 1978.

Table of Acts: Indexes to the Legislation of Tasmania 1996 (annual) contains:

Part 1: Alphabetical table of Tasmanian Acts 1826-1995
Part 2: Subject Index to Tasmanian Statutes
Part 3: Subject Index to Subordinate Legislation.

Electronic form

Online: The Tasmanian Legislation site provides the researcher with its legislation in consolidated form and since 1 February 1997, the enactments made each session.

Since that date it is also possible to view Acts in *point-of-time*. Indeed it was Tasmania that was first in Australia with this facility. The legislation of Tasmania is also available on AustLII. Care must be taken that the electronic source being accessed is current.

9. The legislation of the Territories

(a) Australian Capital Territory

Form of Legislation: The laws are produced in pamphlet form and then in bound, annual volumes. There was a reprint of the laws of the ACT: *Laws of the* Australian Capital Territory 1911-1959. Currently the laws are periodically reprinted.

Citation of ACT Laws: The *Self Government (Citation of Laws) Act 1989* altered the citation of most Ordinances, the name previously given to the laws made by the Legislative Assembly, so that after Self-Government day (11 May 1989) they could be cited as Acts. However there were some areas of law that were withheld from the new Legislative Assembly and these were to continue to be known as Ordinances. See s 34 and Schedule 3, *Australian Capital Territory (Self-Government) Act 1988* (Cth) and the *Reserve Laws (Interpretation) Ordinance 1989*.

Table of Acts: The AGPS-published *Laws of the Australian Capital Territory: tables 1911-1987* (1988) contains a valuable set of tables, arranged alphabetically and chronologically, of the ordinances in force as at 31 December 1987. This is kept up to date by *Laws of the Australian Capital Territory – Tables*, published annually by the ACT Govt Pr.

Electronic form

The *ACT Legislation Register* has now made available all consolidated Acts at <*www.legislation.act.gov.au*>.

(b) Northern Territory

Form of Legislation: Before the establishment of self government on 1 July 1978, the legislation for the Northern Territory, known as Ordinances, was made by the Commonwealth. With self government, and the establishment of a Legislative Assembly, the products of that Assembly are known as Acts. The ordinances have been reprinted: *Ordinances of the Northern Territory of Australia 1911-1960*. Since that date the ordinances and Acts have been produced in pamphlet form and in annual volumes.

Table of Acts: Within volume 1 of the annual volume of legislation, *Laws of the Northern Territory of Australia*, can be found two principal tables: "Alphabetical table of Ordinances and Acts of the Northern Territory of Australia (including Ordinances of the Territory of Northern Australia) made from 1 January 1911 to 31 December 20XX showing the_commencement date to be fixed by *Gazette* notice", and "Chronological table of Ordinances and Acts of the Northern Territory of Australia made from 1911 to 20XX inclusive". The latter table shows the present status and the history of legislation and is updated (twice yearly) by the *Northern Territory Index to Legislation*.

Electronic form

There are three tables – "Current Northern Territory Legislation" (consolidated Acts); "Northern Territory Legislation History" (historical consolidations) and "Register of Legislation" (Bills) – available on the *Hansard & Legislation page of the Northern Territory Government* website at: <*www.nt.gov.au/lant/hansard/hansard.shtm*>.

The legislation of the Northern Territory is also available on AustLII. Care must be taken that the electronic source being accessed is current.

(c) Non-governing Territories

The numbered ordinances/regulations and compiled ordinances/ regulations of Ashmore and Cartier Islands, Australian Antarctic Territory, Christmas Island, Cocos-Keeling Islands, Coral Sea Islands Territory, Heard Island and McDonald Islands and the Jervis Bay Territory are available on ScalePlus at <*http://scaleplus.law.gov.au*>.

10. The legislation of the United Kingdom[19]

Because of the Australian States' initial status as British colonies, searching United Kingdom legislation may be different from finding the current law of other jurisdictions with which we may, for example, trade. Many UK statutes have been influential in the development of our own legal and political institutions and provide a guide to the study of our own history. There have also been dramatic recent changes to the nature of the United Kingdom itself with the devolution of law making to a separate Scottish Parliament (laws enacted since 1999) and a Welsh Assembly (with power to enact subordinate legislation only, since 1999). In addition, after much internal strife, a negotiated settlement was reached, endorsed by a referendum, which created a new Northern Ireland Assembly in 1998. The Assembly was suspended from midnight on Monday, 14 October 2002. Elections to the Northern Ireland Assembly were held on 7 March 2007 and the Northern Ireland Assembly was restored on 8 May 2007.

---

19 "United Kingdom" means Great Britain and Northern Ireland (*Interpretation Act 1978* s 5, Sch 1) and "Great Britain" means England, Scotland and Wales (*Union with Scotland Act 1709* preamble, art 1 *Interpretation Act 1978* s 22(1), Sch 2 para 5(a)) For other material in this field see Woodman, "Legislation in Northern Ireland" (1988) 18 *Law Librarian* 46 and MacQueen, "Scots Law in its Historical Context" (1991) 22 *Law Librarian* 85.

In these various circumstances, there will be different publications consulted. Set out below is a range that should satisfy all researching needs.

Older Series

Statutes of the Realm

This series contains legislation from 1235-1713, with alphabetical and chronological indexes. It was compiled by the Records Commissioners in the early 19th century from over 61 separate private editions of early English legislation. It was granted 'authoritative' status in 1889 and now represents early English legislation. There is a valuable historic introduction in volume 1 which explains the sources in great detail.

Statutes at Large

This series covers the period 1217-1866, and as a private edition had a number of distinguished editors, including Hawkins and Ruffhead. From 1800 it was published by the Queen's Printer, later to become the HMSO.

Current Official Series: Public General Acts 1866+

These are published annually and are similar to our own annual or sessional volumes. They come out in loose parts and later a bound volume is published, the Acts arranged in chronological order.

Updating. The publication *Chronological Table of Statutes* is annual and it sets out all English and UK legislation, from 1235, and section by section indicates the current status. Another publication is *Index to Statutes in Force* which provides the information in subject heading form as to material in the official *Statutes in Force*, the official consolidation of UK legislation.

Current Private Series

Halsbury's Statutes of England and Wales 4th ed (Butterworths)

This is the series usually found in Australian libraries and is similar to our own incorporation of legislation for it has brought together all legislation currently in force. There is one considerable difference. While both the NSW and Australian incorporations are arranged alphabetically by short title, *Halsbury's Statutes* are arranged into major topic areas and all legislation currently in force will be found in one of these subject areas. For example, "Real Property" is in volume 37 and contains all relevant legislation on that topic.

Updating. Those volumes which have been substantially amended are periodically replaced. Thus, volume 37 of the fourth edition was recently reissued in 2003 and the 1998 reissue should be discarded. Legislation that has not yet been incorporated can be found in one of the volumes which make up the *Loose-leaf Current Statute Service*.

A bound Cumulative Supplement shows the effect of new legislation on already published material. This is kept up to date by the *Loose-leaf Noter-Up Service*.

A volume entitled *Is it in Force?*, published annually, is a guide to commencement dates of legislation passed since 1 January 1971.

Current Law Statutes Annotated (Sweet & Maxwell)

The current legislation is set out, together with relevant annotations. Because it is produced shortly after enactment, the annotations are limited to legislative cross-referencing and not to case annotations. However, those annotations are important in observing why the legislation was passed. Where it may be a codification of the common law, there is usually a helpful commentary. This will be invaluable if the Australian law is not yet codified. This is in a bound annual form with looseleaf binders for recent material.

Law Report Statutes

Part of the subscription to the *Law Reports* provides the *Law Report Statutes*. Because of this they are found in many Australian libraries. The only tables provided each year when they are bound are those which show the Acts arranged alphabetically and chronologically.

Electronic form

The United Kingdom Public General Acts, as enacted by the Parliament since 1988, together with a selection of Acts prior to this year, are available at <*www.opsi.gov.uk/acts.htm*>. These are not consolidated. The non-consolidated Acts are also available on BAILLI, organized chronologically and alphabetically.

In order to obtain a consolidated Act, it is necessary to access one of the commercial services. These include Justis.com; Legislation Direct; Westlaw UK and LexisNexis Butterworths.

For a comprehensive overview of aspects of UK legislative research, including electronic retrieval, see Stephen Young, *Researching Primary Legislation of the United Kingdom*, published 19 May 2003 as a LLRX Feature at </*www.llrx.com/features/uklegis.htm*>

The Interregnum

In historic research the period of the Interregnum, 1642-1660, is difficult to find because the legislation of the Commonwealth has been excised from the official series. The ordinances and Acts have been brought together in:

Acts and Ordinances of the Interregnum, 1642-1660, collected and edited by CH Firth and RS Rait, for the Statute Law Committee, reprinted by Professional Books, 1978, in 3 volumes.

Vol I: Ordinances of the Long Parliament from 5 March 1642 to 20 December 1648

Acts of the Long Parliament from 6 January 1649 to 30 January 1649

Vol II: Acts of the Long Parliament from 9 February 1649 to 8 April 1653

Acts of the Little Parliament from 27 July to 3 December 1653

The Instrument of Government

Ordinances and Orders of the Protector and Council from 24 December 1653 to 28 February 1655

Acts of the second Parliament of the Protectorate from 27 November 1656 to 26 June 1657

Acts of the restored Long Parliament from 11 May 1659 to 16 March 1660

Vol III: Introduction, chronological table and indices

Special features of United Kingdom legislation

1. Many Acts are referred to under popular names that may reflect their subject matter or may be connected with a particular person who may have been instrumental in getting it into the statute books. It can be very difficult to trace a piece of legislation if references are only to this popular title. Consequently it is handy to remember that Appendix A of *Craies on Statute Law* 7th ed, 1971, is headed "Some popular titles of Statutes" and there is set out many of these popular titles together with the short title or the official title.

2. *Halsbury's Laws of England,* 4th ed, reissued vol 53, also contains a comprehensive "Consolidated Table of Statutes and Statutory Instruments". Arranged alphabetically and chronologically this can be a valuable aid when tracing legislation when only the date and general subject matter is known.

3. In the citation of UK legislation, reference has been made to the official title of an Act as distinct from a short title. The citation of this legislation was further complicated by the fact that the official title, ie, the chapter and year of the Act, used to be a reference to the regnal session and chapter number. The regnal year is the year of the monarch's reign

and complications arose when there were overlaps between the Parliamentary year, the regnal year and the calendar year.

It is sufficient to draw attention to the fact that UK legislation would, before 1962, be couched in terms of regnal years, but since the *Acts of Parliament Numbering and Citation Act 1962*, the chapter number and calendar year are now the official title of an Act.

Before leaving legislative citation, remember the *Short Titles Act 1896*. This Act retrospectively authorised short titles to UK Acts then in existence which had not been given such a title at the time of enactment.

11. Interpretation of legislation – use of extrinsic aids

One of the major recent changes to the interpretation of legislation in most jurisdictions in Australia has been the use that can be made of matter found outside the Act itself.[20] This is known as extrinsic material.

Until these changes, the courts, and consequently researchers and practitioners, had to attempt to find the meaning of legislation utilising the principles of statutory interpretation that have been developed within the common law. Certainly since the mid-18th century, such aids have not been used in England. But there have always been great problems in the application of many of the common law principles. As one judge noted:

> The duty of the Courts is to ascertain and give effect to the will of Parliament as expressed in its enactments. In the performance of this duty the judges do not act as computers into which are fed the statutes and the rules for construction of statutes and from whom issue forth the mathematically correct answer. The interpretation of statutes is a craft as much as a science and the judges, as craftsmen, select and apply the appropriate rules as the tools of their trade. They are not legislators, but finishers, refiners and polishers of legislation which comes to them in a state requiring varying degrees of further processing.[21]

But the task of finishing, refining and polishing has involved a host of rules, often conflicting, which has caused a great deal of judicial dissatisfaction – particularly as the task of interpreting statutes is

20 The House of Lords in *Pepper v Hart* [1993] AC 593 re-examined the whole question of Parliamentary extrinsic aids and decided to allow their use if it were to assist in the interpretation of statutes. In many ways this will bring all jurisdictions into line, although the Commonwealth and those States which have legislated can possibly use a greater range of material than those jurisdictions (South Australia and Northern Territory) that have not.

21 Donaldson J in *Corocraft Ltd v Pan American Airways Inc* [1968] 3 WLR 714 at 732.

growing.[22] The situation was not helped in the 1970s when the High Court of Australia continually took a narrow view of the *Income Tax Assessment Act 1936*, notwithstanding Government attempts to legislate in a way that would outlaw contrived schemes aimed at avoiding taxation. In order to assist in the interpreting process, the Parliament enacted a number of amendments to the *Acts Interpretation Act 1901*. First of all, in 1981 s 15AA was inserted, which required the purpose or object underlying an Act to be taken into account. Later in 1983, after a Symposium on Statutory Interpretation made the recommendation, s 15AB was included. This provision allows the court to look at designated material not forming part of the Act which is capable of assisting in the ascertainment of the meaning of the provision of the Act, either to confirm that the meaning is the ordinary meaning conveyed by the text of the provision, or to determine the meaning if, in the opinion of the court, the provision is ambiguous or obscure, or the ordinary meaning is manifestly absurd or unreasonable (s 15AB(1)(a) and (b)).

Section 15AB(2) of the *Acts Interpretation Act 1901* then sets out a series of aids which can be looked at:

(a) *all matters* not forming part of the Act that are *set out in the document* containing the text of the Act as printed by the Government Printer;

> [This includes headings, titles, preambles and anything else not appearing in a section of the Act and which has traditionally not been examined. In Victoria, there are some exceptions to this.]

(b) any relevant *report of a Royal Commission, Law Reform Commission, committee of inquiry* or other similar body that was laid before either House of Parliament before the time when the provision was enacted;

> [Where a law reform body has been responsible for legislation which is before the parliament, it has usually been accompanied by a report. Traditionally the law reform report is constructed in such a way that identifies the problem, proceeds to examine how other jurisdictions may have resolved the problem, if any, indicates its own choice, with reasons, and finally drafts the legislation that embodies those ideas. The connection between the legislation and the report is clearly evident. Royal Commissions and other types of commissions work in much the same way, with the exception in many cases of the drafting of the legislation. However, where the recommendations of the report are adopted, it can be assumed that the ideas within the report will be embodied in the recommendations, and consequently in the legislation.]

---

22 In the Report on the Interpretation of Statutes, a 1969 report of the Law Commission and Scottish Law Commission (Law Com No 21; Scot Law Com No 11), footnote 2 (p 3) indicates the growing problem in English courts with statistics back to an arbitrary base year of 1905. There is certainly no reason for believing the situation is different in Australia.

(c) any relevant *report of a committee of the Parliament* or of either House of Parliament that was made to the Parliament or that House of the Parliament before the time when the provision was enacted;

[For much the same reason as (b).]

(d) any *treaty* or other international agreement that is referred to in the Act;

[Traditionally the treaty has been examined for constitutional purposes but not for interpretation purposes. Where the Government has organised for legislation to be enacted to ratify international obligations under a treaty, it would be constitutionally required that the legislation be in reasonable conformity with the treaty and consequently the treaty should be able to be examined.]

(e) any *explanatory memorandum* relating to the Bill containing the provision, or any other relevant document, that was laid before, or furnished to the members of either House of the Parliament by a Minister before the time when the provision was enacted;

[This is one of the most valuable of the extrinsic aids because of the use that is now being made of it in most Australian jurisdictions. It started in the Commonwealth, principally with taxation legislation in the 1970s. Its use was to allow those parliamentarians the opportunity of explanation at the time of enactment. It was particularly useful to non-legal parliamentarians. In the early 1980s the Government noted the use that could be made of the EM by the courts in the interpretation of legislation, particularly where the search for exactness by the draftees led to complexities in language. Since this change to legislation, which allows the courts to look at the EMs, they have become an increasingly valuable aid to legal research, for there is much that can be found within the EM that provides a much clearer picture of the legislative intent. By the use of examples found within the EM, the intention of the parliament becomes much clearer in many instances. A recent alteration to the NSW Act provides for an *Explanatory Note* to be provided by *any member* introducing a Bill.

It must be remembered that the EM only refers to the Bill that is introduced into the house. It could well change and be entirely different from the final product – the Act. If there are many changes to a bill, it sometimes occurs that the government organises a supplementary EM that reflects the (altered) bill after the changes made in another chamber.

Another aspect is that the EMs are now being published in looseleaf services and they are part of the legislative histories that are being collected for use retrospectively.]

(f) the *speech made to a House of the Parliament* by a Minister on the occasion of the moving by that Minister of a motion that the Bill containing the provision be read a *second* time in that House;

[Again the speech made by the Minister who introduces the legislation into the chamber, and found in Hansard, will usually contain valuable information about the problems to be solved by the legislation and other background material that can be most useful in determining the meaning of the legislation. Because the minister has the responsibility for the drafting, it can be reasonably assumed that the legislation reflects her views as to what it meant to achieve. As above, the NSW Act now allows the second reading speech by *any member* proposing legislation to be examined.

Since the inclusion of this term, the date of the second reading speech now appears in the Act, usually near the end. The date also appears in many lists associated with legislation. How to find this material is set out on pp 64-65.]

(g) any *document* (whether or not a document to which a preceding paragraph applies) that is *declared by the Act to be a relevant document* for the purposes of this section; and

[If an Act refers to another document, it is clear that it should also be taken into account.]

(h) any *relevant material* in the *Journals* of the Senate, in the *Votes and Proceedings* of the House of Representatives or in any *official record of debates* in the Parliament or either House of the Parliament.

[Speeches made by any parliamentarian are allowed to be looked at but it must always be remembered that they do appear at the end of this list and after the ministerial second reading speech, and they must be carefully used. It cannot necessarily be assumed that because a parliamentarian voted for a particular provision that the provision actually means what he believes it to mean. Every other parliamentarian might well have had an opposite point of view.]

A number of points should be noted:

First, this is a hierarchical list and the researchers would go initially to the material set out in paragraph (a) before proceeding down the list.

Secondly, note that the material being examined is that material that was available and notionally before the House when the provision was enacted. It is thus assumed to have been known to the parliamentarians at the time of enactment and in a manner accepted by them.

Thirdly, from the Attorney-General's statement made in the House of Representatives at the time of the Second Reading Statement, and from the opening words of sub-s (2), this is not an exclusive list ("non-exhaustive"). However, any other items probably should have the same quality as being before the Chambers, or at least able to have been examined, at the time of enactment.

Finally, the provisions allow this extrinsic material to be used to examine all legislation that has ever been enacted. That is to say that the effects are retrospective and not merely prospective.

Extrinsic material and the States and Territories

Provision has been made for the use of select extrinsic material in the interpretation of the legislation of Western Australia (*Interpretation Act 1984* s 19); the Australian Capital Territory (*Legislation Act 2001* s 142); New South Wales (*Interpretation Act 1987* s 34); Queensland (*Acts*

Interpretation Act 1954 s 14B) and Tasmania (*Acts Interpretation Act 1931* s 8B) in terms practically identical to that of the Commonwealth, while the Victorian legislation (*Interpretation of Legislation Act 1984* s 35) is similar.

The common law applies to the use of extrinsic material in South Australia and the Northern Territory.

12. Legislative histories

The changes to the *Acts Interpretation Act* (Cth) by the inclusion of s 15AB has meant that there is now a whole new field of legal publications. Already in the areas of taxation, the major publishers have included the provisions of explanatory memoranda and Second Reading speeches in the looseleaf taxation services, but more recently Butterworths have published *Taxation Laws of Australia,* a comprehensive collection of available s 15AB extrinsic material relating to the *Income Tax Assessment Act 1936*. Commencing with the *Income Tax Assessment Act 1915* and including some other Acts before the 1936 enactment of the principal Act, all Acts which have amended that Act have been gathered together with the relevant extrinsic material. Researchers now need not search in the larger library holdings for material of years ago but can find it in one place.

If the United States is any guide, there will be an increasing array of such publications.[23] The US Supreme Court from the very early days after Federation did not hesitate to utilise such aids in interpretation, and while in the late 19th, early 20th century, this practice declined, since the 1940s it has been as strong as ever. To facilitate these enquiries such material has been made available for the court and profession. All the official documentation on major pieces of legislation which could be of assistance to understand the problem and the attitude of the legislators in solving that problem are published routinely.

---

23 For an excellent study on the history and use of such material, see Gwendolyn B Folsom, *Legislative History: research for the interpretation of laws,* University Press of Virginia, 1972, reprinted Rothman, 1979.

Finding Second Reading Speeches[24]

The need to be able to locate second reading material should not be underestimated. Contained within the official reports of the parliament, usually referred to as *Hansard*, the Second Reading Speech allows the researcher to find the original intention behind the legislation, including references to reports of commissions of inquiry and law reform agencies as well as cases that may have criticised the existing law. Indeed, in all Australian jurisdictions except South Australia, *Hansards* are formally recognised as an extrinsic aid that can be used in the interpretation of legislation.

But while *Hansard* could be found in most of the larger libraries for the local parliament, and even the parliaments of other jurisdictions, recent inclusion of that material on the Internet has caused many libraries to cancel subscriptions. Researchers are now, at least in some of the university collections, left very much on their own in finding this information. Below are some useful Internet sources:

Commonwealth of Australia

Parliament of Australia, including the Senate and House of Representatives, from 1996: <*www.aph.gov.au/hansard*>

New South Wales

Hansard is comprehensively available from 1984, together with search facilities, at <*www.parliament.nsw.gov.au/prod/web/common.nsf/V3HHBHome*>

Queensland

Queensland Parliament (consisting of the Legislative Assembly), since 1990: <*www.parliament.qld.gov.au/hansard/index.htm*>

South Australia

South Australian Parliament, including the Legislative Council and House of Assembly, from 1993: <*www.parliament.sa.gov.au/Hansard*>

---

24 In November 2006, the Legislative Assembly of the NSW Parliament adopted new standing orders that modernized the terminology used in the passage of a Bill through that Chamber. Noting the antiquity of the phrases First, Second and Third Readings, dating back to the early English Parliament, the Chamber replaced First Reading with the phrase "introduction of the bill"; Second Reading is the stage when the "bill is agreed to in principle" and the previous Third Reading is the declaration by the Speaker "to have passed". The principal debate still occurs when the Bill is agreed to in principle. The Legislative Council still uses the older terminology.

Tasmania

Tasmanian Parliament, including Legislative Council and House of Assembly, from 1992: <*www.parliament.tas.gov.au*>

Victoria

Victorian Parliament, including the Legislative Council and Legislative Assembly, from 1991: <*www.parliament.vic.gov.au*>

Western Australia

Western Australian Parliament, including the Legislative Council and Legislative Assembly from 1999: <*www.parliament.wa.gov.au/ indexn.htm#*>

Australian Capital Territory

Australian Capital Territory Legislative Assembly from 1989: <*http://hansard.www.act.gov.au/welcome.htm*>

Northern Territory

Legislative Assembly of the Northern Territory from 1990: <*http://www.nt.gov.au/lant/hansard*>

Synonyms in working with Legislation and Cases

Acts/legislation/statutes may be passed/enacted/assented to and may come into operation/commences when they are proclaimed/gazetted.

Delegated/subordinate legislation can also be called *statutory instruments* (especially when referring to Commonwealth) and can consist of *rules*, *regulations*, *bylaws* and *ordinances*. This last group are not used interchangeably but will take their name depending upon the body delegated the task of making them.

Be careful that you understand that, while *cases/reports* can be usually used interchangeably, *judgment* and *report* are **not** synonyms. The judgment is as a judge has handed it down. The report is as published, usually with a headnote and (maybe) grouped with the judgments of all of the judges in that case. Thus you read a *judgment* on AustLII but consult the *report* (ie, reported case) in print form or in a commercial service.

Chapter 3

Delegated Legislation

Outline

1. What is subordinate or delegated legislation?

Subordinate or delegated legislation refers to those laws made by persons or bodies to whom Parliament has delegated law-making authority. These laws are referred to collectively under many names: as *statutory rules, statutory instruments,* and the two already used: *subordinate* and *delegated legislation,* taken from their relationship with legislation. Finally, there is the term *regulation* which, while referring to a specific type of subordinate legislation, has come to be used in certain publications to signify all rules of this type.

Notwithstanding which general term is used, it is clear there are several names given to these rules in specific instances. Thus, *Regulation,* probably the most common, tends to be the name given to rules made by a minister or governor or governor-general and which are usually associated with a government department. *By-law* is the term given to the rules made by local councils or statutory bodies like universities. *Rules* tend to be made by courts and historically they deal with matters of procedure, while *Ordinances* tend to be made in situations which indicate that they stand instead of legislation. Thus the law governing the Australian Capital Territory was in the form of ordinances until 1989 when the Legislative Assembly of the ACT was established with the power to make enactments. The product of that body is now known as

"Acts". The term ordinance is also used in local government, particularly in NSW.

Notwithstanding the variety of names, the basis of such delegation lies in the fact that the parliament cannot be expected to legislate for the minutia of government and there will be many aspects which must be changed regularly or which need detailed consideration not amenable to parliamentary enactment. The general power is given to another body, although the power of review is maintained by the parliament. This is usually in the form of having the delegated law laid before the parliament for a period, thus allowing the members of the parliament to scrutinise with a view to control.

2. The enabling Act and the statutory instrument

The Act conferring the law-making authority is referred to as the *enabling (or empowering) Act*. An enabling Act usually stipulates the various conditions under which a person or body shall make delegated legislation. They will usually include the scope of such regulations together with the procedures to be followed for them to become effective. For these reasons, it would be wise, once the Act has been located, to check the regulation-making section to see the extent of the power which may have been given to another person or body to make such a legislative provision.

Example (a)
Section 22 of the *Bank Integration Act 1992* (Vic) provides:

---

22. Regulations

The Governor in Council may make regulations for or with respect to any matter or thing required or permitted by this Act to be prescribed or necessary to be prescribed to give effect to this Act.

There are no restrictions here on the regulation-making power.

Example (b)
Section 60 of the *Marine Administration Act 1989* (NSW) provides:

Regulations

60. (1) The Governor may make regulations, not inconsistent with this Act, for or with respect to any matter that by this Act is required or permitted to be prescribed or that is necessary or convenient to be prescribed for carrying out or giving effect to this Act.

(2) A regulation may create an offence punishable by a penalty not exceeding 5 penalty units.

Note the restriction here on the regulation-making power. A limit has been placed on the amount that can be imposed by penalty. A penalty at a higher rate without more would be outside the power and could not be enforced. Sometimes the restrictions are very detailed.

However, in many Acts, particularly some of the older legislation, it can be difficult when reading the Act to know when the matter is covered by the Act and when there may be related statutory rules and regulations that deal with the matter. There are certain clues within the Act which can assist in this search. One such clue is the use of the word "prescribed".

Citation of delegated legislation

Researchers do have trouble with correctly citing delegated regulations. See E Campbell, LP York and J Tooher, *Legal Research: materials and methods*, 4th ed, LBC, 1996, pp 273-276 for important background material and rules. Two points should be made here. First, always examine the short title within the set of rules to obtain some idea of the mode of citation, particularly of assistance in NSW. Secondly, examine internal references for assistance, particularly of assistance in Victoria.

Example of Citation

If the *Adoption Regulation 2003* (NSW) needs to be cited, the short title indicates a single regulation, broken into clauses:

clause 1	(cl, with plural cll)
sub-clause 1(1)	(sub-cl)
paragraph 1(1)(a)	(para, with plural paras)
sub-paragraph 1(1)(a)(i)	(sub-para and plural sub-paras)

However, the *Life Insurance Regulations 1995* (Cth) is a collection of regulations. Thus reference is made to each separate regulation:

regulation 1	(r or reg, with plural rr or regs)
sub-regulation 1(1)	(sub-r or reg with sub-regs)
paragraph 1(1)(a)	(para with plural paras)

An ordinance is divided into sections, subsection and paragraph.

Rules are divided into rule, paragraph and subparagraph.

Rules of Court are (usually) divided into Order, Part, rule and paragraph.

---

3. The delegated legislation of the Commonwealth

This is an area of law-making which has received a great deal of recent attention. Four reports which have examined aspects of the making of delegated legislation are: *Rule Making by Commonwealth Agencies*, Administrative Review Council (May 1992); *The Cost of Justice Second Report: Checks and Balances*, Senate Standing Committee on Legal and Constitutional Affairs (August 1993); *Clearer Commonwealth Law*, House of Representatives Standing Committee on Legal and Constitutional Affairs (September 1993); and *Access to Justice: an Action Plan*, Access to Justice Advisory Committee (May 1994). In the context of examining problems associated with the making and finding of such law, a number of recommendations have been made, particularly in the Administrative Review Council report which dealt with delegated legislation specifically.

One of the results of this interest in delegated legislation was the need to systematise the various types of delegated legislation found within Commonwealth law. To this end, and after a number of false starts in the early 1990s, the Commonwealth Parliament eventually enacted the *Legislative Instruments Act 2003*. Giving this material the generic name legislative instruments, the Act "introduces a consistent system for registering, tabling, scrutinising and sunsetting all Commonwealth legislative instruments" (Explanatory Memorandum).

However, possibly the most interesting aspect of this development, which commenced on 1 January 2005, was the creation of the Federal Register of Legislative Instruments (FRLI) which is a repository of Commonwealth legislative instruments, explanatory statements and compilations. But, more importantly, the FRLI is an *authoritative* source and if downloaded and printed with the FRLI logo, will be acceptable for court purposes (s 22 *Legislative Instruments Act 2003*).

Locating Commonwealth legislative instrument (or statutory rules)

At the present time the new legislative instruments appear in the *Commonwealth Government Gazette,* are printed in pamphlet form and then in annual volumes.

There is a reasonably complete list of the Commonwealth instruments alphabetically arranged in *Wicks Subject Index to Commonwealth Legislation* – "Index to Regulations", while recent rules are listed in the current awareness services:

- ALMD in the "Table of Subordinate Legislation", and
- *Australian Current Law: Legislation* in "Cumulative Table of Regulations and Rules made and amended".

Federal Register of Legislative Instruments (FRLI)

The ability to browse and search Commonwealth instruments that are of a legislative character is one of the principal benefits of the 2003 Act. If determined to be a legislative instrument by an Act – or if it has the qualities of a legislative instrument according to criteria set out in the Act – it will appear in the FRLI.

All legislative instruments made on or after 1 January 2005 must be registered on the FRLI to be enforceable. However, all legislative instruments made prior to this date must also be registered if they are to remain in force.

The FRLI **is** maintained by the Attorney-General's Department and is an integral part of the of COMLAW. This allows the researcher to search Acts and legislative instruments together on that site. However, while the site provides compilation (that is incorporation of any amendments as at a particular date) for both legislation and delegated legislation, there is one noteable distinction between Acts available on COMLAW and legislative instruments on the FRLI – while the latter are authoritative when marked with the logo, the former are not.

The changes made by the creation of the FRLI are extremely important and there is little doubt that it will have on future developments in the dissemination of legislation electronically. However, care must be taken because there are terms used on COMLAW and in the FRLI that are new and it is strongly urged that the new researcher consult the FAQ (frequently asked questions) link to get a better understanding of this site's scope and limitations.

4. The delegated legislation of other jurisdictions

(a) New South Wales

Until recently NSW legislation, which allowed for delegated legislation to be made, also set out the procedures that should be followed. These were repeated in identical form in all Acts. The provisions for statutory rules, which tend to be the largest group, have now been placed in the *Interpretation Act 1987* ss 39-40, and provide for publication in the *Government Gazette* and tabling before each of the Houses of Parliament. This is always subject to any specific instructions in the enabling Act. See also the material on sunset clauses at the end of this Chapter.

Thus delegated legislation is initially found in the *Government Gazette*, is published in pamphlet form and is brought together annually in a bound volume entitled the *New South Wales Rules, Regulations, By-Laws, Ordinances etc issued for the year ...*

Finding delegated legislation

Finding delegated legislation is one of the more difficult aspects of legal research. In the past this was caused in no small measure by a lack of systematic indexing. This situation has improved tremendously because of a re-examination of all rules, etc, in the mid-1980s, and the repeal of many, leaving only those that were desired to remain in a Schedule. Later even these were subject to staged repeal and replacement where necessary. From this starting point there is no lack of documentation of those rules currently in force. However a second problem is that the researcher is seldom automatically directed to delegated legislation as a source of the law. This is particularly the case if the regulation is being found via the subject approach.[1] The mind tends to go to an Act and unless careful, the regulation made under the Act can be missed.

The starting point in locating delegated legislation must be the "Principal Statutory Instruments" table in *New South Wales Legislation in Force* (Parliamentary Counsel, quarterly). This may be updated using the *Monthly Statutory Instruments Table*, a cumulative publication, in most libraries files with the pamphleted regulations. The current awareness services also update this information:

---

1 *Indexes to Legislation of Tasmania* does contain a subject index to the Tasmanian regulations. It is interesting to read the "Important Note" that accompanies the list. The compilers draw attention to the fact that while legislative indexes are common, indexes to subordinate legislation are rare because of availability, transitory nature and present effectiveness. While the first relates particularly to that jurisdiction, the second and third reasons, as set out fully in the note, apply to most jurisdictions.

- ALMD in the "Table of Subordinate Legislation", and
- *Australian Current Law: Legislation* in "Cumulative Table of Regulations and Rules made and amended".

Reprints: Most of the current statutory rules are being reprinted and are generally available in that form. Use the "Principal Statutory Instruments" table, referred to above, to find the date of the last reprint.

Electronic form

Online: NSW delegated legislation is freely available from the Government of NSW Legislation home page maintained by the Parliamentary Counsel's Office at <*www.legislation.nsw.gov.au*>. It is also available via AustLII and can be effectively searched used the SINO search engine at <*www.austlii.edu.au*>. If the researcher is wanting sessional regulations, this is not available on AustLII but is available on the NSW Legislation home page, at least back to 1990.

Commercially, NSW delegated legislation is available on LexisNexis AU and TimeBase, the latter also including historic details of amendments and commencement dates. It is updated weekly.

Example

The *Noxious Weeds Act 1993* (NSW) requires that agricultural machinery – "of a kind declared, by order of the Minister published in the Gazette, to be agricultural machines to which this section applies" – is to be cleaned before being brought into NSW from Queensland "to the satisfaction of the inspector" situated near the border. Failure to obtain his approval before moving the machinery is, pursuant to s 31 of the Act, an offence. To find what machinery has been so declared it is necessary to find the *Noxious Weeds Regulation 2003*. This can be done by consulting "Principal Statutory Instruments Table" found in *New South Wales Legislation in Force*, published quarterly by the Parliamentary Counsel's Office. Under the name of the Act are set out the regulations made, the original gazettal date, reprint date and any amendments made since the last reprint.

(b) Victoria

Victorian delegated legislation is regulated by the *Subordinate Legislation Act 1962*. By s 2, the definition of a statutory rule is established and while wide, it does restrict them and will not generally include purely local or geographically limited rules.

By s 4 of the Act, notification of the making of a statutory rule must appear in the Victorian *Government Gazette*, together with information as to where copies can be obtained. Section 9B places a duty on the Minister administering the Act under which the statutory instrument is made, to make available for purchase or inspection, a statutory instrument. Failure to do so will mean that at the time of an alleged contravention, if that is the case, no person can be convicted of an offence under that regulation.

The Victorian statutory rules, after notification in the *Gazette*, are published in pamphlet form and in annual volumes and are periodically reprinted.

Finding statutory rules

Victorian statutory rules are found with relative ease using the *Cumulative Statutory Rules Table*, an annual publication from The (official) Law Printer. This contains a number of valuable tables:

1 Unrevoked principal statutory rules (arranged alphabetically by short title of the rule),

2 Table of statutory rules (arranged alphabetically by the name of the parent Act),

3 Instruments declared by the Attorney General to be statutory rules, and

4 Disallowed statutory rules.

This is kept current by the *Statutory Rules Table*, a monthly publication, or the current awareness publications.

Electronic form

Victorian regulations since 1996 are accessible via AustLII (<*www.austlii.edu.au*>) or *Victorian Statutes Book* at <*www.dms.dpc.vic.gov.au*>. If the short title is not known, then the relevant regulation may be found by using the key-word search facility or, alternately, the *Cumulative Statutory Rules Table* (above). The commercial service TimeBase also has Victorian regulations on the net.

(c) South Australia

The text of South Australian statutory rules appears in the *South Australian Government Gazette*, and in pamphlet form.

Finding statutory rules

One of the tables in the annual volume of legislation lists statutory rules, including certain proclamations and notices, with reference to the date they appeared in the *Government Gazette*. This list is an alphabetical arrangement under the short title of the parent Act.

This is kept up to date using the current awareness services.

Electronic form

South Australian regulations as consolidated in 1991 and all subsequent updates are available on the Parliament's homepage at: <*www.parliament.sa.gov.au/dbsearch/legsearch.htm*> and also on AustLII (<*www.austlii.edu.au*>) and the commercial service TimeBase.

(d) Queensland

In the recent changes to the making of legislation, delegated legislation was also affected There is a new Act, *Statutory Instruments Act* 1992, governing subordinate legislation, which came into force on 1 July 1992. Pursuant to s 9, "subordinate legislation" is defined and there are certain exclusions, insofar as not all delegated legislation is covered by the Act.

While the Act requires notification in the *Queensland Government Gazette* and the tabling in the Parliament within 14 sitting days after notification, notification is merely the notice of the making of the subordinate legislation together with details of the places where it can be obtained. It does not now include the text of the subordinate legislation to be published in the *Gazette*. The text will be available through the Queensland Subordinate Legislation series.

Finding statutory instruments

Reference to statutory instruments made pursuant to an Act are shown after the parent Act in *Queensland Legislation Annotations*: "Current Legislation", and updated in *Queensland Legislation Update* Pt 1. References are either to the *Government Gazette,* or *Queensland Subordinate Legislation Series*. This can be updated using the current awareness services.

Electronic form

Online: Queensland subordinate legislation is electronically available from the Office of the Queensland Parliamentary Counsel in the "Queensland Legislation Reprint Series" and annual form since 1991, at <*www* *legislation.qld.gov.au/legislation*>. In the main work, the subordinate legislation is set out following the parent Act in an alphabetical arrangement.

While it also appears to be on the AustLII site, care should be taken to ensure it is current. The commercial service TimeBase also has Queensland regulations on the net.

(e) Western Australia

In Western Australia, the term used is "subsidiary legislation" as defined in s 5 of the *Interpretation Act 1984*, and is quite wide, including any proclamation, regulation, rule, by-law, order, notice, rule of court, town planning scheme, resolution, or other instrument made under any written law and having legal effect. To have such effect, it must, however, be published in the *Gazette*. The subsidiary legislation is published in annual volumes.

Finding subsidiary legislation

In the "Index" volume of the *Statutes of Western Australia*, Table 4 is a "Table of By-Laws, Regulations, Rules, Notices, Orders in Council, and Proclamations". This includes most of the material covered by the term "subsidiary legislation" but not all. It is alphabetically listed under the enabling Act and contains a *Government Gazette* reference for the text.

This is kept up to date using the current awareness services.

Electronic form

Western Australian delegated legislation is available electronically from the State Law Publisher <*www.slp.wa.gov.au*>. There are regulations on AustLII. Care must be taken that the electronic source being accessed is current.

(f) Tasmania

The *Rules Publication Act 1953* s 2 provides for a wide definition of "statutory rule", with s 4 restricting the inclusion of certain specific inclusions. The Act requires the rules to be published in loose form and then in bound volumes with a sequential number relating to the year they are made. There is no general rule as to publication in the *Gazette*, with each Act providing if necessary.

Tasmanian statutory rules, if not otherwise specified, take effect from their publication or notification in the *Gazette* if enacted before 1 January 1982 or on or after 14 May 1985. The statutory rules enacted between those dates take effect one day after their publication or notification in the *Gazette*. These changes were brought about by changes to the *Acts Interpretation Act 1931*.

Finding statutory rules

As has been noted, there is a subject index to the subordinate legislation contained in *Indexes to the Legislation of Tasmania*. "Table 3: Subject Index to Subordinate Legislation".

This is kept up to date using the current awareness services.

Electronic form

Tasmanian statutory rules made from the beginning of 1998 are available on the Internet via the Tasmanian Government's site at <*www.thelaw.tas.gov.au*> in both consolidated, "historic" and sessional volumes. The sessional document is that which appeared in the *Tasmanian Government Gazette*. The stated aim of the Government is progressively to add historic versions as the workload of the Office of Parliamentary Counsel permits.

(g) Australian Capital Territory and Northern Territory

The delegated legislation of the ACT is set out in *Laws of the Australian Capital Territory*: "Table of regulations, by-laws and rules . . ." (1988), and updated by *Table of ACT Laws*, annually. The six-monthly *Northern Territory Index to Legislation* has a table "Acts and Regulations of the Northern Territory ... in force ... listed alphabetically". This is a good place to locate and update regulations.

Electronic form

The *ACT Legislation Register* has now made available current subordinate laws and notifiable instruments of the ACT at: <*www.legislation.act.gov.au*>. The subordinate laws are also available on AustLII. Care must be taken that the electronic source being accessed is current. For Northern Territory subordinate legislation, see the Current Northern Territory Legislation Database at: <*http://notes.nt.gov.au/dcm/legislat/legislat.nsf?OpenDatabase*>. This is also on AustLII. Once again, care must be taken that the electronic source being accessed is current.

5. English delegated legislation

Like Australia, English law consists of the Acts of Parliament, subordinate legislation and case law. The items of subordinate legislation were called statutory rules and orders, but by the *Statutory Instruments Act 1946* the name was changed to "statutory instruments".

There are two principal ways of obtaining information as to statutory instruments:

1. "Statutory Rules, Orders and Statutory Instruments revised to Dec 31st, 1948"

This is a consolidation of all statutory instruments in force at the end of 1948. The arrangement within the volumes is by subject, while index volumes contain a numerical table in chronological order. This is kept up to date by annual volumes (*Statutory Instruments,* in 3 parts) and related publications. It is not considered here in any depth because few Australian collections would have the statutory instruments in this form. By far the most popular is *Halsbury's Statutory Instruments*.

2. Halsbury's Statutory Instruments (Butterworths)

This set of 22 volumes provides a complete classification of all instruments in force but does not set out the text of them all, only those selected rules and orders "chosen from the point of view of the practising lawyer". Recently reissued, the statutory instruments are arranged by subject classification. Additional volumes include an annual consolidated index, bound index volumes and looseleaf services.

Electronic form

United Kingdom Statutory Instruments, published since the beginning of 1987, are available on the site maintained by the Office of Public Sector Information (OPSI) <*www.opsi.gov.uk/stat.htm*>. Note from that page that, while numbered in the same series, statutory instruments of only local application are not usually published and will also not appear on the web. The homepage also states that normally an item will appear on the web simultaneously with the print publication. The instruments are also available on BAILLI from 2002 and on the commercial services WESTLAW and LEXIS.

Citation of statutory instruments[2]

The form of the citation of statutory instruments is set out in s 2(2) of the *Statutory Instruments Act 1946*:

> Any statutory instrument may, without prejudice to any other mode of citation, be cited by the number given to it in accordance with the provisions of this section, and the calendar year.

Example of Citation

By s 2(1), the numbering of statutory instruments shall be made by the HMSO in accordance with regulations made under the Act. They have been provided for in the *Statutory Instruments Regulations 1947*, SI 1948 No 1, reg 3.

---

6. Delegated legislation: sunset clauses and impact statements

One of the features of the age of deregulation has been the concern by government generally of the over-regulation of the community, particularly commerce. From the late 1980s onwards governments have committed to review existing statutory rules, with a view to removing those that were outdated, unnecessary, ineffectual and overlapping. Initially, in 1984 the impetus in New South Wales was the need to tidy the books, to streamline the regulations, before the conversion from legislation and delegated legislation produced from the old "hot lead" to the use of computers both to typeset and store this information. These attitudes went much further and they are accompanied by two related features: the first was to ensure that when regulations were made their impact would cause minimum disruption or dislocation, and, secondly, that there would be an automatic review mechanism, or sunset clause, built into the regulation when initially made, that has meant automatic review at some preordained future time. The idea was to shift the onus from those who need to show why a regulation is not necessary at the time of repealing, to those who must show why it continues to be necessary.

New South Wales: After preliminary work undertaken by the Regulation Review Committee of the Parliament, established under the

---

2 There are further refinements to this topic set out in E Moys, *Manual of Law Librarianship*, 2nd ed, published for the British and Irish Association of Law Librarians by Gower, 1987, p 110.

Regulation Review Act 1987, the *Subordinate Legislation Act 1989* was enacted which made three principal changes. The first was for a staged review of statutory rules, including a timetable for rules in existence to be reviewed, together with the inclusion of a sunset clause whereby all rules made on or after 1 September 1990 are to be repealed on the fifth anniversary of their publication. The second change was the provision of guidelines to be followed in the making of such rules. The third was the requirement for a Regulatory Impact Statement. This would include matters such as objects to be achieved, realistic options available, economic and social benefits arising from each option, economic and social costs arising from each option, qualitative factors necessary to weight impact and evaluation of the net impact of each option. Certain rules have been specifically excluded.

To assist in rules during this process, the Parliamentary Counsel's Office publishes three times a year *Status of Statutory Rules*.

Victoria: The *Subordinate Legislation (Revocation) Act 1984* and *Subordinate Legislation (Review and Revocation) Act 1984* were two of the earliest efforts in the matter of staged review and the use of greater public consultation in the making of subordinate legislation. It is interesting that the sunset clause built into the Victorian legislation is ten years. A Regulatory Impact Statement is required unless the Premier grants an exemption where it is believed a statutory rule should be made without one. Scrutiny of statutory rules is by the Legal and Constitutional Committee of the Parliament which can recommend disallowance where there has been inadequate regard to the preparation of the RIS.

Queensland: The *Regulatory Reform Act 1986* provided for staged review of subordinate legislation and for a sunset clause in new rules. In Queensland it is seven years. One difference in the Queensland situation from the other Australian States that have adopted the consultation and impact procedures is that in Queensland they have not been imposed by legislation. The original study, the Savage Committee report, recommended that a number of key principles and procedures should be applied in the making of new rules. These have now been contained in a Legislative Manual prepared by the Premier's Department in 1986, which set out the matters that should be contained in a "Green Paper" to be released before the adoption of new rules to facilitate public discussion. These follow broadly the matters in the Impact Statements of Victoria and NSW. However, in Queensland it is at the discretion of the Minister whether a Green Paper should be prepared and there is no scrutinising body other than the Minister and Department.

South Australia: The *Subordinate Legislation Act 1987* provides for staged review and for a sunset clause of seven years in new subordinate legislation made after 1 January 1986. To determine the impact of new regulatory, or deregulatory schemes, there is a two-tiered system in place in South Australia, provided by Cabinet direction. The "Green Paper" is to be used as the basis for the discussion of policy matters and need not be elaborate. In many cases the normal paper work that is created could well fill this role. However, if the Minister feels it is necessary, the Green Paper should be formally released and set out the objectives, background, alternative options and their financial and social costs. Where there may well be severe impact upon the community, the Adviser on Deregulation, an officer within the Attorney General's Department, can advise a Regulatory Impact Statement. This would set out the matter in the Green Paper but in greater detail.

Tasmania: There are no stage reviews or impact provisions in Tasmania, although a Deregulation Advisory Board has existed within the Attorney General's Department since 1983 with the aim of slowing down the making of regulations. The Board is a government/public sector venture and has had a reasonably successful impact upon the amount of rule making. They report that in the few years after creation, it was reduced by one third. The Cabinet now requires a Regulatory Impact Statement to accompany any new regulatory proposals before it.

Western Australia: There are no formalised stage reviews or impact provisions in Western Australia although there is a concerted effort to review governmental function. This has been in existence since 1986 with the establishment of the Functional Review Committee. This Committee is working in conjunction with the information provided by the *Financial Administration and Audit Act 1986* which requires annual reporting about their efficiency and effectiveness and impact upon the community in which they operate. At the same time there is a major review of regulatory bodies.

Chapter 4

Law Reports

Outline

1. History and importance

The development of the common law depends largely on the production of reliable law reports. These contain not only the facts, issues and decisions but also, most importantly, the legal principles upon which the judgment was made. Thus, the purpose of a law report can be defined as "the production of an adequate record of judicial decision upon a part of law in a case heard in an open court".

It is not possible to report every case that comes before the courts and such a task is not necessary. A case is selected for reporting if it raises a point of legal significance. The vast majority of the matters that come before the courts involve disputes of fact and do not raise any important issues of law. It is for this reason that it is the decisions of the appellate court, rather than the court of first instance, that tend to be reported.[1] The criteria are set out below.

Law reports have existed in various forms since the time of Edward I. The forerunners of the law report were the year-books of the 14th and 15th centuries. These were far from factual and objective, they were in fact highly subjective, and their purpose is still not totally clear. Legal historians have speculated that their purpose may have been for student use, although others believe they were produced as an aid for the practitioner.

However, by the 16th century the anonymous year-books were replaced by reports of cases collected and written by eminent judges and practitioners. It has been estimated that between 1571, with the publication of Plowden's reports of cases, and 1865 there were over 300 separate series of reports published by reporters. These are the ***Nominate Reports***, the name being derived from the fact that most reports took the name of the reporter.

In order to make this source of law available to the profession, the most important of the pre-1865 reports were brought together and reprinted over the period 1900-1932. These are known as the *English Reports*. Both because of the mixed quality of the original reports and because they are only a republication of the case, the practice is to acknowledge both the original report and the volume of the *English Reports* where it can be found.

2. Official control of reporting

Returning to law reporting in the 1700s, because anyone could enter a court and report the arguments and decisions and subsequently publish them, it has been noted that the standards did differ. In 1785 the courts themselves regulated the activities of reporters by "authorising" certain reporters and would allow only their reports to be cited in their courts. There needed to be some further rationalising of reporting and in 1865 the Incorporated Council of Law Reporting was established to publish a collection of reports of all the superior courts of England.

---

1 This is looked at in greater detail shortly when examining *which* cases are reported.

In Australia there has been systematic reporting in the various colonies from the 1860s.[2] There exists in each State jurisdiction an official body responsible for the reporting of cases, although in the Commonwealth it is still in the hands of the judges.

Modern law reporting is considerably different from the reports of the past. Some series report cases decided by one particular court. For example, the *Commonwealth Law Reports* reports cases decided principally by the High Court of Australia.

Other series report cases decided within a number of courts in the same geographic area exercising the same kind of jurisdictions, such as the *Federal Law Reports* and the *Local Government Reports of Australia*.

There are some series which report cases on a geographic basis such as the *All England Law Reports* and the *Dominion Law Reports* (for the whole of Canada).

Other series report cases decided on particular subjects of law such as the *Australian Trade Practices Reports*, and *Family Law Reports*.

Finally, there are the law reports which are supplied to subscribers of looseleaf, subject specific, services and which, when they take up too much room within the service, are placed into new folders or are replaced by a bound volume of cases. These may carry a new title or still relate back to the original service.

3. Which cases are selected for reporting?

It was noted above that the criteria for reporting was if points of legal significance are raised. This is a little too vague. The publishing director of the *All England Law Reports* stated the criteria of that general series which covers the English superior courts of record:[3]

- (i) it makes *new law* by dealing with a novel situation or by extending the application of existing principles;
- (ii) it includes a *modern judicial restatement* of established principles;
- (iii) it *clarifies conflicting decisions* of lower courts;
- (iv) it *interprets legislation* likely to have a wide application;
- (v) it *interprets a commonly-found clause*, for example in a contract or will;
- (vi) it *clarifies an important point of practice or procedure*.

If it is remembered that the vast majority of cases determined by the courts are those where guilt or innocence is decided, or a penalty is

---

2 For a complete, historic list from the various jurisdictions, see E Campbell, et al, *Legal research: materials and methods*, 4th ed, LBC, 1996, pp 114-135, and Watt, "Sources and literature of Australian law, Part II, The States" [1985] *Lawasia* 40-47.

3 Brown, "Law reporting: the inside story" (1989) 20 *Law Librarian* 15-18.

determined, there is little chance for these cases to fall within the reporting criteria. It does happen, but not (statistically) often. Where the case is on appeal the matter to be decided is usually a point of law rather than a matter of fact. These cases are far more likely to come within the reporting criteria. It is for this reason that the generalisation is often made that cases heard in the "courts of first instance" tend not to be reported while cases from the appellate courts are reported. This is not exactly true, as an examination of the law reports show, but considering the ratio of cases reported in each class, it can be understood why the generalisation is so often made.

4. "Authoritative" and "authorised" distinguished

The published reports are edited by legally trained persons, usually barristers. This makes them *authoritative*. In addition some series of reports are *authorised*. This means that after being reported by the barrister but before publication, the report of each decision is first checked by the judge. Series of reports which are not authorised in this way are still authoritative and acceptable to the courts, but if a case has been reported in an authorised series of reports and also in another series, it is preferable, and sometimes essential if before a court, to cite the authorised report.

Council of Law Reporting for NSW

The Council of Law Reporting was established as a statutory body by the *Council of Law Reporting Act 1969* (NSW) with a general responsibility to select cases to be reported; to report them as speedily as possible; to ensure they are as cheap as possible; and, finally, it must ensure – as far as possible – efficiency and accuracy of reporting, including the preparation of headnotes to reported decisions. The reports put out by this body – *NSW Law Reports* – are "authorised" because they are the product of the Council. Where there is no Council, traditionally the judge will approve page proofs before publication. Such happens with the *Commonwealth Law Reports* and the "authorised" status comes from that fact. See Naida Haxton, "Law Reporting and Risk Management – citing unreported Judgments" (1998) 17 *Australian Bar Review* 84 for a collection of Practice Notes and Practice Directions regarding authorisation from the various Australian jurisdictions.

---

5. Stare decisis or precedent

Legal principles stated in earlier cases are given effect to in later cases by the operation of the doctrine of precedent. For the law student, the examination of the rules and the particular application of the rules to individual cases, tends to be part of their studies.[4] However, suffice it to note here that it is as essential, when about to apply such legal principles, to know the current status of a case decided some time before as it is to determine whether a piece of legislation is still in force. A principle of law established by a case can be just as important as an Act of Parliament in the creation of a legal proposition. It can be just as fatal to litigation to find that a case relied on for a principle of law has been overruled by a superior court, as it is to find that legislation relied on is no longer in force. The name given to this task is "noting-up" and it is essential in the determination of the law. The methods are set out later in this chapter.

6. Current reports of the Australian jurisdictions

Listed below are the current reports series of, or ways of finding electronically, recent cases. For a complete list which includes historic material, see E Campbell, LP York, and J Tooher, *Legal Research: materials and methods*, 4th ed, Lawbook Co, 1996, Chapter 5: "Australian Law Reports". This covers many of the specialist subject series as well.

(a) Reports of High Court, Territories and federal jurisdiction

There are six principal sets of reports that report some of the decisions of cases before courts of federal jurisdiction, the Supreme Courts of the Territories, and the High Court of Australia:

Commonwealth Law Reports (CLR), 1903 to date. This is possibly the most widely used and important of all Australia's report series, both because of the reporting of the decisions of the High Court (and previously the Privy Council decisions on appeal from the High Court and State Supreme Courts) and because it is "authorised" ie, each judge has the opportunity of checking the report after it has been delivered and before it is published. There are index volumes covering the years 1903-1982 (vols 1-150), 1982-1995 (vols 151-184) and 1995-2004 (vols 185-218).

4 For a comprehensive analysis of stare decisis, see A Macadam and J Pyke *Judicial Reasoning and the Doctrine of Precedent in Australia,* Butterworths, 1998. Another excellent book is R Cross and JW Harris *Precedent in English Law,* 4th ed, Clarendon Press, 1991.

This index lists alphabetically all cases in the CLR and those High Court cases not reported in the CLR, together with a subject index.

Federal Court Reports (FCR), 1984 to date. This is the authorised set of reports of the Federal Court of Australia.

Federal Law Reports (FLR), 1957 to date. This series does not report decisions of the High Court but reports those of other courts of federal jurisdiction.

Australian Law Journal Reports (ALJR). Before 1958 these reports were included in the *Australian Law Journal* but not separated from other journal material. Since 1958 the reports have been included in the ALJR section of the ALJ and when the monthly parts are bound, these reports are bound either separately or at the back of the ALJ in the same volume. The ALJR has its own pagination, subject index and case index. This series reports the decisions of the High Court.

Australian Law Reports (ALR), 1973 to date (also contains *Australian Capital Territory Reports* (ACTR)). This publication replaces the Australian *Argus Law Reports* and the previous Argus Law Reports, and reports not only the High Court cases, but also those cases determining Federal law. There are also High Court cases not reported in the CLRs included in this series.

Northern Territory Law Reports (NTLR), 1992 to date. This is an authorised report series of the Supreme Court of the Northern Territory.

Electronic form

There are basically four major suppliers of Federal case material electronically:

- AustLII is freely available;
- LexisNexis AU, Thomson Legal Online and TimeBase are commercial and subscription-based services.

The following case databases are on AustLII (<*www.austlii.edu.au*>)

Commonwealth

- High Court of Australia Decisions 1903+
- Family Court of Australia Decisions 1982+
- Family Court of Australia – Full Court Decisions 2008+
- Federal Court of Australia – Full Court Decisions 2002+

- Federal Court of Australia Decisions 1977+
- Federal Magistrates Court of Australia 2000 +
- Federal Magistrates Court of Australia – Family Law Decisions 2000+
- Industrial Relations Court of Australia Decisions 1994-2001
- Administrative Appeals Tribunal Decisions 1976+
- Australian Industrial Relations Commission Decisions 1983+
- Australian Competition Tribunal Decisions 1997+
- Australian Designs Offices Decisions 1982+
- Australia Domain Name Decisions 2003-+
- Australian Patent Offices Decisions 1981+
- Australian Trade Marks Offices Decisions 1991+
- Copyright Tribunal Decisions 1982+
- Australian Takeovers Panel Decisions 2000+
- Defence Force Discipline Appeal Tribunal Decisions 1999+
- Federal Privacy Commissioner of Australia Cases 2002+
- Federal Privacy Commissioner of Australia Complaint Determinations 1993+
- Human Rights & Equal Opportunity Commn Decisions 1985+
- Immigration Review Tribunal Decisions 1990-1999
- Migration Review Tribunal Decisions 1999+
- Insurance Ombudsman Service Limited Privacy Compliance Committee Complaint Determinations 2004-2005
- National Native Title Tribunal Decisions 1994+
- Refugee Review Tribunal Decisions 1985+

ACT

- Supreme Court of the Australian Capital Territory – Court of Appeal Decisions 2002+
- Supreme Court of the Australian Capital Territory Decisions 1986+
- Administrative Appeals Tribunal of the ACT Decisions 1993+
- Discrimination Tribunal of the ACT Decisions 1998+
- Tenancy Tribunal of the ACT Decisions 1996-1998
- Residential Tenancies Tribunal of the ACT Decisions 1998+

NT

- Supreme Court of the Northern Territory – Court of Appeal Decisions 2000+
- Supreme Court of the Northern Territory – Court of Criminal Appeal Decisions 2000+
- Supreme Court of the Northern Territory Decisions 1986+
- Northern Territory Residential Tenancies Commissioner Decisions 2006+
- Northern Territory Anti-Discrimination Commission Decisions 1995+

LexisNexis AU, Thomson Legal Online and TimeBase

Because federal primary material (including High Court cases back to 1903 and all Federal Court cases back to 1976) is so freely available, the need for the commercial services in this area is limited. Each of these services, however, has some special feature. Thus:

Thomson Legal Online provides a number of its printed reports online, including the *Commonwealth Law Reports, Federal Court Reports* (both authorised) and *Federal Law Reports.*

TimeBase contains High Court cases and Privy Council appeals from 1901-1975, as well as the Federal Court from 1976 to the present. Provision is made for citation and individual page references to the CLR, FCR and ALR. This information, together with catchwords indicating major topic(s) of a case allow reasonable keyword searching of these Federal decisions.

LexisNexis AU has the benefit of having secondary source material online (for example the Australian Corporate Law Library which includes commentary) which can be used in conjunction with the primary material. It is by far the largest of the commercial services and the most comprehensive of the *Unreported Judgments* databases.

Caution when searching online for cases

Many law lecturers have noted a trend developing in the way law students are using the cases they find electronically. Using a word, or Act or case authority, they are locating their search term in a judgment *without checking on the status of that judgment* (is it the view of the court? a majority point of view? or minority view?) and are using it to establish a legal authority. Where it is a judgment of a minority judge and they cite it *as a statement of law*, they are most surprised when they fail that exercise. Always remember, the computer is a wonderful aid in finding specific material but that is only half the job, for the researcher must then determine its status, which may be difficult. Many researchers at this stage return to the reported case and seek the assistance of headnotes and the like.

(b) New South Wales

The *New South Wales Law Reports* (NSWLR), 1971 to date, are now the only authorised series of reports of the superior courts of New South Wales, which cover the common law, equity and appeals from certain tribunals and other courts.

There was a change in their citation in 1985. Before this, concluding with [1984] 3 NSWLR, the year was included in the citation. There has since been a sequential volume number.

There is a consolidated index: 1971-2005 (in 2 volumes).

Electronic form

LexisNexis AU contains the *New South Wales Law Report* series (1971+) which is a complete reproduction of this authorised series, together with unreported judgments from the NSW Supreme Court (1984+). Thomson Legal Online also provides access to the New South Wales Law Reports as well as unreported judgments from 1995.

AustLII also has selected decisions of the Supreme Court available since 1995 (with Appeals Court decisions from 1999).

(c) Victorian Reports

The *Victorian Reports* (VR), 1957 to date, are the authorised reports of the Supreme Court of Victoria. The *Victorian Law Reports Consolidated Index and Tables 1861-1996* (3 vols), together with a cumulative supplement, is available to research all Victorian reports.

Electronic form

LexisNexis AU contains the *Victorian Reports* (1957+), together with unreported Supreme Court decisions since 1984. Thomson Legal Online's unreported judgments start in 1995.

AustLII also has selected decisions of the Supreme Court (1997+) and these can be accessed without cost.

(d) South Australian Reports

The *South Australian State Reports* (SASR), 1921 to date, are the authorised South Australian report series. A number of index volumes have been published: 1921-1971; vols 1-50 (1971-1989), supplemented by a volume for vols 51-70. There is an annual index at the end of each volume of reports.

Electronic form

LexisNexis AU contains unreported Supreme Court decisions since 1987. Thomson Legal Online's unreported judgments start in 1995.

AustLII also has selected decisions of the Supreme Court since 1989 and these can be accessed without cost.

(e) Queensland Reports

The authorised reports of Queensland are the *Queensland Reports* (Qd R), 1959 to date. These contain the decisions of the Supreme Court of Queensland. There is an index of the decisions in this series covering the period 1860-1981. See also the *Queensland Legal Indexes: consolidated 1987-1996*, with "Legislation and Case Table" (vol 1) and "Judgment Service" (vol 2).

Electronic form

LexisNexis AU contains unreported Supreme Court decisions since 1987. Thomson Legal Online's unreported judgments start in 1992.

AustLII (1994+) also has selected decisions of the Supreme Court and these can be accessed without cost. The Court of Appeal judgments from 1992 are available on the Supreme Court of Queensland Library site at <*www.sclqld.org.au/qjudgment*>. Selected decisions are also available on AustLII (1994+).

(f) Western Australian Reports

There are now two authorised sets from Western Australia:

- the *Western Australian Reports* (WAR), 1960 to date, being the authorised reports the decisions of the Supreme Court of Western Australia.

These were cited by year until 1989-1990. The set now has sequential numbering. There is an index volume for the period 1898-1988 which is updated by a cumulative index at the end of each volume of reports.

- the *State Reports (Western Australia)* (SR(WA)), 1979+. This set reports the decisions of the Family Court in the exercise of State jurisdiction, the District Court and others. There is also an index to this: *The State Reports (WA) Consolidated Index, vols 1-25 (1979-2001); 26-40 (2000-2005); 41-50 (2005-2007).*

Electronic form

LexisNexis AU contains unreported Supreme Court decisions since 1987. Thomson Legal Online's unreported judgments start in 1995.

AustLII has selected decisions of the Supreme Court since 1999 and these can be accessed without cost.

(g) Tasmanian Reports

The *Tasmanian Reports* (Tas R), 1979 to date, is the authorised report series for Tasmania. These decisions have been digested and are arranged by subject in *Tasmanian Supreme Court Judgements: a digest of cases, 1897-1988*. These have been compiled and published by MF & CA Lillas. They are supplemented by the *Lillas Digest*, published in looseleaf.

Electronic form

LexisNexis AU contains unreported Supreme Court decisions since 1985. Thomson Legal Online's unreported judgments start in 1995.

AustLII also has selected decisions of the Supreme Court since 1987 and these can be accessed without cost.

7. English law reports

The early report series has already been mentioned, together with the role of the Incorporated Council of Law Reporting for England and Wales. Its reports are the *Law Reports*, unofficially known as the "authorised reports".

They consist of four parts:

Appeal Cases (AC) containing the decisions of House of Lords and Privy Council.

Chancery Division (Ch) containing the cases of the Chancery Division of the High court together with appeals from that Division to the Court of Appeal.

Queen's Bench Division (QB) consists of the cases of this Division of the High Court together with appeals to the Court of Appeal.

Family Division (Fam) includes cases of this Division and appeals but also cases in the Ecclesiastical Courts and Admiralty. This was previously the *Probate Division* (P).

They are called "authorised" reports because each judge has the opportunity of checking the report of his or her decision before it is published. The mode of citation is set out on p 14. When there is a choice, they will be used in preference to the series below.

Several other report series concurrently report the decisions of the English superior courts:

(1) Weekly Law Reports (WLR) 1953 to date

Published also by the Incorporated Council of Law Reporting, these reports are issued weekly and are bound in three volumes annually.

Vol 1 contains cases of interest to practitioners which will not be included in the *Law Reports*, together with practice notes and directions.

Vol 2-3 contain cases that will eventually appear in the *Law Reports*. They have the advantage over the *Law Reports* in that, because the reports once reported do not have to go back to the judge for checking, they are usually available much sooner.

(2) Law Journal Reports

Possibly the least cited of the several law reports mentioned here is this series. It was first published in 1822 and was later combined with the *All England Law Reports* in 1950. It is essential to be careful if you need to use them because in some years there are 3 volumes; each with the same year number but one contains the cases of chancery and bankruptcy, the second decisions of common law and the third in probate and admiralty.

(3) All England Law Reports (All ER)

Delays in the issue of the monthly parts of the *Law Reports* led Butterworths to begin publishing this private series of general law reports. It succeeded and the *All England Law Reports* are now very popular.

Issued in weekly parts, each part can contain cases from any court or Division, unlike the separation found in the Law Reports. The criteria of publication for this series was previously noted on p 83.

This publication has a number of valuable aspects. The first is the cross-referencing to *Halsbury's Laws of England*, the *English and Empire Digest* and *Halsbury's Statutes of England and Statutory Instruments*. Thus the background of relevant law to a case you are reading can be referred to quickly with the aid of these references. The second is the excellent indexing of the materials within the series. This can be either by subject, case name, statute or word and phrase. Finally, there is the speed and general accuracy of the report series.

Electronic form

BAILII (British and Irish Legal Information Institute) commenced in 2000 providing 14 databases of cases from the UK, England, Scotland and Ireland, freely to the public. That has increased to 29 databases by 2004, with various commencement points since 1996. There is also the House of Lords cases, available since 1996, accessible via <*www.parliament.the-stationery-office.co.uk/pa/ld/ldjudinf*>.

However, the commercial services are far more comprehensive. LexisNexis provides English cases via the *Law Reports* back to 1865, tax cases since 1875, *Lloyd's Law Reports* from 1991 and the *All England Law Reports* since 1936. Unreported decisions are available from January 1980. Other commercial services include Justis Law Reports (1865), Westlaw (1865), Butterworths All England Direct (1936) and Lawtel (1980).

(4) Nominate Reports

(a) English Reports

Reference has been made to the proliferation of reports during the 16th-19th centuries. These are extremely important, for within these various report series can be found many of the cases that established and laid down the basic principles of modern law. As it is extremely difficult to collect all of the nominate series, there have been a number of publications which have brought together many of these law report series. Probably the most comprehensive is the *English Reports* reprint. This is a straight reprint from the original reports which number over 265 separate series. There are, in the English Reports, over 100,000 cases reported between 1220-1865.

The *English Reports* consist of 178 volumes with the last two volumes being an index of cases.

Example: *Langridge v Levy* (1837) 2 M & W 519; 150 ER 863.

(b) All England Law Reports Reprint

The publishers of *All England Law Reports* have also collected between 4000-5000 cases together and put them out in the *Reprint* series. This consists of 36 volumes with selected cases from 1558-1935. The criterion for inclusion in this Reprint series is present day relevance or value to the legal profession. This has been further supplemented by the *Extension* series.

8. Finding the "right" case

The researching of the law reports can be one of the most difficult of all tasks facing the researcher. This can be for a number of reasons. The first is that there are just so many cases found in so many law report series in a law library. They come from various jurisdictions, with or without adequate indexes. Where do researchers start, when do they search other jurisdictions, and probably the biggest problem of all, when do they finish?

Secondly, there are mixed reasons for consulting the law reports. Sometimes it will be to find the common law. On other occasions it will be to find cases that relate to a particular word, phrase or section of an Act, while finally, it may be to find out the legal meaning of a word or phrase that appears in a document, for example a contract or will, and so find a decision that may have set out the law.

The third problem is to ensure that the case is still good law, notwithstanding that it may have been decided many years before.

Depending upon the information sought from the reports, so the research strategy will differ. To simplify the examination of the materials to be consulted, we can identify three headings: *Cases by Subject*, *Cases by Legislative Reference* and *Cases by Words and Phrases*.

(a) Finding Cases by Subject

The starting point for finding the common law, or generally cases upon any legal subject, is a ***Digest***. There are digests for most jurisdictions, although in Australia the Australian Digest Service has not separated out the various State and Territory cases. The researcher may have to be careful, therefore, and note the jurisdictional origin of the cases when using this research tool.

(i) Australian Digest

The *Australian Digest* is part of the Australian Digest Service and is published by Lawbook Co. This service covers not only the *Australian Digest* volumes themselves but also the *Australian Digest Supplement* which comes out annually and the *Australian Legal Monthly Digest* (ALMD).

There are three editions: the first edition covered cases reported in Australia between 1824-1933, and its supplement covered the period 1934-1947. The second edition, which started in 1961, was completed in the 1980s. The third edition, commencing in 1988, is now complete.

Online: However, the most important recent development in searching case law is the electronic researching tool: FirstPoint. Using the same taxonomy and case material found in the Australian Digest Service, the publishers of the paper product now facilitate the researcher to browse and search the whole database for specific legal concepts that, while maybe in the *Australian Digest*, can be overlooked. In order the understand the comparison it is necessary that certain finer points of both are examined.

The "Square Bracket" Number ([ ] number)

The inherent value of the *Australian Digest* is that all the Australian cases it digests are arranged in a subject classification. With over 170 topics, each is then broken down in parts, divisions, subdivisions, etc. When each subject is consequently divided down into the smallest (or specific) subject, it is identified with a number. In order to show that this is a specific *Australian Digest* reference, it is placed in square brackets – just as the *American Digest* places a small key in front and this is known as a "key' number. That same [ ] number will be used in linked *Australian Digest* publications like the ALMD as well as selected Thomson law report services.

Problems can exist in how you efficiently locate the [ ] number. In many cases you can use the **subject index** volumes of the *Australian Digest* or, alternately, you can use the volume known as the ***Key***. The difference between the two lies in the very simple proposition that an index tends to be a mere alphabetical list of terms and concepts and without specific knowledge you may miss the exact term or concept. Whereas the Key consists of the table of contents of all the topics, together with many references inserted by the editors which allow the person with a reasonable knowledge of the subject matter to work their way down the subject matter, progressing from the most general to the most particular. Once the cases in a particular area or concept of law are found, they must be updated through the system culminating – in paper – with the ALMD.

FirstPoint

The *Australian Digest* has been replaced online with a new publication which combines the content of the *Digest* with the functionality of the *Australian Case Citator*. The new service is known as ***FirstPoint*** and is available through the ThomsonReuters service Thomson Legal Online. FirstPoint is a new product and does not carry across all the features of the *Australian Digest*. For example the [ ] numbers are no longer identified.

The key element of the *Australian Digest*, that is its very detailed legal classification system, has been included as a dynamic table of contents which enables easy navigation and the ability to find cases related to a topic. The case digest entries include links to all topics a case may be classified under so it is easy to find related cases to any of the issues which may be covered by the respective case. Once a relevant case is found the citatory function will provide information on sunsequent treatment.

FirstPoint is singular because it is the first Australian online publication which has successfully integrated two different but complementary resources to create a totally new service. It represents the potential of online publishing.

Australian Current Law: Reporter

Unlike the Australian Digest Service which provides the researcher with the ability to find a wide range of cases over a considerable time span, this publication provides a far more limited time span. It allows all cases to be found for the year of the service only. The cases are arranged under alphabetical subject headings and by jurisdiction. However, with updates every two weeks of the *Reporter*, and a wide spread of cases including relevant material from overseas common law jurisdictions, this publication has a worthy record in providing case material quickly to the profession.

Example: Finding a Case

There was considerable interest when Justice Bollen of the South Australian Supreme Court, at the time of summing up to the jury in a rape case, said that rougher than usual handling by a husband could be used to get his wife to change her mind.

That case was not reported, being a question of fact, nor would the words of a judge in a summation usually find their way into a public form.

However in this case the Director of Public Prosecution stated a case pursuant to s 350(1a) of the *Criminal Law Consolidation Act 1935* reserving two questions for consideration by the SA Supreme Court (in Banco). In a majority decision, Perry and Duggan JJ, King CJ dissenting, the court held that the trial judge had erred at law in aspects of his summation. (This, of course, would not affect the jury acquittal.)

That case was eventually reported: *Question of Law Reserved on Acquittal Pursuant to section 351(1a) Criminal Law Consolidation Act (No 1 of 1993)* (1993) 59 SASR 214.

This case can be found using the *Australian Digest*, using criminal law as subject, or a keyword search across any of the SA case databases (for example AustLII using the word "rougher").

The Digest *(published before 1982 as* The English and Empire Digest*)*

Like the *Australian Digest, The Digest* brings together all related cases reported, giving a short digest of the facts and the law to aid a reader collecting relevant cases. Unlike the *Australian Digest,* however, it does include a selection of cases from other jurisdictions, including Scotland, Australia, Canada, India and New Zealand. It is therefore a good place for locating either a broad selection of cases or for searching a narrow area of law.

Special Features

(1) *The Digest* purports to digest **all** English cases.

(2) It also includes cases outside the English jurisdiction but which may have a bearing on English law. Thus the publishers conclude: "The inclusion of these cases enables the English lawyer to find many cases or points on which there has been no English decision, and, in some instances, decisions opposed to those of the English courts, which may offer him great assistance in higher tribunals. The legal profession in other parts of the Commonwealth similarly enjoys the opportunity of

comparing and contrasting the decisions of their own courts with those of the courts of England and overseas".

(3) Cross-referring from *The Digest* to *Halsbury's Laws of England* and *Statutes* is included.

(4) It notes-up the digested cases.

Editions

Publication of the original E & ED began in 1919 and the last volume of text was issued in 1932. By 1950 supplementary volumes made the use of *The Digest* unwieldy and in that year there began the issuing of the replacement (blue-band) volumes. They are commonly called the ***"blue-band"*** edition because of the distinctive band on the spine of each volume. However, in 1971 it was necessary that certain of the blue band volumes should be reissued and this was to continue until all that edition had been replaced by volumes which have a ***green band*** on their spine. The green band volumes are now being replaced but with volumes that have a spine marking to indicate a replacement volume but keeping the green band. Most have now been reissued twice and are shown on the spine with notation "2nd Reissue".

How to Use The Digest

Like the *Australian Digest*, each subject contains a table of contents where the subject is split into various divisions and subdivisions with a page reference to where the cases or those parts can be located. Starting with the first case digested on the subject, all subsequent cases are numbered in the order they appear. There is no square bracketing. However, like the *Australian Digest*, all cases are still located together under a specific heading. There is a separate ***subject index*** (2006, in 3 volumes) and alphabetical ***list of cases*** (2006, in 3 volumes).

Notes on The Digest Extract

- Here are selection of cases from the criminal law area. The words in bold after the number are key words which reflect the subject matter of the case. They can be broken down into further sub-headings. Where a dash is used in the second and subsequent cases, the same heading – or sub-headings – used above apply to that case as well. Thus here the cases in paras 7506, 7507, 7508, 7509, 7510 and 7511 all deal with the need to have ownership of the property before it is capable of being stolen. The first and second cases involved a corpse, the third was also a corpse but included a shroud as well. The fourth involved the coffin, while the last case leaves the cemetery and looks at intangible property, namely the confidential information in an examination paper.

- The case in para 7518 has since been considered in a later case, shown under the heading **Annotation**, with its full citation.
- Although we cannot see if there are any Scottish, Irish or Commonwealth cases on this point – for they are digested at the end in a smaller printing font – you can see how they are set out by examining the part of the Canadian case, and the New Zealand case, which relate to the previous section of *The Digest*.
- Finally, on the previous page is cross referencing to *Halsbury's Laws of England* and, at the very top of the page extracted, reference to *Halsbury's Statutes of England*.

How The Digest Cases are Kept Up to Date

Because *The Digest* volumes are now being reissued much sooner than previously, the need for elaborate methods of updating has been eliminated. There is now a two-volume (annual) *Cumulative Supplement* that contains the digests of new cases and updates the material found in the annotations. Care should be taken for while it may show "2003" on the spine, the material contained within it is only as at 1 January 2003. On the next two pages can be found a page from the main work and a page from the *2003 Cumulative Supplement* that updates the information in the main work.

(b) Finding Cases by Legislative Reference

Part of our common law tradition is that while parliament makes the law, the courts interpret it. It is thus very important that we understand the meaning attributed to words in legislation. There are three ways that this information can be determined:

(i) Annotated Acts (specific)
(ii) Annotated Acts (general)
(iii) Words and Phrases

(i) Annotated Acts (Specific)

There are several publications which take an Act and then, section by section, refer to cases, and maybe articles, where that section has been considered. Acts treated in this way include the Australian Constitution, and that legislation in the general practice areas of family law, taxation,

Example from *The Digest*

Vol 14 (2) Criminal Law, Evidence and Procedure 4 Cases **7505–7519**

STATUTE See Theft Act 1968 s 4, 12 Halsbury's Statutes (4th edn) Criminal Law

A In general

7505 Must be of some value Though to make a thing the subject of an indictment for larceny, it must be of some value, and stated to be so in the indictment, yet it need not be of the value of some coin known to the law, that is to say, of a farthing at the least.
R v Morris (1840) 9 C&P 349

7506 Must be subject of ownership
R v Westbear (or Westbeer) (1739) 2 Sess Cas KB 233; 2 Stra 1133; 1 Leach 12; 2 East PC 596; 93 ER 235

7507 —— No property in corpse
Handyside's Case (undated) 2 East PC 652

7508 ———— Neither does our law recognise the right of any one child to the corpse of its parent. Our law recognises no property in a corpse (*per curiam*).
R v Sharpe (1857) Dears & B 160; 26 LJMC 47; 28 LTOS 295; 21 JP 86; 3 Jur NS 192; 5 WR 318; 7 Cox CC 214, CCR

7509 ———— Property in shroud
Haynes's Case (1614) 12 Co Rep 113; 2 East PC 652; 77 ER 1389

7510 —— Property in coffin In an indictment for larceny in stealing from a private vault in a public church, the lead which had composed a coffin therein deposited, the property in the lead is well laid in the churchwardens and overseers of the parish or township to which such church belongs, though it may be locally situated out of such, and in another parish or township, and though it may have been long disused for every other purpose than the burial of the dead.
R v Garlick (1843) 1 LTOS 479; 1 Cox CC 52

7511 —— Intangible property — Confidential information An information was preferred against a university student who had acquired the proof of an examination paper, alleging that he had stolen certain intangible property, namely, confidential information being the property of the Senate of the university. It was agreed that the student had not intended permanently to deprive the university of the proof itself. The justices dismissed the charge on the grounds that confidential information was not intangible property within the Theft Act 1968 s 4: rather, the confidence consisted in a right to control publication of the proof, which was a right over property. The prosecutor appealed by case stated: *Held* there was no property in the confidential information capable of being the subject of a charge of theft. The appeal would be dismissed.
Oxford v Moss (1978) 68 Cr App Rep 183; [1979] Crim LR 119, DC

7512 Goods abandoned
R v Peters (1843) no 8031 post

7513 —— *R v Thurborn* (1849) no 8022 post

7514 —— *R v White* (1912) no 8037 post

7515 —— *Digby v Heelan* (1952) 116 JP Jo 312

7516 —— Intention to abandon — Burial of dead animal A mad dog having bitten three pigs, the owner ordered the latter to be killed and buried on his own land, not intending ever to disturb them. E dug up the bodies by night and sold them. The jury found that the owner did not intend to abandon the property in the pigs: *Held* E was properly convicted of larceny of the dead bodies of the pigs.
R v Edwards & Stacey (1877) 36 LT 30; 41 JP 212; 13 Cox CC 384, CCR

7517 Sale of pirated music The mere sale of pirated music is not larceny at common law, notwithstanding 5 and 6 Vict c 45 s 23.
R v Kidd & Walsh (1907) 72 JP 104

7518 Documents in archives of foreign embassy Appellant was employed as code clerk at a foreign embassy to this country. He was dismissed by the ambassador and immediately arrested on charges under Official Secrets Acts, and of larceny of documents at the embassy: *Held* although the documents were part of the archives of the embassy they could be the subject-matter of a charge of larceny in an English court, or of a charge under Official Secrets Acts.
R v AB [1941] 1 KB 454; 165 LT 382; sub nom *R v Kent* 110 LJKB 268; 57 TLR 307; 85 Sol Jo 315; 28 Cr App Rep 23, CCA
ANNOTATION **Apld** R v Madan [1961] 1 All ER 588

7519 Property converted or exchanged — Savings stamps A number of savings stamps were stolen and converted for their cash value. Some of the Bank of England notes received for them were handed to appellant who knew that the money was part of the proceeds of the theft and conversion of the stamps: *Held* the money received by appellant fell within the definition of property into which other property has been converted or for which it has been exchanged in Larceny Act 1916 s 46(1) (repealed), and appellant was rightly convicted of receiving the money, contrary to Larceny Act 1916 s 33(1) (repealed).
D'Andrea v Woods [1953] 2 All ER 1028; [1953] 1 WLR 1307; 117 JP 560; 97 Sol Jo 745; 37 Cr App Rep 182, DC

233

From the cases 7506–7511, the researcher can see that there is need for ownership before goods can be stolen. The first case from 1739 shows this and the following case shows further extensions of this rule. Recently this point of law was raised again in *R v Kelly* [1998] 3 All ER 741 and the editors of the *Supplement* have decided that this case rightly belongs with these cases. Consequently, it has been given the paragraph number 7511a to indicate it will follow *Oxford v Moss* next time the main volume is reprinted. Further, at the very end of the page are two references to the case extracted at 7673. Those two references indicate that that earlier case has been both disapproved (by Lord Widgery) and applied in later cases. Before that earlier case was now cited, it would need to be carefully checked to see that it was still good law.

Example of Cumulative Supplement of *The Digest*

515 Vols 14(1)-15(2) — CRIMINAL LAW

7399a Child abduction — Meaning of 'taking' a child

A, a man in his thirties, had a relationship with a 15-year-old girl. On two occasions, she went away with him, but was returned by the police. After the second incident, the girl's mother told A that she wanted her daughter at home. The following month, A arrived at the girl's house in the early hours of the morning. Her mother told A that he could not take the girl away, and he responded by saying that he did not intend to do so. Nevertheless, later that morning he took her to London in his car, allegedly in response to the girl's pleas. After living rough with A in his car for nine days, the girl was returned to her parents by the police. A was charged with taking a child under the age of 16 without lawful authority or reasonable excuse, so as to remove her from the lawful control of a person having such control over her, contrary to s 2(1)(*b*) of the Child Abduction Act 1984. Under s 3(a) of the 1984 Act, a person was to be regarded as taking a child if he caused or induced that child to accompany him. At trial, A's counsel submitted that there was no evidence of 'taking' as defined by s 3(a) and that accordingly there was no case to answer. The judge rejected that submission, and A was subsequently convicted. On appeal, A contended that he had not taken the girl within the meaning of s 2(1)(*b*) because she had wanted to go with him. *Held*, for the purposes of ss 2(1)(*b*) and 3(a) of the 1984 Act, the defendant's acts did not need to be the sole cause of the child accompanying him. Rather, it was sufficient that those acts were an effective cause of the child accompanying him, and it was immaterial that there were also other causes, such as the child's state of mind. A conclusion to the contrary would render s 3(a) unworkable since, in many cases, the child's consent was likely to be a cause of the child accompanying the defendant. In the instant case, there was ample evidence to leave to the jury on the question of whether A's acts were a cause of the girl accompanying him. Accordingly, the judge had been correct to reject the submission of no case to answer, and the appeal would therefore be dismissed.

R v A [2000] 2 All ER 177; [2000] 1 WLR 1879; [2000] 1 Cr App Rep 418; [2000] Crim LR 169; [1999] 40 LS Gaz R 42; 143 Sol Jo LB 240, CA

Part 4 — OFFENCES AGAINST PROPERTY

7511a Property belonging to another — Parts of corpses removed from Royal College of Surgeons — Whether parts of corpse capable of being property

K, an artist, had privileged access to the Royal College of Surgeons where he was permitted to draw anatomical specimens which were used by doctors training to be surgeons. L was employed at the college as a junior technician, and K asked L to remove a number of body parts. Approximately 35 to 40 body parts were removed, and K made casts of them. Most of the body parts were buried in a field; part of a leg was found in K's attic and the remaining parts were found in the basement of a flat belonging to friends. K and L were charged with theft, contrary to s 1 of the Theft Act 1968. At the trial, the defence submitted at the close of the prosecution case (i) that parts of bodies were not in law capable of being property and therefore could not be stolen, and (ii) that the specimens were not in the lawful possession of the college at the time they were taken because they had been retained beyond the period of two years before burial stipulated in the Anatomy Act 1832, and so did not belong to it. The trial judge rejected those submissions, ruling that there was an exception to the traditional common law rule that there was no property in a corpse, namely that once a human body or body part had undergone a process of skill by a person authorised to perform it, with the object of preserving it for the purpose of medical or scientific examination, or for the benefit of medical science, it became something quite different from an interred corpse and it thereby acquired a usefulness or value and it was capable of becoming property in the usual way, and could be stolen. K and L were convicted, and they appealed against their conviction. *Held*, parts of corpses were capable of being property within the meaning of s 4 of the 1968 Act if they had acquired different attributes by virtue of the application of skill, such as dissection and preservation techniques, for exhibition and teaching purposes. It followed that the trial judge was correct to rule as he did. Further, he was right to hold that the college had sufficient possession for the purposes of s 5(1) of the Act, since such possession was not dependent on the period of possession, whether it be for a limited or indefinite period. Moreover, there was evidence before the jury which illustrated the fact of the college's possession and it was not necessary for the judge to direct the jury further. Accordingly the appeals against conviction would be dismissed.

R v Kelly and another [1998] 3 All ER 741, CA

7672 Disapprvd (dictum Edmund Davies LJ) R v Dubar [1995] 1 All ER 781

7673 Disapprvd (dictum Lord Widgery CJ) R v Dubar [1995] 1 All ER 781

administrative law, trade practices and conveyancing. They may be either in book form or part of a looseleaf service. When Acts associated with courts and their procedures are dealt with in this way, those publications are referred to as "practice books". There are many Acts that are annotated and researchers should keep them in mind. The amount of references, ie, depth of annotation, does vary from service to service.

Updating: It may be necessary to update the Act using one of the current awareness services (ALMD or *Australian Current Law: Legislation*).

(ii) Annotated Acts (General)

There are a number of general services:

Australia	*Commonwealth Statutes Annotations* (Lawbook Co) *Federal Statutes Annotations* (also online, LexisNexis AU)
NSW	*New South Wales Statutes Annotations and References* (Lawbook Co) *New South Wales Statutes Annotations* (Butterworths)
Victoria	*Victorian Statutes Annotations* (also online, LexisNexis AU)
South Australia	*South Australian Statutes: Index* (Attorney-General's Dept)
Queensland	*Queensland Legislation Case Annotations* (also online, LexisNexis AU)

There are other sources: the *Australian Digest* (3rd ed) contains such a list in each subject volume, while many law reports, both jurisdictional and specialised subject reports, contain lists of cases decided under legislation in that volume. These lists are occasionally consolidated.

Updating: To update this information (when using paper) use one of the current awareness services (ALMD or *Australian Current Law*).

(c) Words and phrases

To find cases via words and phrases involves a choice of approaches. There are three main ways that the problem can be approached:

(i) The Words and Phrases Dictionary

There is a particular type of dictionary which contains the legal definition of words and phrases, as they have been defined in legislation or in the courts. Because the exact words of the primary sources of law are used, and the authorities set out, this can be an invaluable aid. These are dealt with more fully with other dictionaries (at pp 118-119).

(ii) Specialised Australian Services

There are two services which are of particular assistance to the Australian researcher: *Australian Legal Words and Phrases* (3 vols, Butterworths) and *Consolidated Words and Phrases Table to* The Australian Digest, *titles 1-83* (looseleaf) Lawbook Co.

(iii) Index to Specialised Law Reports

Many of the specialised law reports and services have their own indexes. In these, either separately or within the subject index, are references to words and phrases referred to in the cases reported in that service. This is a valuable starting point if the word is likely to be considered in a particular area of law.

Administrative Law Decisions, consolidated index (Butterworths)
"constant care and attention"; "married person"; "persons aggrieved"; and "special circumstances"

Australian Tax Cases; index and tables (CCH)
"eligible person"; "business"; "gift"; "manufacture"; and "public benevolent institution".

Intellectual Property Reports (Butterworths)
"goods of the same description"; "person aggrieved"; "special circumstances"; and "tit for tat".

Research tip: which order?

When there is the need to find the legal meaning of a word, a good thing to remember is that if the word is in legislation, start searching by *using the Act* for as long as possible, either in specific annotation services or the general annotation services. Having finished that line of enquiry with the current awareness services, you might then go to the index volumes often provided for specialised law report series. After these approaches have been exhausted then go to *Australian Legal Words and Phrases* or *Consolidated Words and Phrases Table* where in most cases the legislation which is being defined is also identified. This will save time and it is only after these avenues have been exhausted that in order to obtain a complete picture the researcher will consult the general dictionaries.

9. Noting-up Australian, English and American cases

In a common law environment like Australia or America, it is essential that the researcher can rely on the decided cases to determine both the common law as well as the meaning of words in legislation. Thus, having found references to a relevant case using the subject approach, or the legislation approach or the word approach, and been satisfied that the case is relevant, it will then be essential to note-up the decision to make sure that its status as an authority has not been altered by later decisions. The researcher needs to be totally satisfied that it has not been reversed on appeal or subsequently overruled by a superior court. Merely because a case appears in a digest cannot guarantee that the whole decision, or parts of it, have not been overruled or doubted by later cases.

Example of finding cases where words in legislation have to be examined

Assume that two young persons, 17 and 18 years old, wish to marry. They are told that they cannot and they seek assistance to find out the full legal position. Having determined that it would be governed by Commonwealth legislation, the task of the researcher then is to locate the relevant Act by consulting a subject index.

From that (sometimes difficult to get to) starting point, the researcher can then quickly locate s 11 of the *Marriage Act 1961*, which provides that persons are of marriageable age if they have attained 18 years of age. However, this is subject to s 12 which provides that a person between 16 and 18 years old can be granted permission by a judge or magistrate to marry a specific person who is of marriageable age if "the circumstances of the case are so exceptional and unusual as to justify the making of the order" (s 12(2)(b)).

But what use is it to tell the young couple those rather cryptic words? The next task in fully informing them of the legal situation is to find a case(s) where those words may have been considered by a court and the criteria to be used by the court set out. This is a situation where to examine the words "exceptional and unusual" in a words and phrases dictionary might get you results, ultimately, as would a search of the *Australian Digest* approach, but by utilising either of the two Commonwealth legislation annotation services, the researcher can quickly find reference to a number of cases including *Re Z* (1970) 15 FLR 420. In that case Joske J set out a number of factors which he considered relevant. The researcher must be satisfied that there are no later cases which change or add or subtract from that information and, once satisfied, using *CaseBase* or *FirstPoint* can confidently give advice with regard to those words and the young couple are in a better position to consider their options with regards to court permission.

The term ***noting-up*** [5] comes from the time when the actual report itself was physically marked in the margins with references to later cases which referred to it. The remnants of periods when this was done can still be seen in the older sets, particularly those that may have once been used by judges, many of whom were supplied with the labour to carry out this task. Recently this process has been replaced by published citators.

In setting out the method and terminology used in noting-up of cases, it is always presupposed that the researcher has a knowledge of the rudiments of *stare decisis* or the *doctrine of precedent*. Suffice it to note here that it is necessary that you be aware of how a case has been dealt with in the courts after it was decided. Thus if you are relying on a case as an authority for a proposition of law, it is necessary that you know whether that case has been subsequently overruled by the same or "higher" court in the hierarchy of courts. In the same way it would also be of immense interest to know if it had been favourably commented upon in a later decision by other courts, either of the same level in the hierarchy, but particularly by superior courts.

(a) Method of noting-up Australian cases

Just as we have come a long way in using the citator in preference to physically noting up the law report, so the electronic citator has now effectively replaced the paper citator as the preferred way of carrying out this task. The researcher does not always have the choice and so the various options should be understood. There are three principal services:

Australian Case Citator (Law Book Co), FirstPoint (Thomson Legal Online) and *CaseBase* (LexisNexis).

---

5 In the American context, this is called shepardising after the firm that produces the books which allows it to be done.

General Noting-Up Terminology

Followed (*F*)	Used when a court is expressing itself as bound by a previous decision of a court of co-ordinate or superior jurisdiction in a case where the facts were the same or substantially the same.
Applied (*Appld*)	Used when a court is applying the principle of a previous decision to the present case, the facts of which are materially different from those of the earlier case.
Approved (*Apprd*)	Used when a court approves the previous decision of an inferior court.
Explained (*Ex; Expld*)	Used when a court interprets a previous decision and states what it means.
Adopted (*Adopt*)	Used rarely, usually when the reasoning of a judge in one case, which is not binding authority, is used in arriving at a decision in a later case.
Distinguished (*Dist*)	Used when a court decides that it need not follow a previous case by which it would otherwise be bound because there is some salient difference, eg of fact or the terms of a document, between the previous case and the present.
Overruled (*Ov; Overld*)	Used when a court decides that the previous decision of a court of inferior jurisdiction is wrong.
Doubted (*Dbtd*) Disapproved (*Disap*) Dissented from (*Diss)* or Criticised (*Crit*)	Used when a court disagrees with a previous decision, but (a) it is not necessary for the purpose of the present decision or to overrule the earlier case, or (b) both courts being of co-ordinate jurisdiction, the latter court has no power to overrule the earlier decision. A court may disapprove or criticise a previous decision and yet be compelled to follow it.
Not followed (*NF*)	Is similar to (b) in previous definition, ie: both courts being of co-ordinate jurisdiction, the latter court has no power to overrule but also is not bound to follow.
Considered (*C*; *Consd*) Discussed (*Discd*) Referred to (*Refd*)	Used when the court considers, etc a previous decision, but does not actually apply, disapprove, follow, etc, it.
Affirmed (*Affd*) Reversed (*Revsd*)	Indicates the fate of a case when it goes to appeal.

Restored (*Restd*) Varied (*Varied*)	Usually refer to quantum of damages on appeal.
Certiorari Denied (*Cert den*)	An American term that indicates that the Supreme Court has denied the writ of certiorari for the case to be quashed and reheard by that Court.

Australian Case Citator

This service is available both in paper (seven non-cumulating volumes) and as part of Thomson Legal Online, as an element of *FirstPoint*. This service provides, first, citations to cases reported since 1825 and, secondly, references to those subsequent cases where a court has discussed the case, using language of stare decisis – followed, not followed, applied, etc. It also provides reference to journal articles where the case has been discussed.

Because of the need to go to the various (paper) volumes to track down the history of the case decided some time ago, use of the electronic product may be easier than using the paper copy. However, as with many of the electronic products the casual user will have to spend time perfecting their skills is using that software initially.

CaseBase Case Citator

This service commenced its life as a paper product (*Australasian Current Case Annotator*) but now is offered only electronically on LexisNexis AU. In this form it provides a very large database of information. Currently it has over 410,000 primary case entries covering over 60 Australian and overseas law reports, together with the unreported decisions of most superior courts of Australia. It additionally has over 40,000 annotated and digested article entries from the major Australian and overseas legal journals. Each entry includes, where appropriate, case names and citations, annotations, catchwords, judicially considered words and phrases, and statutes.

There are a number of features that make *CaseBase* extremely attractive to the researcher. These include:

- the comprehensive coverage of local and some overseas material;
- the relative ease of searching the database; and
- the fact that the database is updated frequently.

(b) Methods of noting-up English cases (in later English cases)

A number of methods can be used in noting-up English cases:

The Digest (formerly English and Empire Digest)

As noted, the *Digest* includes at the conclusion of the digested case, a list of subsequent cases which have judicially considered the digested case. This is updated using the *Cumulative Supplement* of that publication.

The Current Law Citator

This publication provides citations for all cases reported since 1947 and includes references to subsequent cases where a reported case has been judicially considered. This is currently done using four volumes: 1947-1976; 1977-1997; the two annual volumes since; and is brought right up to date using the table "Cumulative Case Citator" in *Current Law*, a monthly publication not dissimilar to our own ALMD.

Law Reports Index

The reports of the Incorporated Council of Law Reporting, including all the English authorised reports, are subject indexed here, and these volumes, extant since 1951, include a table: "Cases Judicially Considered". The latest consolidation covers the years 1981-1990, with annual cumulations and cumulative quarterly issues bringing it up to date.

All England Law Reports

The publishers of this series brought out a three volume subject index and Noter-Up in 1981. This Noter-Up contains all cases since 1936 and subsequent annual issues keep them up-to-date.

(c) English cases in Australia and New Zealand

There are then four ways of noting-up an English case to see if it has been judicially noted in subsequent English cases. To see if an English case has been judicially considered in Australia or New Zealand, the *Australian Case Citator* is of limited assistance except, as has been noted, for recent years. For a far more complete list, the researcher can consult *Australian & New Zealand Citator To UK Reports [latest year]*. *CaseBase* is also useful in this regard.

This publication contains the decisions of English superior courts upon which judicial opinion has been expressed by Australian & NZ superior courts. It is available via Butterworths Online where it is updated annually, or as an annual paper product. If using the latter, it will be necessary to update using either of the two annotators previously mentioned.

(d) Shepardising American cases

The term "to Shepardise" a case is derived from the American *Shepard's Citator*, which is a procedure whereby all subsequent cases citing the initial decision are found. The process is the same as noting up. However, the special feature of the *Shepard's* services is that they have been extended to include legislation and even journal articles.

In fact *Shepard's* case citators now exist for the reports of every State, the District of Columbia and Puerto Rico, every part of the National Reporter System, the Supreme Court and lower federal courts. They also exist for all State and federal statutes, federal administrative rules and regulations, journal articles, court rules and for certain publications in specialised fields of tax and labour law. For those using the *Shepard's* publications for the first time, there tends to be a period of anxiety – particularly for the innumerate amongst us – as the researcher is looking at a page of numbers. The *Shepard's* publications seem to be all numbers, and yet when it comes time to use them they are surprisingly simple.

Understanding Shepard's

The secret of understanding how to use the *Shepard's Citators* is to transpose them to the Australian situation. Say you wanted to find the present status, or validity, of *D'Emden v Pedder* (1904) 1 CLR 91. In the Australian environment, as we have seen above, one uses the *Australian Case Citator*. Using the alphabetical sequence, and the various volumes that cover cases from 1904 to the present, the subsequent cases which have significantly commented upon *D'Emden v Pedder* will be cited. And the references will be all full citations, ie, parties name as well as date, and where it can be found in the law reports.

But why cite the case fully? The case could be found if it were to be cited only as *1 CLR 93*. And if there were a citator for the Commonwealth Law Reports, it could just as easily be cited as *1: 93*. And that is how *Shepard's* works. There is a *Shepard's* service for each set of law reports or statutes. Full citations are not used, but rather a truncated form of citation – the volume and page number. The case name is unnecessary.

Thus, to shepardise an American case the researcher finds the service, usually with the law report, and proceeds to find the subsequent case citation, but without the party names.

Important points to note

(i) The researcher is able to use the *Shepard's* services to find parallel citations, the history of the case on appeal and even references to the case in professional journals.

(ii) There is very little selectivity in the material that is placed in a *Shepard's* service. The researcher has to be prepared to examine many irrelevant cases before finding anything really worthwhile. With most citators, this irrelevant material has been already rejected by editors. The *Shepard's* services tend to be the raw material, although abbreviations are used to indicate the traditional terms of criticised, distinguished, explained, followed, harmonised and overruled.

Electronic: Because of the cost and (in)frequency of use in many Australian law libraries, there is a tendency for many of the *Shepard's* services to have been recently cancelled and the researcher is encouraged to finish the search using the online service, available through LexisNexis. Online Shepardising removes all the technical complexity of the hard copy approach.

Westlaw's KeyCite: While much has been said above of Shepard's, a similar facility of obtaining subsequent information about a case can also be obtained by Westlaw's KeyCite facility. In many ways the facilities are similar, each with the ability to find easily those subsequent cases referring to the case you have entered and both providing flags to draw attention quickly if the subsequent case has treated the earlier case in a positive or negative way. Unlike Shephard's, there are no backsets to consult before going online.

Example of Shepard's Service

FEDERAL REPORTER, 2d SERIES

Vol. 639

Vol. 639

—1—
US cert den
in451US913
Cir. 1
782F2d[3]4
f853F2d[3]2
N H
127NH421
503A2d767

—6—
a453US916
a69LE999
a101SC3151
s453FS1272
453US[4]509
f453US511
453US531
69LE[4]816
f69LE817
69LE829
101SC[4]2893
f101SC2894
101SC2904
Cir. 1
665FS114
d692FS[4]14
Cir. 3
e709F2d877
752F2d[2]869
542FS[4]186
d545FS[2]1295
Cir. 6
d822F2d[4]593
Cir. 9
682F2d852
557FS55
Cir. 10
622FS[2]699
Ark
280Ark417
660SW905
Calif
237CaR825
Colo
634P2d57
Fla
415So2d1314
421So2d1085
Me
458A2d1237
488A2d481
Mass

—29—
Cir. 1
678F2d[11]4
678F2d[12]4
711F2d[14]1101
732F2d[4]19
732F2d[8]19
760F2d[11]351
815F2d[4]788
Cir. 2
770F2d[3]338
533FS[1]1105
63BRW[2]1008
Cir. 4
690FS[14]1453
Cir. 5
814F2d[2]1014
Cir. 6
525FS[14]822
Cir. 7
d655F2d[15]786
772F2d[4]332
776F2d195
e851F2d[9]935
594FS154
642FS1055
Cir. 9
d639FS[9]74
Conn
192Ct276
471A2d641
Fla
439So2d275
Idaho
105Ida567
671P2d480
Mass
392Mas106
465NE1208
N Y
121NYM87
467NYS2d
[179

—42—
US cert den
in451US970
Cir. 1
e651F2d[4]74
672F2d[1]234
672F2d[3]235
e687F2d532
f711F2d[1]460
e711F2d[3]461
717F2d[2]655
676F2d[3]203
676F2d[4]204
704F2d[4]342
j704F2d344
Cir. 7
675F2d[2]134
j745F2d1055
545FS[5]351
551FS[1]403
Cir. 8
700F2d469
705F2d[2]988
705F2d[4]989
Cir. 9
f654F2d1362
j654F2d1363
e663F2d[4]938
e761F2d[4]541
Cir. 10
670F2d914
Cir. 11
709F2d661
Me
430A2d555
Mass
384Mas765
13MaA198
429NE1010
431NE589
Mich
424Mch74
378NW465
Ore
62OrA806
62OrA810
662P2d741
662P2d743

—49—
US cert den
in452US917
s489FS650
Cir. 1
643F2d899
668F2d10
681F2d[1]51
j792F2d1210
634FS1445
Cir. 2
542FS[1]902
Cir. 3
f657F2d[1]1369
j657F2d1377
Cir. 6
531FS[1]1147

—54—
s486FS368
Cir. DC
713F2d[8]844
713F2d[3]845
713F2d[2]855
e750F2d[8]980
750F2d[9]989
750F2d[9]999
j750F2d1020
589FS1220
Cir. 1
574FS1569
d574FS[3]1570
Cir. 2
f759F2d225
781F2d[3]307
842F2d[8]622
844F2d959
513FS1386
570FS[2]153
e570FS[5]187
570FS[2]188
596FS1172
596FS[1]1186
596FS[9]1227
599FS[6]554
599FS[9]584
603FS[2]991
603FS[3]991
e606FS937
609FS[1]1295
616FS[4]1435
f618FS[8]156
618FS[1]167
631FS[2]970
631FS[9]971
634FS[3]308
d641FS478
665FS270
677FS245
88FRD[4]563
Cir. 3
577FS[9]330
Cir. 4
829F2d1287
557FS[3]954
Cir. 5
650FS[3]772
690FS548
Cir. 6
645F2d1233
j645F2d1247
842F2d[9]847
Cir. 7
Calif
220CaR855
Colo
659P2d1357
675P2d751
685P2d258
Conn
193Ct325
477A2d1011
D C
472A2d48
Ill
83Il2d159
111IlA1016
111IlA1062
153IlA984
419NE357
444NE1102
445NE18
505NE718
527NE1306
Mass
395Mas36
478NE724
512NE260
512NE264
512NE271
Mich
137McA54
169McA253
357NW802
425NW527
Mo
637SW269
690SW783
690SW787
Nev
99Nev412
664P2d343
N J
89NJ72
444A2d1091
N M
97NM245
98NM292
638P2d1090
648P2d331
N Y
59NY13
68NY289
84NYAD241
84NYAD477
449NE719
501NE553
445NYS2d
Pa
544A2d1357
R I
497A2d327
520A2d150
S D
378NW880
Tex
743SW679
Wash
42WAp684
713P2d741
RLPB§ 1.04
20Æ3988s
37Æ41116n

—72—
s493FS192

—75—
US cert den
in454US1083
in102SC639
s563F2d54
s579F2d126
Cir. DC
735F2d[5]1488
Cir. 1
850F2d[12]841
534FS[5]1293
623FS[1]1450
667FS[10]45
Cir. 2
662F2d[3]941
662F2d[6]941
662F2d[8]944
677F2d[3]952
677F2d[9]953
d685F2d[9]45
f685F2d46
700F2d[10]817
737F2d[17]245
737F2d[19]245
742F2d[10]58
769F2d[12]924
812F2d[1]793
812F2d[15]795
500FS[5]1363
518FS[1]1105
554FS[1]847
559FS[1]965
571FS[1]586
582FS[5]775
590FS1436
590FS[17]1449
Cir. 8
671F2d[10]1171
671F2d[10]1172
712F2d1237
712F2d[9]1238
j712F2d1240
722F2d[1]1384
513FS[3]997
Cir. 9
709F2d[9]1262
709F2d[15]1267
Cir. 10
663FS[5]1484
Cir. 11
851F2d[5]1286
95FCC293
Calif
137CA3d720
187CaR805
Mass
14MaA419
440NE45
W Va
357SE778
AABA§ 9.18
LASB§ 1.02
RLPB§ 6.02
41ÆRF175s

—82—
s33FRD540
cc581F2d1045
Cir. 1
e691F2d[7]22
691F2d[8]23
Cir. 2
662F2d[6]919
769F2d[2]78
769F2d[7]79
833F2d[7]438
600FS[8]249
625FS756
629FS[8]281
f629FS[9]283
650FS[2]1001
650FS[5]1002
650FS[8]1003
659FS[5]1010
683FS335
100FRD[3]806
101FRD[8]14
101FRD[8]15
105FRD[8]623
110FRD[8]692
111FRD450

—101—
Cir. 2
d678FS[2]403
Cir. 3
775F2d[2]519
621FS[1]1063
Cir. 4
f674F2d266
Cir. 6
774F2d[1]730
Cir. 8
697F2d[1]235
Cir. 9
706F2d[1]915
803F2d[1]440

—107—
s679F2d1032
s487FS539
Cir. 1
683FS[1]287
Cir. 2
d647F2d[3]232
e693F2d[3]248
513FS218
535FS260
535FS[1]261
f535FS[3]262
Cir. 4
577FS[1]1244
Cir. 5
792F2d534
c792F2d[3]535
Cir. 7
738F2d826
738F2d[3]827
d745F2d[3]469
d745F2d[1]470
d845F2d[3]137
c563FS[3]1087
c563FS[1]1088
e665FS[3]708
690FS[3]643
Cir. 8
d755F2d[3]631
787F2d397
Cir. 9
685F2d[1]1096
54ÆRF752s

—113—
s494FS314
N Y
cc44NY658
cc56NYAD

Chapter 5

Secondary Source Material

Outline

1 Current Awareness Services
2 Dictionaries
3 Legal Encyclopaedias
4 Legal Periodicals
5 Textbooks
6 Law Lists, Directories and Almanacs
7 Forms and Precedents
8 Practice Books
9 Law Reform Publications
10 Research Strategy Using Secondary Source Material

Legal research is underpinned by the notion of authority. In legal writing an author cannot make a statement about what the law is without a reference to the primary source of the law, that is, either case law or legislation. However, a legal researcher cannot come to an understanding about what the law is simply by finding the relevant primary sources. Unless the researcher is already an expert, the primary sources may be difficult to find, or if relevant materials are found the context or value of the resources may not be easy to understand.

Secondary sources, that is commentary about the law rather than the law itself, are useful for either providing an overview of the topic of law being researched, providing the detail of how the primary sources fit together, or providing an explanation of the meaning or significance of primary sources.

The discussion in this chapter introduces types of secondary source and sets out possible methods of using these sources for legal research in worked examples.

The chapter considers both hard copy and online methods in searching secondary sources. The medium used makes a difference to the approaches used. In using hard copy the researcher tends to adopt a structured, systematic approach whereas when using an online resource, because it is more likely that various resources are integrated and more particularly they are not indexed in the same way, there is the temptation to rely on a less formal approach relying on serendipitous outcomes, rather than by applying a comprehensive disciplined approach.

Secondary sources can have a range of objectives. Some sources are simply compilations of information which indicate the status of the primary sources such as current awareness services; other sources can be seen as concise expressions of the law based on primary sources such as encyclopaedias and text books; others can be practice works which compile and summarise the law in such a way to enable a solicitor to discover the law and offer advice by simply referring to a single source—for example looseleaf services; others can be an in depth evaluation of the primary law which may be provided for example in academic law journals. This chapter considers each of these sources.

To find the law, that is to say, to find the relevant section of an Act, clause of a regulation or case where a judge has set out the common law or explained the meaning of words, it has been seen that the researcher has to go to legislation, delegated legislation or the law reports. But what quickly becomes apparent is that there is no way that the relevant material can be located without the assistance of secondary sources: be they **subject indexes to legislation**, **citators**, **annotators** or **digests**. These have already been examined. But there is one more to add to this list – current awareness publications. These types of publications, as already seen, allow the latest Act or case to be located and used when writing a legal opinion. They will be examined here in some more depth.

However, there is another real problem for the researcher – particularly the novice who may just be embarking on their legal studies. In many cases, the researcher will have little, if any, real knowledge of the topic that is being researched. It is difficult to research the topic *riparian rights* when you don't even know what *riparian* means. Gaining that knowledge by reading an Act or a case can be challenging and not really satisfactory. It is at this stage that the researcher must appreciate that there are *types of publications* which can assist in gaining a general understanding of the law that can underpin research in specific areas of law.

To gain this knowledge, you work from the very general, through to the very particular. Some of the publications used are:

legal dictionary ➘
legal encyclopaedia ➘
textbook ➘
journal article ➘
thesis

Now we can exclude the last form – the thesis. Researchers don't usually have access to higher degree theses where some very fine point of law may be examined. And, anyway, that information usually makes a public appearance in journal articles or books at some point in time. And so what is examined below are the remaining four types of publications in more detail.

Always remember that the material contained within these types of publication is never the law. It might be advisable for the new researcher to re-read the first chapter for the explanation of the basic division of legal materials into primary and secondary. What is being examined here is secondary, and whatever it contains can seldom replace the actual law found in the legislation or the report. Yet teachers will persistently find students expounding the law and citing as an authority the author of a textbook or journal article. It must always be remembered that when a statement of law is being expounded there must be an authority and it must be a reference to a section of an Act, or delegated legislation or the judgment contained within a case. The only time secondary legal materials are given as source material is when the opinion of an author is being submitted in support of a particular interpretation of the law. It can never be used to replace the authority itself.

1. Current awareness services

While most of the looseleaf services perform the task of keeping the practitioner aware of recent changes in the law – either legislative or case – they do tend to be subject specific.

Also in this discussion it is important to note the impact of online research. It is in the area of current awareness that there is the greatest disparity between hard copy and online research. A systematic and structured approach to updating the law in hard copy is being replaced by easy access to a large range of online materials that can be navigated without a sense of context. While online research can be faster and more convenient there can also be the risk of missing crucial information.

There are two services that aim to give a broad coverage of recent Australian material, and which cover all Australian jurisdictions. These are:

Australian Legal Monthly Digest (Lawbook Co) and

Australian Current Law (LexisNexis)

In practically every law collection, government department, chambers and legal practice one or both of these publications will be found. Already they have been referred to in locating the latest Act (p 38); finding the latest rule or regulation (p 59); and latest *[ ] number* case (p 80). They provide a broad spectrum of information essential to any person who needs to find the latest law or material written about the law.

Australian Legal Monthly Digest

A service which both stands alone and complements the *Australian Digest*. Since the beginning of 1994, monthly parts are filed into a folder with a separate table of contents. To indicate the diversity and value of this publication, the various tables are listed below:

List of Titles
List of Reports
Abbreviations
Updater to the Australian Digest
Table of Cases
Judgments Handed down by the High Court
Judgments Received by the High Court
Special Leave hearings in the High Court
Legislation Judicially Considered
Words, Phrases and Maxims
General [case] Index
Chronological Table of Statutes
Acts Passed, Amended, Repealed, or Commenced
Subordinate Legislation
Table of Bills
Table of Reprinted Legislation
Legislative Index

Elements of this service are available on Thomson Legal Online. Current awareness of particular areas of law can be gained by using a combination of FirstPoint for cases and Alert24 for cases, news and legislation. Alert24 is a service which provides current awareness information on a regular basis but is not a way to look up changes to specific legislation.

Australian Current Law

This service closely resembles ALMD and has done so for a number of years. There are some differences, however. Unlike its competitor which brings out monthly a new and complete brochure of cumulative tables that is used with the monthly issues containing the numbered paragraphs of new legal information, *Australian Current Law* has the cumulative tables in the monthly issues themselves. And sometimes they are not cumulative. Thus, the researcher needs to follow closely the instructions on each issue as to how to update. This can cause confusion for those who are first or infrequent users of the publication.

However, the biggest difference is that legislative and case information is split into two groups. The legislation issue arrives monthly, the case information arrives fortnightly.

Legislation:

Title Scheme
Cumulative Table of Proclaimed Legislation
" Table of Acts Passed
" Table of Amended Acts
" Table of Parliamentary Bills
Table of Reprinted Acts
Cumulative Table of Regulations and Rules made and Amended
Table of Reprinted Regulations/Rules
Cumulative Table of Miscellaneous Orders/Notices
Abbreviations
Legislation

Reporter:

Title scheme
Abbreviations
Cumulative Table of Cases
Table of Cases Judicially Considered
Table of Statutes Judicially Considered
Table of Books, Articles and Other Materials
Cumulative Halsbury Updating Table
Cumulative Index
Table of Sentencing Decisions
Table of Quantum of Damages
Reporter

At the end of the year, the material is brought together and released in book form, with most of the tables in the monthly issue being included.

Australian Current Law is available on LexisNexis AU, however, its presentation is fragmented and if used online exclusively it is difficult to get a sense of its structure. For occasional online users the most useful elements are the legislation tables and the case digests (which may appear in a general case search anyway). The notes on legislation amendments are also useful but it is necessary to know the exact name of the legislation update first. *Australian Current Law* would be a better service online if it were possible to browse through a cumulative consolidation of the year's legal updates in the respective subject areas. This is a strength of FirstPoint in regard to cases.

Which is better: Australian Legal Monthly Digest or Australian Current Law?

This is an extremely difficult question to answer. If you ask the librarians, the chances are that they will split about 50:50. With the ALMD keeping the *Australian Digest* updated, and the *Australian Current Law* doing the same task for *Halsbury's Laws of Australia*, most practitioners may well have to subscribe to both. They certainly could do worse. But if the choice has to be made, the only really practical way to go about making that decision is for the decision maker to select an area where they have expertise and evaluate, in that area, over a 3-4 month period. Note the delays, coverage, errors and quality of digesting. Using that information, but appreciating that there can be a lack of uniformity in quality over various subject areas, the person who has to make the decision has at least something to work with.

In the online environment, as a case law current awareness resource FirstPoint is superior to *Australian Current Law Reporter* because of the legal classification scheme and the combination of the citator content. The legislation content of ALMD is not available online and the *Australian Current Law Legislation* service is imperfectly realised online.

For an effective legislation current awareness service which also provides full text links Lawlex is a product which was exclusively designed for online research. Lawlex is a service which has set up a common interface for searching legislation across all Australian jurisdictions but relies on the respective government sites for its content. The interface enables easy access to current awareness information. It is a very efficient approach to developing a legal research service.[1]

1 See <http://my.lawlex.com.au>. Lawlex is part of the Anstat group owned by SAI Global. Anstat is predominantly a Victorian legislation publisher but also provides online access to Australian legislation. See <www.anstat.com.au>.

2. Dictionaries

Having noted what was written about finding background information from the secondary sources, what must be studied now is that type of publication on the very bottom rung – the legal dictionary.

Never underestimate the need to consult the legal dictionary. There are many words and phrases which have been introduced into our legal vocabulary. That this has occurred is not strange. Until the 1500s, all law spoken in the common law courts of England was a type of French (law French), and all documents used in the court process were written in Latin. Consequently, it is readily understandable why those two languages are found so often in law. To obtain the meaning of words used in the study of law, it is thus preferable to use a law dictionary rather than a common English language dictionary. It is the source of the most abbreviated form of information and, consequently, will provide the novice researcher with the place to start researching.

Every law student and legal practitioner needs a legal dictionary. The one that should be purchased will depend principally upon the amount that is to be spent. For the students just starting their studies, the following are suitable:

Osborn's Concise Law Dictionary, 10th ed by M Woodley, Sweet & Maxwell, 2005

Butterworths Concise Australian Legal Dictionary, 3rd ed 2004

A more comprehensive Australian dictionary is the:

Butterworths Australian Legal Dictionary (paper 1997 and online and linked to cases and legislation)

The online version found on LexisNexis AU is titled the *Encyclopaedic Australian Legal Dictionary* and is an expanded version of the 1997 publication. It last had a major update in September 2004. There is not a direct correlation between the two although much of the material is the same. While both versions are comprehensive the quality of the definitions are variable and there are some key terms missing.

While one has been on the market for some time and is highly respected is:

Jowitt's Dictionary of English Law, 2nd ed, 1977, in 2 vols with supplements.

An American dictionary can be most useful because of extensive references to US cases and the inclusion of a great number of Latin word and phrase translations. Two that dominate the US student market, which are therefore relatively inexpensive, are:

Black's Law Dictionary, 8th ed, 2004 (West)

Ballentine's Law Dictionary, 3d, 1969 (Lawyers Cooperative)

Special legal dictionaries: Words and phrases

Certain dictionary-type publications have gone beyond being a mere source of the meaning of a word. They provide the law itself – complete with legislative and/or case authority. These are distinguished from the dictionary in that they contain the law rather than editorial commentary about the law. Most of the traditional dictionaries fit into the latter category and consequently may have limitations in finding the law. Yet the introduction to *Words and Phrases* (US) includes the observations of one of America's greatest jurists on the use of words: "A word is not a crystal, transparent and unchanged, it is the skin of a living thought and may vary greatly in colour and context according to the circumstances and the time in which it is used" (Justice OW Holmes). The "words and phrases" publications provide the context and circumstances to allow flexible use. Examples of them include:

Australia

Australian Legal Words and Phrases (3 vols, Butterworths). Now contains over 100,000 words and phrases from Australian case law and legislation. This work is available on LexisNexis AU.

Consolidated Words and Phrases Table to the Australian Digest, titles 1-83 (looseleaf) (Lawbook Co)

England

Words and Phrases Legally Defined, 4th ed (Butterworths, 4 vols) Updated by cumulative supplement.

Stroud's Judicial Dictionary, 7th ed (Sweet & Maxwell 3 vols) 2006 Updated by cumulative supplement.

Canada

Words and Phrases Judicially defined in Canadian Courts and Tribunals, (Carswell, 8 vols) Updated annually by cumulative supplement.

United States

Words and Phrases (West over 130 vols) Updated by annual pocket parts.

3. Legal encyclopaedias

In the common law world, there are three principal legal encyclopaedias:

Halsbury's Laws of England, 5th ed (LexisNexis)

American Jurisprudence, 2nd ed (West Publishing)

Corpus Juris Secundum (West Publishing)

Australia has two major legal encyclopaedias: *Halsbury's Laws of Australia* (Butterworths) and *Laws of Australia* (Lawbook Co).

Encyclopaedic style of writing

Before examining specifically the relevant encyclopaedias for Australian legal research, always keep in mind the value that legal encyclopaedias provide in our gradation of information about the law. This is principally because of the style of writing. First, it is written in what can be described as a "propositional" style. Thus, an exact statement or proposition of law is made in the text and the footnote carries the authority. This style by necessity limits the inclusion of related historic and law reform material. Secondly, it is a narrative style, usually adopting numbered paragraphs within broad subject headings. Thirdly, the encyclopaedic style tends to provide a broad overview of the subject, with succinct legal analysis of the current law and reference to all leading authorities. Other aspects of the style dictate that extracts of cases are minimal, although examples are used to explain difficult points of law. Where there is uncertainty, the differing views are explained with necessary analysis, leaving hypothetical and personal views as to what the law *should be*, severely restricted. The authorities, both case and legislative, are usually found in detailed footnotes.

For both the novice and seasoned researcher, it can be the perfect starting point and in many ways preferable to a textbook in order to get a quick overview and to understand the principal problems of the topic. They all have, additionally, good methods of keeping the information up to date in preference to the traditional textbook.

Example of the entry in the "Cumulative Halsbury Updating Table" in *Australian Current Law: Reporter*

Cumulative Halsbury Updating Table

Important Note At the beginning of each title of *Halsbury's Laws of Australia* there is a statement of currency. Subscribers can search for developments subsequent to the currency date in the *Halsbury Updating Table*. The emboldened paragraph numbers are those in published titles of *Halsbury* affected by recent cases appearing in the Australian Current Law Reporter. The Australian Current Law Reporter reference follows. The *Halsbury Updating Table* is cumulative – subscribers need only consult the latest issue of the Reporter

For legislative development for particular titles, subscribers should consult Australian Current Law Legislation.

Updates to *Halsbury* titles will be made by service issues as the need arises.

Method of Citation

Cases in the Reporter are cited: [5-20] ... [2004] (Iss 1) ACL Rep 90 HC 1

[5-20] — refers to the *Halsbury* paragraph

[2004] — refers to the year of the Reporter in which the case digest appears

(Iss 1) — refers to the Reporter issue number if the case is digested in the current year. Cases for previous years will appear in the yearbook for that year.

90 — refers to the subject classification

HC — refers to the court, ie High Court

1 — refers to the number of the digest

5 — Aboriginals and Torres Strait Islanders

[5-80] . . . . [2000] 5 FC 11
[5-85]-[5-95] . . . . [1998] 5 FC 7
[5-85] . . . . [2003] (Iss 1) 5 FC 1
[5-95] . . . . [2003] (Iss 8) 5 FC 44
[5-110] . . . . [1998] 5 FC 6
[5-170]-[5-335] . . . . . . [2003] (Iss 12) 5 NT 2
[5-170] . . . . [2000] 5 FC 11
[5-180] . . . . . [2001] 5 FC 4, [2002] 385 HC 2
[5-195] . . . . . . [2001] 5 FC 4, [2002] 5 FC 19
[5-260] . . . . [1997] 5 NT 1
[5-320] . . . . [2002] 385 HC 2
[5-335] . . . . [2001] 5 FC 11
[5-345] . . [1997] 5 NSW 2, [1998] 5 NSW 1, 5 NSW 2, [2002] 5 NSW 1
[5-410] . . . . [1997] 120 NSW 45
[5-1005] . . . . [1997] 5 WA 1
[5-1055] . . . . [1996] 5 FC 10
[5-1255] . [1999] 130 NSW 10, [2002] 5 NSW 2, 5 NSW 3
[5-5070] . [2002] 5 HC 2, [2003] (Iss 1) 5 HC 1, 5 FC 1
[5-5075] . . . . [2002] 5 HC 2
[5-5085] . [2002] 5 HC 1, 5 HC 2, [2003] (Iss 1) 5 HC 1, 5 FC 1
[5-5090] . [2002] 5 HC 2, [2004] (Iss 2) 5 FC 7
[5-5145]-[5-5315] . . . . [2003] (Iss 12) 5 FC 58
[5-5145] . [2002] 5 HC 1, 5 HC 2, [2003] (Iss 1) 5 HC 1
[5-5155] . . . . [2002] 5 HC 1, 5 HC 2
[5-5160] . . . . [2002] 5 HC 2
[5-5165] . [2002] 5 HC 1, 5 HC 2, [2003] (Iss 1) 5 HC 1, [2004] (Iss 1) 5 FC 4
[5-5170] . . . . [2002] 5 HC 2
[5-5175] . . . . [2002] 5 HC 1, 5 HC 2
[5-5180] . . . . [2002] 5 HC 2
[5-5190] . [2002] 5 HC 2, [2004] (Iss 2) 5 FC 8
[5-5195] . . . . [2002] 5 FC 11, 5 HC 1, 5 HC 2
[5-5200] . . . . [2002] 5 HC 2
[5-5205] . . . . [2002] 5 HC 1, 5 HC 2

(i) Halsbury's Laws of Australia (LexisNexis)

After the success of the principal English work, it was only a matter time before an Australian version became a reality. The *Pilot* to the 3rd ed of *Halsbury's Laws of England*, and the *Australian Commentaries* to the 4th ed, were always useful but would never replace the need for specifically written product for the Australian market. The aim of the publisher was to produce a totally local product with little need to consult the English work for local law.

Updating: Beside the constant section replacement required by changes in the law, there is a table in the *Reporter* part of the *Australian Current Law*: "Cumulative Halsbury Updating Table", which allows monthly updates to be noted.

Halsbury's Laws of Australia was designed from the outset to be accessible electronically. The paragraphs are short and can be easily read on a computer screen. The tagging in the editorial process has enabled comprehensive linking throughout the publication itself and to other LexisNexis AU sources. This legal encyclopaedia online is a far more powerful research tool than the hard copy version. The *Australian Current Law* update is embedded at paragraph level, the footnote references are linked to the full text of the respective authority where available, and there are also direct links to CaseBase.

(ii) Laws of Australia (Lawbook Co)

This publication commenced in 1993. Written in the traditional encyclopaedic style, the law has been divided into 36 distinct topics and the publication has been well received by the profession. *Laws of Australia* does not attempt to be as comprehensive as *Halsbury's Laws of Australia*. It is seen by the publisher more as a collection of high level texts on each of the topics. In fact some of the key topics are available as individual publications.

Update: Until 2002, the current awareness publication *Australian Legal Monthly Digest* was linked to the *Laws of Australia* by paragraph and a researcher was able to keep abreast of subsequent changes relatively simply. However, when that link was removed from the ALMD, it meant that there could well be periods when *Laws of Australia* is somewhat out of date and in hard copy there is no clear way of updating the information.

In such a case the researcher should consult a current awareness publication and a citator: the former to find new legislation and cases on the topic generally, the latter to check the status of specific cases mentioned within the paragraph.

On Thomson Legal Online footnoted case authority is linked to the full text of the case where available as well as to FirstPoint which can be used to note up the reference.

(iii) Halsbury's Laws of England (5th ed) (LexisNexis)

Historically this publication has served the Australian legal profession well. The Halsbury-style of writing has become synonymous with good encyclopaedic writing and is in many ways the benchmark for all legal encyclopaedias.

Even though the local encyclopaedias are now completed, this work will still have a place in all Australian law collections but will be a luxury for many firms in the near future. There will always be a place for it in any of the larger collections which need to have the full common law collection.

Updating: In addition to the various editions, there is an annual *Cumulative Supplement*, now in 2 volumes. There is also a monthly *Current Service*, in two looseleaf binders. These services provide a wide range of new primary and secondary material to the subscriber, as well as detailed noter-up material for cases and legislative information.

Halsbury's Laws of England is now available online through LexisNexis AU. It should be noted that because the new LexisNexis online platform is a global platform any online publications from any LexisNexis publisher in the world will theoretically be available on a local subscription. In Australia this means now many LexisNexis UK publications and soon Canadian sources. *Halsbury's Laws of England* on LexisNexis AU may be a more cost effective proposition than subscribing to the hard copy.

4. Legal periodicals

As in other disciplines, the periodical has assumed an important role in legal research and keeping up to date with the changing law. The pace of law reform allows the legal periodical to reflect both the changes and any reaction that may arise because of those changes. With the publication of letters and short notes, together with the longer, reasoned and well documented articles, the legal periodical provides a forum for both academic and practitioner.

Contemporary information

There are various types of legal periodicals and publications which are aimed at different readers: thus certain English journals, including the *Solicitors' Journal* and the *New Law Journal*, have as their aim to keep practitioners up to date with the day-to-day developments in both legislation and case areas. Such journals are an ideal source of contemporary information, particularly regarding legislation. Both contain extensive correspondence sections. In Australia this role is filled by *Australian Law News,* published by the Australian Law Council, and such publications that emanate from all of the Law Societies in the States and Territories. In New South Wales, the monthly *Law Society Journal* has not only journal articles of the type noted above but also Legal Profession Disciplinary Tribunal Reports, Law Society Rulings and extensive coverage of recent legislation and cases concerning the practitioner. An annual index allows these to be found quickly. The NSW Bar puts out *Bar News* which serves much the same purpose.

Analytical review

On the other hand we have another range of journals that caters for the academic and the person interested in "reasons for change" rather than the mere, commercially pressing, "change" itself. Thus, the *Modern Law Review, Cambridge Law Journal* and the *Harvard Law Review* can be slotted into this type of journal. Yet even with this range you find that the *Modern Law Review* is slanted towards the sociological and reform, while in the *Law Quarterly Review* you can find some excellent articles on historical developments. These types of leanings can, however, be transitory and be due to a particular editor rather than established editorial policy. Into this general category, however, and usually without any of this type of "editorial bias", can be placed the bulk of legal periodicals, particularly the various journals and reviews put out by law schools. The *Australian Law Journal* cannot be fully categorised and may be thought of as keeping the profession up to date, as well as providing a vehicle for deeply reasoned, academic-type articles.

In addition to the above, there are also those journals which cater for a definite interest, for example, *Australian Tax Review* and *Australian Business Law Review.*

Indexes

Without some type of index the wealth of material in the many hundreds of legal periodicals would be lost, and while certain publications like the *Australian Law Journal, Modern Law Review, Law Quarterly Review, Harvard Law Review* and *Yale Law Review* have indexes, they are the exception.

To facilitate searching legal journals the ideal starting point is the *Index to Legal Periodicals.*

1. Index to Legal Periodicals (1908+),

Produced by HW Wilson in the US with a strong North American bias, it indexes the articles in over 620 legal periodicals in the English language.

In many libraries, the paper copy is being replaced by a subscription to the electronic product. Available back to 1981, the WilsonDisc allows the researcher a speedy way of locating recent articles, using key words. This is far preferable to searching some of the broad categories in the hardcopy. An example is *Legal History* which might run into pages and consequently difficult to research manually. It is also available via the Westlaw and LexisNexis online services where it is included in the particular subscription. This will not include most academic deals.

Example from Index to Legal Periodicals

Capital imports *See* Foreign investments
Capital punishment
Barbarism in the plastic bubble: an application of existentialist theory to capital punishment in the United States. 1990 *Det. C.L. Rev.* 1011-83 Wint '90
A beyond a reasonable doubt standard in death penalty proceedings: a neglected element of fairness. L. E. Carter. 52 *Ohio St. L.J.* 195-221 '91
Capital sentencing after Walton v. Arizona [110 S. Ct. 3047]: a retreat from the "death is different" doctrine. 40 *Am. U.L. Rev.* 1389-429 Summ '91
Challenging the death penalty: a colloquium. Foreword. J. Abady, J. M. Lane, W. Tymas; The chiropractor as brain surgeon: defense lawyering in capital cases. V. Berger; The decline of executive clemency in capital cases. H. A. Bedau; Law and reality in the capital penalty trial. W. S. Geimer; Prosecutors' closing arguments at the penalty trial. W. S. White; Innocence, federalism, and the capital jury: two legislative proposals for evaluating post-trial evidence of innocence in death penalty cases. E. M. Freedman; Understanding Teague v. Lane [109 S. Ct. 1060]. J. Blume, W. Pratt; Chipping away at the great writ: will death sentenced federal habeas corpus petitioners be able to seek and utilize changes in the law? S. M. Goldstein; Habeas corpus as a safety valve for innocence. B. Ledewitz; Suspending justice: the unconstitutionality of the proposed six-month time limit on the filing of habeas corpus petitions by state death row inmates. M. Mello, D.

Cappello, A. Barry
Lender liability. What lies ahead: by A. B. Cappello, F. E. Komoroske. 27 *Trial* 68-9+ My '91
Capra, Daniel J.
Discretion must be controlled, judicial authority circumscribed, federalism preserved, plain meaning enforced, and everything must be simplified: recent Supreme Court contributions to federal civil practice. 50 *Md. L. Rev.* 632-741 '91
Carlson, David K.
Significant recent developments in estate planning: by B. M. Abbin, D. K. Carlson, R. W. Nager. 22 *Tax Adviser* 590-4+ S '91; 669-81 O '91
Carnevale, Anthony P.
Schooling and training for work in America: an overview; by A. P. Carnevale, H. Goldstein. 42 *Lab. L.J.* 563-8 Ag '91
Carpinello, George F.
Testing the limits of choice of law clauses: franchise contracts as a case study. 74 *Marq. L. Rev.* 57-89 Fall '90
Carriers
See also
Airlines
Communications
Railroads
The 1980 Motor Carrier Act: a ten year retrospective by traffic executives. J. C. Johnson, K. C. Schneider. 58 *Transp. Prac. J.* 356-72 Summ '91

Note:

(a) It is important that you appreciate that *not* everything that appears in a periodical is in the *Index to Legal Periodicals*. Articles of less than five pages and book reviews of less than two pages are not indexed; but case notes are indexed regardless of length. Insubstantial articles, annual surveys of the law of a jurisdiction are not indexed and statutes on foreign, comparative and international law may not be indexed.

(b) It indexes only legal periodicals.

(c) It indexes only English language legal periodicals.

2. Current Law Index and LegalTrac/Legal Resource Index (Gale Group)

These companion publications have been published since 1980. The *Legal Resource Index* is published in paper and indexes more than 700 legal periodicals and is issued monthly.

LegalTrac and *Legal Resource Index* are electronic facilities that have a larger base of materials, including legal newspapers and legal newsletters. *Legal Resource Index* is available on LexisNexis and Westlaw. The advantage of these electronic products over some of the other bibliographic indexes is that a growing percentage of material that can be located will be full text. Initially only about 5 per cent, in many areas this is now between 10-12 per cent of references found that can be downloaded and read.

3. Attorney-General's Information Service (AGIS)

This is a very popular database of references to legal journals. Because the material comes from the journals received by the Lionel Murphy Library of the Attorney-General's Department, Canberra, it has a predominant Australian focus. It has a comprehensive coverage of Australian, New Zealand and Pacific materials, but includes the principal law journals of the common law world.

AGIS Plus is electronically available on the Informit Internet Services. The index is also published online by Thomson Legal Online as the Australian Legal Journals Index. The Lawbook version has the advantage of including links to FirstPoint and The Laws of Australia.

4. Index to Periodical Articles relating to Law (1958+) (Glanville Publishers, NY)

This is an index to legal articles published in non-legal periodicals and, consequently, not included in the *Index to Legal Periodicals*. Some of the journals indexed here are legal newspapers, others are Bar Association publications but most are periodicals in the fields of economics, sociology and political science which occasionally publish articles relating to law. This index is also available online on HeinOnline <*http://heinonline.org*>

5. Index to Foreign Legal Periodicals

Headquartered at the University of California Berkeley School of Law, Law Library and published by University of California Press, for the American Association of Law Libraries, it covers nearly 500 legal periodicals not published in the United States. While some Australian and Canadian periodicals are included, this is basically a valuable index of non-English material. The entries are in the language of the article, although where in a non-Roman alphabet, the title is translated into English. This is available on Westlaw and Ovid.

Other places to find journal references

- *Australian Digest*, 3rd edition volumes, and ALMD
- *Australian Current Law Reporter*, especially "Table of Books, Articles and Other Materials"
- *CaseBase* entries include a list of journal articles which refer to the case cited.
- *Index to Canadian Legal Literature* (1956+) is a subject and author index of books, articles and government publications published in Canada. Part of the *Canadian Abridgment* (Carswell), it is also available online through LexisNexis Quicklaw service and Westlaw*e*CARSWELL.

5. Textbooks

There is an extensive literature on the rise and development of the law treatise and more latterly the law textbook. But these do tend to provide a number of specific types of information. They both are an excellent source of information about both what the law is and, in many of the current texts, what the law should be. The author, with extensive experience and expertise in the area, has usually delved deep and provides the user with detailed and comparative material. And a particular feature of many of the common law treatises produced earlier in the 20th century is the extensive historic introductions which provide the new researcher with a wealth of such material. The Sweet & Maxwell *Common Law Library* series is a good example covering the traditional common law areas of torts, contracts, contempt, agency, damages, negligence and restitution. Finally, a feature of the late 20th century is the movement to take the law treatise out of book or monographic form, and turn it into a looseleaf or serial format. This does have the advantage of being able to be kept up to date with least inconvenience to the user, but it does appear to add considerably to its price.

To find the older and current law treatises and texts, the library catalogues are an excellent starting point. In Australia the courts were the early repositories of law materials and in all States the libraries of the Supreme Courts are well placed concerning as historic legal material of the jurisdiction. The older universities in each State have excellent historic materials as well. But it is in the university collections generally, particularly those established in the 1960s, that the greatest repositories of legal books can be found. In the past 40 years, with increased budgets, aggressive collecting and expanding university curricula, the Australian university collections have become impressive. They are certainly equal to the average UK university law library but they still have some way to go before they reach the average standards of the Canadian and the US university law collections. Specialised law collections can be found in government departments and in private law and accounting firms.

To locate specific books, the holdings of many of the larger libraries are in electronic form in the Australian National Bibliography which can be searched. The catalogues of Harvard University, Columbia University and the Squires Library at Cambridge University, have all been published. Many others are now in electronic form and can be accessed online.

6. Law lists, directories and almanacs

Law lists give information as to solicitors and barristers who are located in a particular area.

Australia

Probably the most important was the *Australian and New Zealand Law List,* which ceased publication in 1975. This was replaced by the *Australian Legal Directory,* published by the Australian Document Exchange Pty Ltd for the Australian Law Council. It was an annual publication. It is now published biennially by DXMail, part of the Toll Priority business ... AustLII have expressed an interest. In the meantime FindLaw's *Australian Legal Directory* is probably the most comprehensive. It is at <*www.findlaw.com.au/wld/advancedsearch.asp*>.

United Kingdom

The English equivalents, Sweet and Maxwell's *Law List* and Butterworths' *Law List,* have also stopped publication, although recently published was *Havers' Companion to the Bar* (Sweet & Maxwell), which lists the services offered by individual members of the Bar, showing areas of particular interest and specialisation. However, because of fragmentation, an excellent starting point are the lawlinks maintained by the University of Kent at Canterbury at <*www.kent.ac.uk/careers/siteslaw.htm*>.

United States of America

The *Martindale-Hubbell Law Directory* (12 volumes) lists American lawyers, by State, city and town, together with a list of special services offered to the lawyer in the United States. This work is principally used for this extensive coverage but the researcher should be aware of the material in the final volume. Here is contained material relating to the court calendar of each State together with digests of those areas of the law of most use to out of State practitioners.

Because of the size and expense, few of the latest editions are in Australia. However, as *Martindale-Hubbell Law Directory* is on LexisNexis, and <*www.martindale.com*> sophisticated searching of American lawyers can be done by geographical location, size of firm, law school attended or special interests, or permutations of all four, using that service. The functionality of the Martindale web site has been enhanced by a partnership with LinkedIn enabling professional networking.

Another similar publication is *The American Bar – the Canadian Bar – the International Bar: lawyers of the world*, two volumes, published by Forster-Long, Sacramento, California, which provides a similar, if much less intensive, coverage of a wider area. The online version can be found at www.americanbar.com.

Internet: Findlaw/*West's Legal Directory* is a free internet service provided by West Information Publishing Group and has more than 800,000 profiles of lawyers and law firms in the United States and Canada. The URL is: <*www.findlaw.com*>.

Canada

As well as the publication noted immediately above, there is a special *Martindale Hubbell Canadian and International Lawyers*, which provided an extensive list for Canada, and many other countries.

Canadian Law List. Published annually by Canada Law Book Inc, it provides a comprehensive listing of all Canadian courts, judges, lawyers in Canada by province, municipality and firm, ministries, legal aid offices and more. Online, see www.canadianlawlist.com.

New Zealand

Brookers *Law Directory*, published annually, provides a comprehensive guide to New Zealand legal professionals, including practitioners by name and location, together with information about the courts and Parliament. A limited content service is available at <*www.brookers.co.nz/ lawdirectory*>.

International

Lawyer's Register International by specialties and fields of law including a directory of Corporate Counsel, Lawyer's Register Pub, Solon, Ohio.

Australian State directories and almanacs

These are valuable government publications which list those matters which are of vital interest in the day-to-day activities of the profession. They include: Court sittings of the High Court, Supreme Court and various county divisions, calendars of legal events, all judicial personnel, legal and associated legal bodies; all solicitors and barristers and the various legal firms, both city, suburban and country. These tend to be annual publications.

NSW Law Almanac (published by Supreme Court)

Law Calendar (Victorian Attorney-General's Department)

Western Australian Law Almanac (Government Printer)

South Australian Law Calendar (Court Services Dept)

Queensland Law Calendar (Department of Justice and Attorney-General).

7. Forms and precedents

Form books and other types and variety of precedents exist to assist the lawyer in drafting a legal document. Thus a solicitor who is preparing a conveyance or a will usually on each occasion does not sit down and draft the wording afresh out of her head. Instead she uses a standard form and this is adopted to suit her immediate situation.

This is not a characteristic of a lazy or unprofessional solicitor if they are used carefully and not indiscriminately. In legal drafting the form of words can be critical and in some cases all can be lost if there is only a slight divergence from an established and recognised sequence; note particularly in drafting a will. In these cases a precedent is an *aide-memoire*. Examples of some of the publications available include:

Comprehensive and general

Australian Encyclopaedia of Forms and Precedents (LexisNexis Butterworths). The advantage of this work is each topic is preceded by a concise overview of the relevant area of law so the context of the precedent being referred to is completely understood.

Practical Forms and Precedents (NSW), ed Ian Salmon (2 vols looseleaf), Lawbook Co.

Specialised precedents (examples only)

Wills:	*Hutley's Australian Wills Precedents*, 6th ed by C Rowland, LexisNexis, 2003
Computer:	Gordon Hughes and Anna Sharpe, *Computer Contracts: Principles and Precedents* (3 vols, looseleaf/online), Lawbook Co

8. Practice books

These books have been published to aid the practitioner who is appearing in a particular Court. They sets out all relevant legislation and rules which govern the jurisdiction and practice in that Court. However, they also contain "informal" rules set down by the Court which must also be followed. For example, on 30 September 1986, the Supreme Court of Victoria, through the Chief Justice, issued Practice Note No 4 of 1986, entitled *Citation of Unreported Judgments*. This set down the rule that unreported judgments were not to be cited in that Court unless leave was first obtained. This Practice Note was in turn revoked by Practice Note No 1 of 2006 which now enables the citation of unreported judgments if made available to the court and opposing counsel with sufficient time for proper consideration. These practice notes appear in the practice books for that Court. They are also known in some jurisdictions as "Practice Directions".

There will thus tend to be practice books for each court in each jurisdiction. In many instances, because of the similarity of court rules and procedures, the practice books of other jurisdictions are used in a supplementary fashion.

Principal superior court practice books, by jurisdiction

High Court & Federal Courts	*Practice and Procedure – High Court and Federal Court of Australia*, J West and others (4 vols, looseleaf/online) LexisNexis
	Federal Court Practice, GA Flick (2 vols, looseleaf/online) Lawbook Co
	Federal Magistrates Court Guidebook, M Steele (1 vol looseleaf/online) Lawbook Co
ACT	*Civil Procedure ACT*, R Refshauge and P Ward (2 vol, looseleaf/online) LexisNexis. To be used in the ACT Supreme Court and Magistrates Court (civil jurisdiction)

New South Wales	*NSW Civil Practice & Procedure,* Hamilton & Lindsay (3 vols, looseleaf/online) Lawbook Co
	Ritchie's Uniform Civil Procedure NSW, P Taylor and others (2 vols, looseleaf/online) LexisNexis
Victoria	*Civil Procedure Victoria,* N Williams, (3 vols, looseleaf/online) LexisNexis
	Victorian Courts, G Nash (2-5 vols, looseleaf) Lawbook Co
Queensland	*Civil Procedure Queensland* J Douglas and others (2 vols, looseleaf/online) LexisNexis
	Queensland Civil Practice PA Keane and others (4 vols, looseleaf/online) Lawbook Co
South Australia	*Civil Procedure South Australia* RM Lunn (2 vols, looseleaf/online) LexisNexis
Western Australia	*Civil Procedure – Western Australia* Seaman P (2 vols, looseleaf/online) LexisNexis
Tasmania	*Civil Procedure Tasmania* A Shott and others (1 vol, looseleaf/online) LexisNexis
New Zealand	*McGechan on Procedure* (1 vol, looseleaf/online/CD) Brookers.
	Principles of Civil Procedure, Andrew Beck, 2nd ed, Brookers
England	The White Book Service 2008*, Lord Justice Waller, (2 vols, looseleaf/CD/online) Westlaw 2008*
	Civil Procedure Online, LexisNexis Butterworths (UK)
	Blackstone's Civil Practice OUP (1 vol, annual publication)
Australia generally	BC Cairns, *Australian Civil Procedure,* 4th ed, LBC, 1996
	Civil Procedure – commentary and procedures, SE Colbran and others 3rd Ed LexisNexis

English practice books in Australian jurisdictions

The principal practice book for English superior courts, as noted above, is Jacob's *Supreme Court Practice,* commonly called the *White Book.* It has value to Australian practitioners generally, but to NSW practitioners specifically. This is so because, since the *Supreme Court Act 1970,* by fusing the common law and equity jurisdiction in the Supreme Court,

NSW court practice was brought back into line with the other Australian States and England. Consequently, where there were no local precedents, those of England were relevant and the *White Book* was consulted extensively for guidance. Over time this reliance has weakened in NSW but it is still used for supplementary authority. The same happens in practically all Australian jurisdictions as well.

District/County Court jurisdictions

NSW	*District Court Practice (NSW)*, EJ O'Grady (1 vol, looseleaf/online) Lawbook Co See Hamilton & Lindsay, above See Taylor above
Victoria	See Williams and Nash, above
Queensland	See Douglas and Keane, above
SA	See Lunn, above
WA	See Seaman, above

Local/Magistrates courts

NSW	***NSW Civil Practice & Procedure – Local Courts***, MF Morahan (looseleaf) Lawbook Co See Taylor above
Victoria	See Williams and Nash, above
Queensland	See Douglas and Keane, above
South Australia	*Magistrates' Court Practice (South Australia)*, A Cannon and G Hiskey (1 vol, looseleaf/online) Law-book Co See also Lunn, above
Western Australia	Civil Procedure Western Australia – Magistrates Court, *PWN Nichols (1 vol looseleaf/online) LexisNexis*

Criminal practice books, by jurisdiction

Federal	*Federal Offences*, Watson & Watson (2 vols, looseleaf/online) Lawbook Co
ACT	*Criminal Law and Practice (ACT)*, Michael Ward (2 vols), published by author, 1996 (ISBN 0 646 27685 9)
NSW	*Criminal Law NSW*, RS Watson and others (2 or 4 vols, looseleaf/online) Lawbook Co

	Criminal Practice and Procedure NSW & Criminal Law News, RN Howie & PA Johnson (4 vols, looseleaf/online) LexisNexis
	Local Court Criminal Practice NSW, N Dugandzic and others (1 vol, looseleaf/online) LexisNexis
Victoria	*Criminal Law Victoria*, D Grace and others (3 vols, looseleaf/online) LexisNexis
	Criminal Law Investigation and Procedure Victoria, I Freckelton (1-5 vols, looseleaf/online) Lawbook Co
Queensland	*Summary Offences Law and Practice Queensland*, N Jarro and others (1 vol, looseleaf/online) Lawbook Co
	Carter's Criminal Law of Queensland, MJ Shanahan and others (16th ed, 2007) LexisNexis
South Australia	*Summary Justice*, PMStL Kelly (1 vol, looseleaf) Lawbook Co
	Criminal Law South Australia, RM Lunn (3 vols, looseleaf/online) LexisNexis
Western Australia	*Criminal Law Western Australia*, Ian Weldon (3 vols, looseleaf/online) LexisNexis
New Zealand	*Summary Proceedings*, Gerald Orchard and others (1 vol and online) Brookers

English criminal practice books in Australian jurisdictions

As in the case of civil procedures, so in the criminal area are English practice books used to supplement the Australian material. Probably the most extensively used is:

Archbold: Criminal Pleading, Evidence and Practice Sweet & Maxwell, 2008

However, a new publication on the market, at much less cost, is:

Blackstone's Criminal Practice 2008 ed D Ormerod, OUP

9. Law reform publications

The value of the publications which emanate from law reform agencies should never be under-estimated. The scholarship which can be found in them is usually of the highest order and the topic upon which they are written usually of importance and of current interest. In many cases the recommendations which such reports contain are accepted by the executive government and become the basis of future legislation.

History: The law reform movement had a spectacular growth in the 1970s and early 1980s. While there has tended to be a consolidation more recently, there is still excellent work being undertaken. For some interesting background material to the law reform movement, see William H Hurlburt, *Law Reform Commissions in the United Kingdom, Australia and Canada*, Edmonton, Juriliber, 1986.

Terms of Reference: Few law reform agencies have the ability to initiate their own investigations into matters of law reform. The usual practice is for the Government, via the Attorney-General, to refer a matter to the agency. That reference is usually quite formal and can either be in very general terms or might well, in a politically sensitive area, be limited. Once the agency receives the reference it will, depending if any time limit is found in the reference, work out its own priority with respect to reporting.

The Nature and Format of Law Reform Publications: Most law reform agencies in Australia publish working papers (also called issues papers or discussion papers) before publishing a final report. They also publish an annual report.

The Working Paper: On many occasions, and particularly when the matter is controversial, the agency will wish to determine all of the arguments associated with the particular legal problem. One excellent way of achieving this end is to conduct initial research which identifies all of the major questions associated with the problem, together with the solutions that may appear obvious or which have been suggested by interested parties and interest groups. To a limited extent the reasons associated with these solutions are also included. This is put into a document and published as a "working paper". These are not the settled views of the agency but are distributed in an effort to focus the debate in a particular direction and elicit as much comment as possible from all interested groups in the community. The terms of reference may specifically direct the debate in a particular direction or the agency may give a preliminary view or it may present merely a number of options. In any case the aim is to encourage debate and response to the agency. There is usually a time limit placed upon that response.

In much the same way, an "issues paper" tends to be published quickly at the beginning of a researching task and includes little research.

The "discussion paper" is produced later on the process and is closer to the traditional working paper.

The Report: Once the agency has received the terms of reference, researched the topic, consulted where necessary and formulated a view, that view is formally communicated to the executive government in its report. In many ways the report mirrors the process of writing the report. In the beginning of the report can be found the terms of reference setting out the problem. Then the report usually sets out the options, either raised by interest groups or adopted in other jurisdictions. At that point the agency usually sets out its preferred view as a solution to the problem. The final task of some, but not all, is to draft the required legislation to achieve this end.

Because of the traditional manner of setting out the report in this fashion, the researcher can see that consulting the report has two distinct advantages. The first is to allow the casual researcher quickly to get an idea of the problem and suggested solutions that have been thoroughly examined by experts in the field. Usually there are extensive lists of authorities and secondary source material that have been consulted. There may well be extensive quoting from experts in the field who have responded to a working paper. However, another invaluable aid of the law reform report is to provide greater understanding of any legislation which may result from the law reform agency's recommendations. This has indeed been formally recognised in those Australian jurisdictions[2] which have legislated[3] to allow the report of a Royal Commission, Law Reform Commission, committee of inquiry or other similar body which is the basis for legislation. The *Interpretation Acts* all require that the report be laid before either House of Parliament before the legislation is enacted and that the words in the legislation contain an element of ambiguity.

The Annual Report: In keeping with good administrative practice or a statutory requirement, most law reform agencies produce an annual report. A particularly valuable feature found in many is a schedule or annexure which sets out the working papers and reports but also includes information as to whether or not the recommendations of the agency have been accepted. At this point details of the legislation are given together with case citations where there have been references to

2 The Commonwealth, the Australian Capital Territory, New South Wales, Queensland, Tasmania, Victoria and Western Australia

3 *Acts Interpretation Act 1901* (Cth) s 15AB(2)(b), (c); *Interpretation Act 1987* (NSW) s 34(2)(b), (c); *Acts Interpretation Act 1954* (Qld) s 14B(3)(b), (c); *Acts Interpretation Act 1931* (Tas) s 8A(3)(b), (c); *Interpretation of Legislation Act 1984* (Vic) s 35(b)(iv); *Interpretation Act 1984* (WA) s 19(2)(b), (c); *Legislation Act 2001* (ACT) s 142(1).

that report. These can be particularly helpful as they are often difficult to find elsewhere.

Dissemination of LRC Publications: To assist in the task of disseminating the views of law reform agencies as contained in their reports and working papers, a number of agencies have entered into formal reprinting exercises with publishers: thus the Law Commission of Great Britain reports are made available by Professional Books, Abingdon. However, a more recent trend is to place agency materials on the internet. Recent publications of the following agencies can be located at:

- Australian Law Reform Commission<*www.alrc.gov.au*>
- NSW Law Reform Commission <*www.lawlink.nsw.gov.au/lrc*> and <*www.austlii.edu.au/au/other/nswlrc*>
- Law Reform Committee of Victoria < *www.lawreform.vic.gov.au*>
- WA Law Reform Commission <*www.lrc.justice.wa.gov.au* >
- ACT Community Law Reform Commission (disbanded) <*www.jcs.act.gov.au/eLibrary/lrc_reports.html*>
- Law Reform Database, British Columbia Law Institute <*www.bcli.org*>

For a range of links go to either the AustLII Law Reform page at <*www.austlii. edu.au/au/special/lawreform*> or the NSW government Law-Link site <*www.lawlink.nsw.gov.au/lawlink/lrc/ll_lrc.nsf/pages/LRC _links*>.

Law Reform Agency Libraries: While not public libraries in the normal sense, the researcher should never forget that the local State law reform agency usually is an excellent source of information relating to the topics which have been dealt with by that agency, together with working papers and reports of other law reform bodies. Where there is an established library, researchers can well expect that many of the reports from other law reform agencies, indeed not only in Australia but from around the common law world, will also be found. One should, however, always make contact before arriving because there is seldom much space for members of the public.

Keyword Index of Law Reform Publications: One of the most useful of publications concerning law reform reports comes from the British Columbia Law Institute. Entitled the *Law Reform Database*, it has recently been placed on the internet. With over 7000 publication references from law reform agencies around the world, all searchable by keyword, this is an invaluable resource. Of particular interest for Australians is the fact that there are over 900 local entries from all Australian law reform agencies. However the best aspect of this database is that is freely available on the internet and while at the moment the database has to be totally downloaded and used locally (on PCs) the Commission is working on providing an online search facility in the near future. The *Database* can be found at: *<www.bcli.orgirlg/law-reform>*.

10. Research strategy using secondary source material

Until Chapter 5 of this book, readers were shown primary sources of law. Chapter 5 has introduced a hierarchy of secondary source materials that allow the researcher to locate, and update, the law.

Readers should be able to see various types of publications and understand their function.

Try it with the words listed below:

- digest
- citator
- (legal) dictionary
- annotator
- index
- (legal) encyclopaedia

However, that still does not tell us a great deal about how to go about extracting the information needed to write an essay or a legal opinion. There have recently been a number of books that have gone to great lengths to assist students more effectively to use the material that has been presented so far. Going under the general heading of "problem-solving" approaches, the idea is to present to the student a mnemonic that will assist the student to remember a few basic steps.

The most simple that will be mentioned here is **IRAC**:

I = identify the issue(s)
R = review the law
A = apply the law to the facts
C = to come to some conclusion

You will see that most of what is set out in this book relates to that step of finding, and updating, the law once issues have been identified. That indeed is the aim of this book and in most introductory subjects of legal research little law will be known by the student that would allow them to go much further. Thus, the dictionary, encyclopaedia and text will be the most commonly used tools to find the law.

But as students progress through a course, or as they spend more time in a law library assisting the client to find the law, so their knowledge of the substantive law will increase and they will then start to identify more complex issues that need to be researched and, consequently, more complex law. Then digests will be used to find cases without recourse to secondary sources. And citators will be used to update those cases found.

In the various examples that follow, the issues are relatively simple and take little legal expertise to understand the researching process. Thus, most emphasis here is on locating and updating the law. Once these skills are mastered, and while studying specific subject areas like contract, or torts or tax, the emphasis shifts from finding the law to being able to determine exactly what the legal issues are that need to be researched and which may be the subject of an opinion, or casenote or essay.

Set out below are seven questions. The choice of what material to use will be very much bound up with the type of question asked. The emphasis here is not on the answer but the methodology of researching.

(i) Where can an official description of the Australian Flag be found?

(ii) Does standing up in a court room, during a hearing, and shouting at the judge constitute contempt of court?

(iii) When is a person dead?

(iv) What is meant by "ought" in s 7 of the *Family Provision Act 1982* (NSW)?

(v) What is meant by "trover"?

(vi) Do NSW dentists have to be officially registered, and, if so, what does it cost?

(vii) Does counsel have to be robed when appearing in the Family Court?

Finding the answers to these seven problems involves using a variety of secondary source material before the answer can be found in legislation or in one of the law reports.

Australian flag

This problem involves statutory material. How do we know that? Simply because a court would not, or could not, be involved in determining such a matter. Thus to find the Act or regulation, we will have to use one of the subject indexes that were previously discussed. Before we could choose between the subject index to the State Acts and the Commonwealth Acts, we would have to know which parliament has the power to determine such an issue. In this example, it is reasonably clear that it would be the Common wealth Parliament and not the State, and so it would be *Wicks Subject Index to the Acts and Regulations of the Commonwealth of Australia* that would refer you to the *Flags Act 1953* s 3. Until you have a thorough grasp of constitutional law you will not always be sure, and will on many occasions in your legal career have to consult both before you find what you want. In this instance the definition is in the Act itself, but it could well be in a regulation made pursuant to the Act. For this reason the regulation-power should always be examined when searching legislation. See the **Dentists** problem below.

As the *Wicks Index* is not available electronically an online search will require a different approach. The phrase search "Australian flag" will not result in relevant hits because the legislation refers to the "Australian national flag". A single term search "flag" will result in scores of hits including the *Flag Act 1953* which may or may not be easily found, depending on the way results are ranked. Relevance ranking should have the *Flag Act* near the top in this particular search but in other types of legislation searches this may not be the case. The point that should be made is there is an assumption that Boolean searching in online databases make indexes irrelevant. This will not always be the case. A good index creates a hierarchy of legal concepts and includes cross references which makes it easy to narrow down a search. Online searching can be hit or miss, or provide hits which may be relevant but allow the researcher to overlook essential material. This is not a debate about whether one approach is superior to another but advice about the importance of considering the correct strategy in formulating a search.

Contempt of court

This question involves no legislation at all but is answered purely from the common law. To determine that fact you can do one of two things: first you can use all the legislative indexes to try to find references in legislation dealing with contempt of court, and, if finding none, make the assumption that it is a matter of common law, or, secondly, you can use one of the legal encyclopaedias or text books to establish the fundamentals of the area of law that interests you. More will be said below about legal encyclopaedias, but in this case once you have decided or read that it is a common law issue, then it is necessary to find all cases that relate to the subject. The way that is done is by consulting the digests, using the subject indexes to find the specific relevant material. In this instance, **Contempt** is a major heading in its own right.

Online research enables browsing through a table of contents as well as text searching. Both *Halsbury's Laws of Australia* and *FirstPoint* have discrete contempt topics, Halsbury in the *Contempt* title and FirstPoint under the *Procedure* category. In the latter it was necessary to do a text search of the table of contents to find where contempt was covered.

Legal definition of death

Sometimes an assumption will allow the researcher to go straight to legislation, completely ignoring the common law. That assumption will be based upon reasoning associated with other developments, particularly technology. This would be such a situation. Before technological advances in medical science, the nature and fact of death were relatively simple. It could be observed, felt, even smelt. Now, with death being not necessarily evident in this fashion, there needs to be a legal definition before many activities can proceed. Legislation has provided those answers.

This then becomes a straightforward legislative reference question, although because of the way the subject has been introduced into the law, there may well be more than one legislative reference to be found.

There would be a number of ways of approaching this. Looking up "death" in a legal dictionary, or referring to a legislation index or doing a text search in an online database which might be in the form of something like death w/5 defin*. The results of the latter approach would be a good demonstration of the power of online searching—a range of contexts of the legal concept of death would found, for example, in relation to organ donation, succession, criminal liability for homicide and indigenous rights.

Section 7 of the Family Provision Act 1982 (NSW)

Section 7 of the *Family Provision Act 1982* allows an eligible person to go to the court and show that that he or she has been left without adequate provision for proper maintenance, education and advancement in life by a person who "ought" to have so provided in their will. In such a case like this what does the word "ought" mean?

It is reasonably clear that a dictionary may give some assistance but it will go beyond a mere dictionary definition. Thus, what is needed is a statement either by the Parliament (usually in the Act itself or in an *Interpretation Act*) or by a court. In this case, without the benefit of the former, we must turn to the latter – the courts. We can find in the Digests general cases on family provision law but here we have an additional element – we know the exact section of the Act where the word can be found.

This enables the researcher to use an annotator where cases are arranged according to the sections of Acts. There are five basic steps:

(a) The new third edition of the *Australian Digest* has such a list at the beginning of each topic

(b) *NSW Statutes Annotations and References* (Lawbook Co)

(c) *New South Wales Statutes Annotations* (LexisNexis)

(d) "Legislation Judicially Considered" – for a particular year to part of a year within the *Australian Legal Monthly Digest*

(e) "Table of Statutes Judicially Considered" – for a particular year or part of a year within *Australian Current Law: Legislation.*

The one consulted will depend on a number of factors, including availability, comprehensiveness and currency desired.

An online approach might be to simply use an online version of an annotator or construct a search in a cases database which finds every case which refers to the specific section. The latter approach would find a greater range of sources than an annotator will provide but in many cases the reference might be simply incidental or a decision of a lower court. The advantage of an annotator is the editorial process which will select the most important cases.

Trover

What does it mean? Where do you start to look? While an ordinary dictionary may be of assistance in some cases, in this particular instance it is not. Indeed if you were looking for the common law offence of blasphemy, an ordinary dictionary may well lead you astray. Thus, you need to go to a legal dictionary or a legal encyclopaedia. Two such encyclopaedias are *Laws of Australia* and *Halsbury's Laws of Australia*. In this case, by use of the index, you should at least be told where to find a little about the topic. Footnotes provide reference to relevant cases where the law of trover has been settled and those jurisdictions where legislation may have been enacted to affect the doctrine. You may wish to know more. For example, should this aspect of the common law be removed by legislation? Not much on this point is found in the encyclopaedia, However, the researcher is now aware of the area of law (torts) and should go to a general torts textbook. At this stage the various references to where it still exists as part of the law are shown, where it has been modified by legislation and references to law reform agencies which may have considered, or be considering, the matter.

The interesting aspect of this problem is that because trover is an archaic term and now referred to as "conversion" it is a situation where a legal dictionary may be more useful than a legal encyclopaedia. This is because the legal encyclopaedias do not concern themselves with history. So there may be references to trover but no complete explanation of it. Nevertheless with the help of the dictionary or encyclopaedia, you are on the right track in starting your research.

There is effectively no difference between searching using these sources online or in hard copy.

Dentists

Need NSW dentists be registered and, if so, what does it cost? Once again we must start our research making some logical deductions. We must be looking for some type of legislation. It would not be appropriate for an ordinary court of law to make such a finding.[4] But which Parliament – State or Commonwealth? In this case, either by trial and error or otherwise, we determine that it is a matter of State concern. But can the NSW Parliament spend all its time determining such relatively unimportant issues, and particularly issues that involve money that must be dealt with every few years?

As we saw when we examined the primary sources of law and noted the existence of delegated legislation, the answer is obviously to be found in the rules and regulations made by the executive arm of government pursuant to a power delegated by Parliament.

To complete our task involves three steps:

- use the subject index to find the Act dealing with dentists;
- check to ensure that it has given the power to the Governor to make rules and regulations relating to registration, together with the power to set the fees; and
- find the latest fees in the regulations.

As with the Australian flag search, the *Wick's Subject Index to NSW Legislation* is not online, so approaching this problem online would involve constructing a text search in a NSW legislation database. The form of the search could be something in the form of dentist w/5 regist* depending on the database used. This search will find the relevant Act and regulations. An aspect of the problem which makes an online

4 We must sometimes be a little careful in determining what courts can and cannot do. There are some tribunals, often called "courts", that have power to determine awards in the industrial area. They are exercising an arbitral function rather than court function and are outside our immediate concern in finding the law.

solution simple is that the combination of the terms dentist and Registration is a rare one in law and will result in limited as well as relevant hits. This will not always be the case in a research problem.

Robing for the Family Court

The choice between the various sources of law here is interesting. The common law is unlikely to provide any answers beyond stating that the courts of record have the power to establish their own procedures. Implied in that is that courts established by legislation must have their procedures established by legislation. The starting point would be the practice books associated with the family court. The researcher would be looking for legislation, regulations or practice notes – directions from the court itself to practitioners.

If the researcher wanted to go beyond the actual rule and look for material associated with robing and the effect this may have upon the people appearing before the court, the journals would be consulted. Initially those journals that are put out for the barristers should be consulted because the profession would be writing of its own experience and ideas, and then a wider search made in the more academic publications.

As court practice books are available online as well as in hard copy there is really no difference in the strategy used but simply in the medium.

Conclusion

From these seven problems, we can see that legal research involves a very few basic tools; *legislative indexes, digests, legal dictionaries, legal encyclopaedias, practice books, journal indexes* and *current awareness services*. For the sake of completeness one further item is added: the precedent, either general or court form. When all these are mastered, there is no reason that a law student should not be able to find all relevant materials. How that material is assimilated and interpreted will require more knowledge of the law, but the skill of finding the raw material is definitely more than half the battle.

Research strategy

Using the mnemonic IRAC and initially *identifying* the legal issue, you then must *research* that issue. But the starting point is not always easy. Is it a case you are looking for (being a legal issue that is still part of the common law)? If a legislative provision, is it State or federal? What is clear is that the novice researcher should be able to get a complete picture of how researching is done in order to get a better way to start.

There are two approaches. The first is the **flowchart**. This allows the problem to be placed within a general framework and the researcher enters the chart at the most appropriate stage. An example of how the flowchart can be used is set out on p 211 in showing the way that United States federal legislation can be found. The flowchart is an ideal researching tool when the starting point is not always the same. In that instance the researcher might want to start with the subject and find US legislation on that point, or, alternatively, the starting point might well be a legislative citation found within a book or a short title or common name. There needs to be a way that the material can be found with a variety of starting points and all then that needs to be done is to work on down through the chart.

The second approach is to construct, using the various guides provided by the publishers, a **schematic chart** which sets out the various tools available for the various researching needs. Three are set out below. They are basic and only relate to NSW and the Commonwealth but they allow a NSW researcher to quickly comprehend the problem, choose the best approach and work their way through. There is nothing new in these charts that has not been previously discussed but it is arranged in an order that brings it together. There are many other charts that could be created in the same way. Thus charts showing how to find articles, how to update cases, how to find and use the extrinsic aids in statutory interpretation are but a few examples. When the researcher has created such a chart, there is far more chance that the material stays in the mind and they are more likely to be correctly used.

Electronic legal resources

These strategy guides are not static affairs. They will change as the researcher develops knowledge of law and gains confidence. Another aspect that will be of critical importance is the availability of, and expertise in the use of, electronic legal databases.

The availability of online services in legal research will change how the researcher will approach any particular task. Decisions will have to be made whether one immediately examines the unedited text of case law or legislation, or whether secondary sources will be used which will usually have taken the raw legislative and case data and re-organised it. This can occur via a subject index, or legislation annotation service or words and phrases compilation. The temptation of easily accessible online resources is to dive in and gather information without any strategy or without regard to the structure of a work relied upon or where a particular resource may sit in the legal hierarchy. Online access does not free a researcher from the discipline of organising a formal research approach.

HOW TO FIND ... LEGISLATION

Locating an Act when you know the subject matter:

NSW and Australia

- Indexes – Contemporary: *Wicks' Subject Index*
  – Recent: ALMD and *Australian Current Law*
- Encyclopaedias, etc – *Halsbury's Laws of Australia*
  – *Laws of Australia*
  – *Australian Encyclopaedia of Forms and Precedents*
- Electronic – searching the text of NSW legislation on *NSW Legislation* homepage at (<*www legislation.nsw.gov.au*>), the text of the Commonwealth legislation on ComLaw at (<*www.comlaw.gov.au*>) or both on AustLII (<*www.austlii.edu.au*>))

Having found a reference to an Act, you need to find, and update, it

Updating Procedure

New South Wales

•**Reprints** (contains all pre-1980 principal Acts, and some after that date)
Sure you have latest? See *NSW Legislation in Force* (Parliamentary Counsel)

then go to

Current Awareness publications:
ALMD ("Acts Amended, Repealed ... in (year)" or
Australian Current Law Legislation ("Table of Amended Acts")

•**Electronic**

– Internet: *NSW Legislation* homepage (<*www.legislation.nsw.gov.au*>) or on *AustLII* (<*www.austlii.edu.au*>)

Australia

•**Reprints** (some still missing, may need to go to ...
Acts of the Australian Parliament, 1903-1973

Up-dating Services
Commonwealth Statutes Annotations (Lawbook Co), or
Federal Statutes Annotations (Butterworths)

then go to

Current Awareness publications
ALMD ("Acts Amended, Repealed ... in (year)" or
Australian Current Law: Legislation ("Table of Amended Acts")

Interpretation: Assistance in interpretation can always be found in *Interpretation Acts*, extrinsic aids (*Acts Interpretation Act 1901* (Cth) s 15AB; *Interpretation Act 1987* (NSW) s 34) and annotation services.

HOW TO FIND ... DELEGATED LEGISLATION

How to Locate by subject:

Manual: NSW and Commonwealth: As no subordinate or delegated legislation can come into existence without enabling legislation, the convention is to list all such material under the name of the enabling or parent act. Thus the first task is to determine that Act. For recent subordinate legislation, the **"Cumulative Legislative Index"** of the ALMD or *Australian Current Law* does provide a good subject approach.

Electronic: Full text allows key-word searching

Update:

New South Wales

- Schedule 1 to the *Subordinate Legislation (Repeal) Act 1985*
- Reprints (incomplete)
- "Principal Statutory Instruments in Force" in *NSW Legislation in Force*

  then go to:

- ALMD's "Table of Subordinate Legislation" **or** *Australian Current Law Legislation*

  finally ending by checking

- Government Gazette

Electronic:

– Internet: *NSW Legislation* homepage (<*www.legislation.nsw.gov.au*>) or on AustLII (<*www.austlii.edu.au*>).

Australia

- *Commonwealth Statutory Rules 1901-1956*
- Reprints (incomplete)
- *Table of Statutory Rules 1901-1988*
  Select Legislative Instruments Tables 20XX
  (Published monthly on a cumulative basis.
  Arranged alphabetically and also under name of parent Act).

  then go to:

- ALMD's "Table of Subordinate Legislation" **or** *Australian Current Law Legislation*

  finally ending by checking

- Government Gazette

Electronic:

– Internet: AustLII (<*www.austlii.edu.au*>) or ComLaw (<*www.comlaw.gov.au*>)

HOW TO FIND ...CASES

A. Locating by subject

Australia

- The *Australian Digest* (3rd edition)
  Subject Indexes (vols 49 & 50) **and/or**
  Key and Research Guide
- ALMD or *Australian Current Law Reporter*
- textbooks
- encyclopaedias
- subject indexes in general or specialised law report series

Electronic: FirstPoint or free text searching on:

– Internet: AustLII (<*www.austlii.edu.au*>), and the cases found on the commercial services of LexisNexis AU and Thomson Legal Online.

England

- The *Digest* (Green band edition)
  Consolidated Index 1 volume
- *Current Law*
- textbooks
- encyclopaedias
- subject indexes in general or specialised law reports series

Electronic: full text searching on:

– LexisNexis, Westlaw

B. Locating by legislative reference

- Specialised annotated Acts in loose leaf services
- Relevant title in the *Australian Digest*, third edition only
- General annotated legislative services:

NSW
- *New South Wales Statutes Annotations and References* (Lawbook Co)
- *NSW Statutes Annotations* (Butterworths)

Aust
- *Commonwealth Statutes Annotations* (Lawbook Co)
- *Federal Statutes Annotations* (Butterworths)

Recent cases:

- "Legislation Judicially Considered" in ALMD **or** "Table of Statutes Judicially Considered" in *Australian Current Law*
- Consolidated indexes and loose volumes of law reports

Electronic: FirstPoint or CaseBase or free text searching on:

– Internet: AustLII (<*www.austlii.edu.au*>), or the cases found on the commercial services of LexisNexis AU and Thomson Legal Online

C. Locating by word or phrase

- *Australian Legal Words and Phrases* (3 Vols (Butterworths)
- "Consolidated Words and Phrases", *Australian Digest Service*
- *Words and Phrases Legally defined* (5 vols + supplement)
- *Stroud's Judicial Dictionary* (4 vols + supplement)
- Indexes to specialised report series.

Electronic: free text searching on:

– Internet: AustLII (<*www.austlii.edu.au*>), ComLaw (<*www.comlaw.gov.au*>) and the cases found on the commercial services of LexisNexis AU and Thomson Legal Online

---

Chapter 6

Finding the Law in New Zealand, Canada and India

In an article,[1] Justice Michael Kirby, then the President of the NSW Court of Appeal and later a Justice of the High Court, commented upon the increased use of Australian authorities in English courts but also drew attention to a number of recent Australian cases that have specifically rejected following UK decisions. This is leading, his Honour thought, to a change in our perceptions insofar as these decisions are nothing more than "a source of comparative law. None of them is now binding on any court in Australia. The gradual realisation of this fact releases the minds of Australian lawyers to revel in the treasure house of the common law as it flourishes in Canada, New Zealand, the United States, India and elsewhere".[2]

More recently the former Australian Chief Justice Murray Gleeson also acknowledge the trend demanded of the Australian legal profession by globalisation even from civil law countries:

> But I believe there is a growing awareness, within the Australian profession, of the importance of looking beyond our own statutes and precedents, and our traditional sources, in formulating answers to legal problems. Our law is increasingly aware of, and responsive to, the guidance we can receive from civil law countries. Ultimately, the issues that arise, and the problems that require solution, are in many respects the same throughout large parts of the world. The forces of globalisation tend to standardise the questions to which a legal system must respond. It is only to be expected that there will be an increasing standardisation of the answers.[3]

The push to force the profession, and through the study of the cases, the universities and students, into these other jurisdictions, is to a marked degree being led from the bench. In Australia the increased use of US, Canadian and other jurisdictions was notable during the tenure, on the

1 "In praise of common law renewal: a commentary on PS Atiyah's 'Justice and predictability in the common law'" (1992) 15 *UNSWLJ* 462.
2 At 464.
3 "Global Influences on the Australian Judiciary" Australian Bar Association Conference, Paris 8 July 2002 <www.hcourt.gov.au/speeches/cj/cj_global.htm>

High Court, of Justice Lionel Murphy. More recently, Justice Michael Kirby deliberately and aggressively raised the issue of non-traditional authorities with counsel appearing before him. The results, as they percolate down, can only lead to a better legal system.

It is with these trends in mind that in this and the following chapter the legal materials of some of those "treasure house" jurisdictions are examined. Necessarily the degree of penetration is not the same, although the length of time spent is not a true guide to importance. The New Zealand system is unitary and familiar and so it is only necessary to spell out the major features and recent changes. Canada is a federation and, while many of the law-making procedures tend to be the same, the need to cover provincial material will make any exposition longer. Indian material is little cited and virtually unknown in Australia. This is a great shame because in the public law area there is a great deal that is of benefit. However, the exposition of Indian material will be restricted to a brief overview of the legal environment and the finding of case law. Finally there is the law of the United States. Because of the unfamiliarity with the law-making process, its federal nature and the relative commercial importance, the legal materials are set out in some detail.

The use of English material will not quickly disappear, but the continual development of the European Union and the effect of it on our traditional common law "reservoir" must mean that far more reliance will be placed upon our own and other common law jurisdictions.

New Zealand

Key references

M McDowell and D Webb, *The New Zealand legal system: structures, process and legal theory*, 4th ed, LexisNexis, 2006. This is a basic text for students and contains a thorough description and analysis of the New Zealand legal system, theory and method. It is comprehensive and particularly useful in its coverage of constitutional law, the courts, and sources of law.

Margaret Greville, Scott Davidson, Richard Scragg, *Legal Research and Writing in New Zealand*, 3rd ed, LexisNexis, 2007.

Bethli Wainwright, *E-Research for New Zealand Lawyers*, Butterworths, 2001

Internet: Those in the information business have come a long way very quickly in establishing attractive and information-valuable homepages. The University law library is no exception. While it maybe difficult to chose only one website, one that could be useful is that maintained by the University of Waikato Law Library at <*www2.waikato.ac.nz/lawlib*>. With excellent links to a wide variety of NZ law sites, and providing simple instruction for the finding of New Zealand case law to a wide variety of court and tribunal decisions, this is an excellent starting point. Australians may find the absence in New Zealand of sites like AustLII and BAILLI (offering free access to basic legal information) a surprise in a jurisdiction which traditionally has been the social laboratory in legal matters. It is hoped that this changes in the future.

An excellent overview of New Zealand law, with numerous links, is a feature provided by Margaret Greville, Law Librarian at the University of Canterbury, for GlobaLex is "An Introduction to New Zealand Law and Sources of Legal Information", August 2005 at <*www.nyulawglobal.org/globalex/New_Zealand.htm*>.

Outline

1. Legal Environment
2. Legal Materials
   (a) Legislation
   (b) Delegated Legislative Material
   (c) Reports
   (d) Secondary Source Materials
3. Electronic Legal Material of New Zealand

1. Legal environment

There is a number of interesting features about the legal environment of New Zealand that sets it apart from the Australian one. The first is that New Zealand only recently enacted a constitution: the *Constitution Act 1986*. Before enactment, the mechanical provisions associated with their parliament and courts were scattered in New Zealand and English Acts. These were brought together and placed in "one Act of constitutional significance". However, it retains a rare distinction of not having a Constitution that is entrenched and that spells out the powers of the various arms of government. Another aspect of this enactment was that, notwithstanding some murmurings from academics to the contrary, the

Constitution maintained the situation that has existed since 1950, that there be only one legislative chamber, the House of Representatives. The concept of review, fulfilled by the upper chamber in all Australian parliaments but Queensland, is in New Zealand carried out by parliamentary committees, usually after the first reading stage in the legislative process.

The second major area that has recently changed is the enactment of the *New Zealand Bill of Rights Act 1990*. This Act came into force on 25 September 1990 and, as the long title explains, affirms New Zealand's commitment to the International Convention on Civil and Political Rights. The taking of this step was not done without a great deal of public examination and debate and is of particular importance to Australia in view of the debate during the 1980s of such a possibility for this country. Released in the form of a White Paper in April of 1985, the draft was not dissimilar to the Canadian Charter of Rights and Freedoms insofar as it would be entrenched and the courts would have considerable power under it. The 1990 Act does not go so far. It is an "ordinary" piece of legislation which in no way guarantees protection of rights. It is a requirement, under s 7 of the Act, for the Attorney-General to report to the House of Representatives where a bill being introduced appears to be inconsistent with the Bill of Rights. Another important difference is that the Act does not set out the remedies for a breach of the Bill of Rights. This has the important effect of allowing the courts some latitude in handing down an order which best reflects the spirit of the Bill of Rights.

The fact that the Australian and New Zealand societies are so similar, and also that there has been a reasonable degree of acceptance of the legislation in New Zealand, will probably have some effect eventually in Australia. The case law that is being generated is being reported[4] and will be of considerable interest, not only in Australia but in Great Britain and Canada as well.

The Treaty of Waitangi

The final aspect of the New Zealand legal situation considered here is the place of the Treaty of Waitangi in that legal environment. In a speech to law students, the former Prime Minister, Sir Geoffrey Palmer, referred to the three legs of the great tripod on which New Zealand public law rests – the *Constitution Act 1986*, the *New Zealand Bill of Rights 1990* and the Treaty of Waitangi.

4 *New Zealand Bill of Rights Reports* 1992+ (Oxford UP).

The Treaty was concluded on 6 February 1840 between Lieutenant Governor Hobson on behalf of Queen Victoria and, over time, nearly 500 Maori Chiefs, and since then there have been two questions which have dominated the debate in New Zealand concerning the Treaty. First, is the Treaty the source of British title to New Zealand? Secondly, what are the rights of the Maori people under the Treaty? The present problems arise because the legal pronouncements as to the cession of sovereignty made in the late 1800s do not necessarily correspond with the de facto status that the Treaty has, both internally and internationally, in the late 1990s.

There is extensive literature upon the subject, due in part to the 150th anniversary of its signing, including:

IH Kawharu, Waitangi: Maori and Pakeha Perspectives of the Treaty of Waitangi, Oxford UP, 1989

C Orange, *Treaty of Waitangi*, Allen & Unwin, 1987

H Yensen (ed), *Honouring the Treaty: An Introduction for Pakeha to the Treaty of Waitangi*, Penguin, 1989

PB Temm, The Waitangi Tribunal: The Conscience of the Nation, Random Century, 1990

P McHugh, *The Maori Magna Carta*, Oxford UP, 1991, together with its review by N Jamieson, "The Maori Magna Carta – fact and fiction, myth and reality" [1992] *NZLJ* 101

R Boast, "The Treaty of Waitangi and the Law" [1999] *NZLJ* 123

Among the considerable recent literature in New Zealand law journals is the debate as to the merits of including the Treaty within the *Bill of Rights Act*. In the end, notwithstanding the auspicious coincidence of timing, it was not so included. However, in these debates, a great deal of material that can be useful in Australia with respect to Aboriginal land rights and the international community can be found.

Court structure

After the *Report of the Royal Commission on the Courts* in 1978, the New Zealand court structure was radically altered. During the early 1990s, it was expected that the last link would be inserted in the chain of court reform and appeals to the Privy Council would cease. That did not come about at that time. Indeed, it would not be until the enactment of the *Supreme Court Act 2003* on 14 October 2003 (coming into force on 1 January 2004 with the court to begin hearing appeals on 1 July 2004) that New Zealand would finally get its own court of final appeal (s 3).

This final step did not come easily and was not without considerable opposition, including from the legal profession, commerce and academics. At the core of the opposition was the appointment process of the new court.

These changes should be placed in the context of New Zealand's legal history and development, well set out in P Spiller, J Finn and R Boast, *A New Zealand Legal History*, Brookers, 2nd ed, 2001, while an excellent source of contemporary New Zealand constitutional and political affairs is contained in Phillip Joseph, *Essays on the Constitution*, Brookers, 1996.

At the bottom of the court hierarchy is the District Court, with a civil and criminal jurisdiction and a separate Family Law division. The next court is the High Court of New Zealand, with an original and appellate jurisdiction in civil and criminal matters, and then the Court of Appeal, with an appellate jurisdiction only in both criminal and civil matters. Finally, there is the Supreme Court, although in certain cases only by leave of that court.

2. Legal material

(a) Legislation

Governing legislation

After an adverse review by the Law Commission in its Report No 17, *A New Interpretation Act: to avoid "Prolixity and Tautology"* (1990), the *Acts Interpretation Act 1924* was repealed by the *Interpretations Act 1999*, which came into force on 1 November 1999.

Unicameral legislature and types of legislation

The Zealand Parliament has one chamber, called the House of Representatives. The second chamber, the Legislative Council, was abolished in 1951. And unlike most Australian jurisdictions where there are basically only two types of legislation, the public and the private Act, with the latter now rarely enacted, New Zealand has four types. Three are reasonably common, while the fourth, Provincial Acts and Ordinances, dates from a time when New Zealand was divided into Provinces. Those still in force are set out in Table V in "Table of New Zealand Acts and Ordinances and Statutory Regulations in Force". They are the public, the local and the private Acts. (See D McGee, *Parliamentary Practice in New Zealand*, esp Chapters 16-20 for methods of enactment.)

Finding New Zealand Legislation

Index to the New Zealand Statutes (LexisNexis) is a looseleaf service, consolidated four times a year, allowing a researcher not only to find legislation by subject but also containing a list of words and phrases defined in New Zealand Acts, together with the regulations by subject and parent Act. Other features include a list of Acts repealed since 1984 by reference to the repealing Act and with replacement provision references. There is also a chronological and alphabetical list of public Acts, private Acts and local Acts, that are all currently in force.

Key word searching of the electronic database is limited to those who have subscriptions to the commercial services set out via *The Knowledge Basket* (see below).

Current New Zealand Legislation

The legislation of New Zealand is published in pamphlet form and annual volumes, and is periodically incorporated in reprinted form. New Zealand legislation was consolidated, in the true sense, in 1908, and reprints since that consolidation have been issued as sets in 1931, the *Public Acts of New Zealand, 1908-1931*, and in 1957, *New Zealand Statutes Reprint, 1908-1957*. The current set, *Reprinted Statutes of New Zealand*, was commenced in 1979 and reprints the Acts on a rotation basis or when amendments make the principal Act unwieldy.

To find the latest reprint consult "Table of New Zealand Acts and Ordinances and Statutory Regulations in Force". This is an annual publication and provides information about amendments subsequent to the reprinting. It contains a number of valuable tables associated with the various types of legislation and Imperial Acts still in force.

Updating

Status Annotated Statutes (30 looseleaf vols, LexisNexis) containing the current Public Acts of New Zealand, including history and editorial notes, with six-monthly services and monthly updating bulletins.

Butterworths Current Law (looseleaf, 25 issues per year, LexisNexis) is a current awareness service that allows the researcher to obtain information about recently enacted legislation. The current legislation is in a table at the beginning of each issue and cumulates every quarter, in issues 6, 12, 18 and 25.

Electronic form

After some delay, in January 2008, the Public Access to Legislation (PAL) Project was completed by the Parliamentary Counsel Office, replacing the *Interim Website of New Zealand Legislation.* "The new website provides free access to Acts, regulations, Bills, and Supplementary Order Papers. The legislation on the website is at present an unofficial version of New Zealand legislation. The PCO will now undertake a process of "officialising" the legislation, so that the website can ultimately become an official source of New Zealand legislation. This process is expected to take around three years."

The New Zealand Legislation site can be located at <*www.legislation.govt.nz*>.

Additionally, both Thomson Brookers (*New Zealand Statutes*) and LexisNexis (NZ) (*Status Statutes*) provide online access to New Zealand legislation in consolidated form. However, as is pointed out in their documentation, neither come from the official government source and should be treated with some caution. Both are fee-based services.

(b) Delegated legislative material

The delegated legislation of New Zealand is published in an annual volume, *Statutory Regulation*. Each volume contains a broad subject index. For a more complete list of all such material see *Table of New Zealand Acts and Ordinances and Statutory Regulations in Force*, published by their Parliamentary Counsel Office.

Updating

Butterworths Current Law lists the new regulations made during the period covered by that issue. These are listed at the front. Every quarter a cumulative list is published. Also available online.

Electronic form

The same approach as to legislation (above).

(c) Reports

The principal and authorised report series of New Zealand is the *New Zealand Law Reports*, 1881+. There is also a series covering the lower courts, the *District Court Reports*, 1980+, previously known as the *Magistrates' Courts Decisions*, together with specialised report series in town planning, taxation, administrative law, family law and Maori land cases.

Some of these specialised case reports are available electronically via The Knowledge Basket, see below. However, one report series which is of particular interest to Australians and, because of their own Bill of Rights, the Canadians, is the *Human Rights Reports of New Zealand* (Thompson Brookers). This series commenced in March 1995 and incorporates the *New Zealand Bill of Rights Reports* (1992-1994, vols 1-3, Oxford UP). While covering significant cases on the *Bill of Rights Act 1990*, it will also include cases on the *Human Rights Act 1993*, the *Privacy Act 1993* and the *Official Information Act 1982*, together with decisions of the Human Rights Committee and other significant international tribunals. See also Alan Edwards, "New Zealand Law Reports: a bibliographical survey" (2002) 10 *Australian Law Librarian* 37. This material must be supplemented by the inclusion of the appeal cases from the new Supreme Court after 1 July 2004.

Electronic form

One of the most important recent changes (September 2006) has been the acceptance by the NZ courts to allow the publication of their judgments and decisions freely online via *Judicial Decisions Online* *<http://jdo.justice.govt.nz/jdo/Introductiotn.jsp>*. Subject only to some legal restraints, the guiding principle is to be that all decisions are made available. Available now are Supreme Court decisions (2004+); Court of Appeal (1999+) High Court (decisions after August 2005) and a variety of additional courts and tribunals.

These judgments are now available via Brookers Judgments Service and LexisNexis Butterworths Judgment Services and NZLII.

The two commercial services have additional coverage. Thus **Brookers** have coverage of Court of Appeal from 1986; High Court from mid-1980s and District Court decisions when discussed in Brookers publications. Judgments from other courts and tribunals can also be arranged.

LexisNexis (NZ) provide access online via the *New Zealand Law Reports*, 1861+ and in their *New Zealand Unreported Judgments* (High Court 2002+); Court of Appeal 2000+; Supreme Court 2004+ Privy Council 1984+ and Employment Court 2003+).

Finding cases

By Subject

The Abridgement of New Zealand Case Law (LexisNexis (NZ)). This contains a digest of all reported cases since 1861 determined in the superior courts of New Zealand and on appeal to the Privy Council, and reported in the *New Zealand Law Report* series.

The Abridgement of New Zealand Case Law

Volumes 1-16 covers the period 1891-1967
Volume 17 contains a consolidated table of cases and subject index
Volume 18 was added later and covers the period 1861-1873, and contains cases annotated together with a list of words and phrases judicially considered

There are now five permanent supplements providing new cases up to 1994 and annual supplements since.

Butterworths Current Law Digest (New Zealand)

Extending back to 1979, this publication consolidates the cases originally reported in *Butterworths Current Law* which were not subsequently reported (and thus included in the *Abridgement*). It is a looseleaf volume bound every three years.

The Digest (Previously known as The English and Empire Digest)

This also contains references, although not a huge number, to New Zealand cases. It is included here because it may well be that the works above may not be available in many Australian law collections.

New Zealand Law Reports, Index

This contains, by subject, reference to the relevant cases appearing in the series.

Electronic form

There is one particularly useful electronic digesting service widely used in New Zealand – BRIEFCASE (Thompson Brookers). This digests cases that are noted in a wide variety of publications including *Butterworths Current Law* and *New Zealand Case Law Digest* as well as all cases that are reported in the various New Zealand law reports. It is updated weekly. Another Brooker service is ***New Zealand Case Law Digest.*** Although ceasing in 2004, it has been archived and is still searchable and includes case summaries back to 1885. Another searchable database by subject keyword is LexisNexis' ***Linxplus.*** This is a database of over 70,000 case summaries of NZ's major courts back to 1986. Where available it also includes full text judgments. The publishers are proud that the service is also hyperlinked to sections of statutes and regulations. It also includes secondary source material as well that can be searched.

By legislative reference

The principal publication available is *Butterworths Annotations to the New Zealand Statutes* (2nd ed). Unreported cases which examined legislation are listed in *Butterworths Current Law Digest*. However, available in most Australian collections are the index volumes to cases contained in the *New Zealand Law Reports*, which, under the heading "Statutes", list the legislation considered in the cases in that series.

By word or phrase

New Zealand Words and Phrases (Butterworths) provides a comprehensive collection of words defined by statutes and by cases since 1958. This is cumulated annually. See also the index volume to the *New Zealand Law Reports*, "Words and Phrases".

(d) Some other secondary source materials

Digests and citators

The *Abridgement of New Zealand Case Law* has already been examined as a means of finding cases via the subject approach. Using the various principal and supplementary indexes, New Zealand cases can be located and citations found. It is also, of course, necessary to be able to update or note up the case to ensure that it is still good law. Here the *Abridgement* must give way to a citator. In this area the Australian researcher will find that many of the citators traditionally used to update the cases of the various Australian jurisdictions also allow New Zealand cases to be updated. Thus, *CaseBase* includes the *New Zealand Law Reports*, while the *Australian Case Citator*, especially since the early 1980s, includes some New Zealand cases, as does the relevant table in the *Australian Current Law: Reporter*.

The subsequent fate of English cases in Australian and New Zealand courts is set out in *Australian and New Zealand Citator to the UK Reports*.

Encyclopaedia

The Laws of New Zealand (LexisNexis), which commenced in 1992, was completed in September 2003. There are 147 titles in 36 volumes plus 4 volumes of tables and supplements. Updating will occur four times a year. Also available on CD-ROM.

Electronic: *The Laws of New Zealand* is available on LexisNexis (NZ) Online.

Current awareness publications

The principal current awareness publication is *Butterworths Current Law*. It contains:

Table of Statutes
Table of Regulations
Bills Introduced
Cases to be Reported in the NZLR
Cases in the issue
Index

This is a fortnightly publication that is arranged by subject. It appears slight compared to the Australian equivalent because of the single jurisdiction and relative size of the jurisdiction. The issues tend to have only tables relevant to the material in that issue but cumulative tables appear quarterly, in issues 6, 12, 18 and the final annual issue. It is reasonably easy to see from the table of cases to be reported in NZLR which cases will remain unreported, and sufficient details are given to allow them to be purchased through the court registry. This is also online.

Although not exactly of the same type as *Butterworths Current Law*, the *New Zealand Law Review* (previously *New Zealand Recent Law Review*) is published by the Legal Research Foundation, Auckland. This is a quarterly journal and its contents are articles but it is more like an annual survey type publication. Yet because this publication appears so early, it is far more valuable in many instances.

Journal Articles

Articles from New Zealand legal periodicals, and about New Zealand law generally, can be obtained using most of the indexes already mentioned in Chapter 5. However there are some specific New Zealand publications which provide greater depth of coverage for that jurisdiction.

JF Northey (ed), *Index to New Zealand Legal Writing 1954-1981*, Legal Research Foundation, 1982

KA Palmer (ed), *Index to New Zealand Legal Writing 1982-1985*, Legal Research Foundation, 1987

Linxplus (LexisNexis (NZ) and Auckland, Wellington and Canterbury District Law Societies) contains an index of all major New Zealand, Australian and UK law journals from 1986 onwards.

3. Electronic legal material of New Zealand

Unlike sites like Cornell's Legal Information Institute (LII) and UNSW and UTS' Australasian Legal Information Institute (AustLII) which have quickly acquired much legal information to be freely made available, the New Zealand Legal Information Institute (NZLII) – a joint project of the University of Victoria, University of Wellington and AustLII – has had a tougher battle. With early indications that New Zealand was going to go down the "user-pay" route, it was welcome news when in late 2006 the decisions of the Supreme Court, Court of Appeal and High Court were made freely available. At that time it was also announced that other jurisdictions would be extended to include the District Court, Employment Court and Environmental Court. Consequently two years later we have 16 courts and tribunals on the NZLII site < *www.nzlii.org*>.

However, reliance upon the two major legal publishers – **Thomson Brooker** and **LexisNexis (NZ)** and their online facilities is still probably more necessary than in, say, Australia and Canada.

There is one uniquely New Zealand player – **The Knowledge Basket** <*www.knowledge-basket.co.nz*>. This is a commercial service that provides access to a number of services for which payment is necessary in most cases although there are some that are freely available.

Canada

Key references

Margaret A Banks, Banks on Using a Law Library: A Canadian Guide to Legal Research, 6th ed, Carswell, 1994.

JA Yogis & IM Christie, *Legal Writing and Research Manual*, 6th ed, by Michael Iosipescu, Butterworths, 2004.

Douglass T MacEllven et al, *Legal Research Handbook*, 5th ed, Butterworths, 2004.

JR Castel & OK Latchman, *The Practical Guide to Canadian Legal Research*, 2nd ed, Carswell, 1996.

Internet: Any researcher of Canadian electronic materials should not go past Ted Tjaden, "Doing Legal Research in Canada", a feature for the *Law Library Research Xchange* (LLRX) at <*www.llrx.com/features/ca. htm*>. As part of a world-wide service of "Doing Legal Research in …", this overview is comprehensive with links kept current. It is currently dated 1 April 2008. The same author also provides a good narrative guide, together with links, to the Globalex site: "Researching Canadian Law" at <*www.nyulawglobal.org/globalex/Canada1.htm*>.

Another feature within the LLRX series is Louise Tsang's "Overview of Sources of Canadian Law on the Web", currently in its fourth update (December 2003) at <*www.llrx.com/features/canadian4.htm*>.

Another similar guide is Catherine Best, *Best Guide to Canadian Legal Research,* at <*www.legalresearch.org*>. This guide does not so much provide links (which it does)) as explain the methodology of research. This it does very well.

Finally, reference must be made to the Canadian Legal Information Institute (CANLII), developed for the Federation of Law Societies of Canada. CANLII has many of the same aims as Cornell's Legal Information Institute (LII) and the Australasian Legal Information Institute (AustLII). It seeks to provide primary legal documents free of charge to those interested while, at the same time, allowing the material to be enriched by basic searching facilities. Using the SINO search software developed by AustLII, and supported by the Canadian Government and LexUM team at the University of Montreal, Canada at last has a site that take its place with LII and AustLII, as well as Britain and Ireland's BAILII and WorldLII.

Outline

1 Legal Environment

2 Legal Materials
   (a) Legislation
   (b) Statutory Instruments
   (c) Reports

3 Secondary Sources

4 Electronic Legal Research in Canada

5 The Law of Quebec

1. Legal environment

Canada as a federation and member of the Commonwealth with a common law system, has played a significant part in the development of our law. Apart from the close connection between our nations because of this cultural and legal heritage, Canadian law is particularly relevant to Australia in the public law area, specifically constitutional law, criminal law, family law, human rights and native title; and in the private law area, particularly in the equity area of unjust enrichment.

The Canadian Constitution: In 1982 there were extensive changes to the Canadian Constitution. After a protracted struggle to achieve agreement between the central and provincial governments,[5] resulting in two Canadian Supreme Court decisions,[6] a request was finally made to Britain to provide for a domestic amending formula to terminate the power of future UK Parliaments to legislate for Canada and to provide for certain fundamental rights and freedoms by the enactment of a Charter of Rights. These requests were agreed to when the Parliament at Westminster enacted the *Canada Act 1982*. The patriation of the Constitution had finally been achieved.

Like the way the *Commonwealth of Australia Constitution Act 1900* (UK) contained the Australian Constitution as s 9 and schedule, so the Canadian *Constitution Act 1982* was Annexure B to the *Canada Act* (UK).

However, it should be noted that there is not one document which can be referred to as the Constitution of Canada. Section 52(2) of the *Constitution Act 1982* defines the term "Constitution of Canada" to include the *Canada Act 1982*, Acts and orders referred to in the schedule and future amendments to those Acts and orders. That definition thus covers the (UK) *Canada Act* to which the *Constitution Act 1982* is annexed, but it also covers 30 other Acts and orders contained in the schedule, and a number have since been amended.[7] This fragmentation of the Constitution has led to some public disquiet. There has been some attempt to modernise the Constitution. The basic constituent instrument that confederated the original three colonies and provided the framework for the other colonies and territories to join was re-named. Thus, the *British North America Act*

5 The history of the movement to have the Constitution "patriated" to Canada was first seriously considered in the 1920s, but it was not until 1960 that the movement gained momentum within governmental circles. The documents associated with the protracted negotiations from 1960 and leading up to 1982 have been gathered together in AF Bayefsky, *Canada's Constitution Act 1982 and Amendments: A Documentary History*, McGraw-Hill, 1989.

6 *Re Resolution to Amend the Constitution* [1981] 1 SCR 753 when eight of the Provincial Governments challenged the right of the Federal Government to make the request to Britain without their consent. The Court found a "legal" right but it would be "unconstitutional" being a break with the conventions of the constitution. After an agreement was reached between nine Provinces but not Quebec, the Supreme Court in *Re Objection by Quebec to Resolution to amend the Constitution* [1982] 2 SCR 793 determined that Quebec's agreement was not necessary for the requisite "substantial agreement" necessary by convention to changes requested of Britain.

7 Many of these are set out in Appendix II "Constitutional Acts and Documents" of the *Revised Statutes of Canada, 1985*.

1867 is now the *Constitution Act 1867*, together with the renaming of all amendments, and all are included in the legislation list in the schedule.

Many Canadians would have preferred a document more in keeping with the document revered in the United States. But considering the history of the movement to get the changes that have been achieved, it would surely have been well nigh impossible to have marshalled the wide public acceptance that such a change would have required.

Electronic: The Constitutional Laws of Canada (1867-1982), both annotated and consolidated and including the *Charter of Rights and Freedoms*, is set out on the Canadian Department of Justice's homepage: <*http://canada.justice.gc.ca*>. On that site also is extensive historical material together with an overview of Canada's court system and changing justice system.

2. Legal materials

(a) Legislation

Federal

Annual Volumes

Canadian federal legislation is printed in annual volumes before it is periodically consolidated into the Revised Statutes. Before that revision, there are certain problems with the **citation** of the Acts within the annual volumes. The question of the mode of citation is open to doubt because the volumes themselves carry both a regnal citation as well as a calendar year citation. In keeping with the general rejection of regnal citation, "[t]eachers of legal method in Canadian law schools generally favour citation by calendar year, and this practice is also recommended in the standard Canadian guides to legal citation" (Banks, 6th ed p 59).

Electronic: The *Annual Statutes of Canada*, since 1995, are also available at <*http://canada.justice.gc.ca*> and CANLII at <*www.canlii.org*>.

Revised statutes

The problem of citation of annual volume legislation is not a long term one because there is a statutory body, the Statute Law Revision Commission, charged with the obligation to periodically revise and incorporate any amendments.[8] The latest Revision, *The Revised Statutes of Canada 1985* includes laws enacted on or before 31 December 1984, although

8 Revisions of Canadian federal legislation have occurred in 1886, 1906, 1927, 1952, 1970 and the latest, 1985, published in 1988.

amendments enacted but not in force at that date tend to be excluded. Once the revision is complete, a proclamation will bring it into force. It can be seen that like Victoria's revisions, this is also a true consolidation.

The **citation** of legislation thus refers to the latest Revision. Since the 1970 Revision, this has been included an alph-numeric notation:

Example

Before the latest Revision, the following Acts were cited:

Patent Act, RSC 1970, c P-4

Copyright Act, RSC 1970, c C-30

Tax Court of Canada Act SC 1980-81-82-83, c 158

Since the Revision, they are cited:

Patent Act, RSC 1985, c P-4

Copyright Act, RSC 1985, c C-42

Tax Court of Canada Act, RSC 1985, c T-2

Supplements

Since 1 January 1985, new legislation has been included in the *Revised Statutes of Canada, 1985* by supplements. The citation to such material will appear as:

Example

International Centre for Ocean Development Act RSC 1985, c 17 (1st Supp)

International Centre for Human Rights and Democratic Development Act RSC 1985, c 54 (4th Supp)

Appendices

The *Revised Statutes of Canada, 1985* contains a volume with three Appendices:

Appendix I: Schedule of Acts and portions of Acts repealed as of the coming into force of the *Revised Statutes of Canada, 1985*;

Appendix II: Constitutional Acts and Documents;

Appendix III: Canadian Bill of Rights.

Bilingual Text

Pursuant to s 133 of the *Constitution Act 1867* and s 18(2) of the *Constitution Act 1982*, federal legislation must be published in both French and English. Since RSC 1970, and continued in RSC 1985, this has been done by placing the two languages beside each other, in columns, on the same page. Before 1970, separate volumes were published.

Electronic: The *Consolidated Statutes of Canada*, arranged in alphabetical order are also available on the Internet at Internet at the Department of Justice site <*http://laws.justice.gc.ca*> and CANLII at <*www.canlii.org*>.

Provincial revisions

The same revision method of presenting legislation tends to have been adopted in the provinces:

Revised Statutes of Alberta Statutes 1980 (8 volumes plus annual vols 1981+). This set states the law as at 31 December 1980.

Revised Statutes of British Columbia Statutes 1979, (8 volumes plus annual vols 1980+). This set states the law as at 31 December 1979.

Re-enacted Statutes of Manitoba Statutes 1987 (5 volumes plus annual vols 1987-88+). This set consolidates and revises the statutes of Manitoba from and including the 1986-87 Session.

Revised Statutes of New Brunswick 1973, (6 volumes plus annual vols 1975+) This set is a consolidation to 31 December 1973.

Revised Statutes of Newfoundland 1990, (8 volumes plus annual vols 1991+).

Nova Scotia Revised Statutes 1989, (12 volumes plus annual vols 1989+). This set represents the law as at 1 October 1989.

Revised Statutes of Ontario 1990, (12 volumes plus annual vols 1991+) This set represents the law as at 31 December 1990, and for the first time is published in both French and English.

Revised Statutes of Prince Edward Island 1988, (3 volumes plus annual vols 1988-1990+) This set represents the law as at 31 December 1988.

Revised Statutes of Quebec 1977. (English edition) (10 volumes plus annual vols 1979+). There is a French edition also available. Since 1978 the annual volumes are also published in separate French and English editions.

Revised Statutes of Saskatchewan 1978, (11 volumes plus annual vols 1979+).

The three territories have followed:

Northwest Territories *Revised Ordinances of the Northwest Territories* (1988) (2 volumes)

The Revised Statutes of the Yukon (1986) (2 volumes). Further Revised Statutes have appeared in 1988 (1 volume) and 1989-90 (1 volume).

Nunavut: the Legislative Assembly of Nunavut met initially on 1 April 1999, adopting over 100 Acts of the North West Territories. These are gradually being altered to reflect the government's direction. These consolidated statutes, together with enacted legislation since April 1999, are electronically available at <*www.assembly.nu.ca/english/bills/ index.html*>.

There is considerable information about finding legislation within the various provincial revised **sets**, together with commentary on citation problem, in Banks 6th ed, pp 69-81. See Quicklaw databases for easy retrieval online.

Electronic: Not all provincial legislation is on the internet nor on CANLII. While some legislation (Canada, Ontario, Alberta and British Columbia) is available on the commercial service LexisNexis Canada, there is a diverse mixture of free and commercially available sites which can easily confuse.

One place where that provincial legislation that is available is very conveniently set out, with additional references to (*Hansard*) debates, Bills and Regulations, is Tjaden's "Doing Research in Canada" Chapter 2: "Canadian Primary Legal Resources" at <*www.llrx.com/features/ca.htm*>. The information is set out there in tabular form with links showing those Provinces where it is on the internet, that which is freely available and that for which a fee must be paid.

(b) Statutory instruments

Federal

The *Statutory Instruments Act*, RSC 1985, C S22, s 2(1), provides a comprehensive definition of both "statutory instruments" and the narrower term "regulation". When made under the authority of a parent Act, the regulation will appear in the Part II of the *Canada Gazette*, and most libraries will then keep it in that form. There is a quarterly, cumulative, index to the regulations which accompanies issues of Part II.

Consolidated Regulations of Canada, 1978 (CRC 1978)

The regulations were consolidated in 1978, and published in 19 volumes. This consolidation formally came into force on 15 August 1979. A two-volume, special edition of the *Canada Gazette Part II* was released shortly after:

Consolidated Index of Statutory Instruments March 31, 1979

It contained three tables:

- I Table of regulations, statutory instruments (other than regulations), and other documents (an alphabetical list by title);
- II Table of regulations, statutory instruments (other than regulations), and other documents by statute (alphabetical list by Statutes of Canada title, showing delegated material, etc, by date etc);
- III Table of regulations exempt from registration and publication in the *Canada Gazette* arranged by statute (alphabetical under name of Statute).

This index is supplemented by a quarterly issue of the *Canada Gazette Part II* which lists the regulations in the *1978 Consolidation*, those made since in the *Gazette* and also lists those regulations not in the Consolidation. This is not a subject index but an alphabetical listing by name.

Canada Regulations Index (Carswell)

The finding of Canadian regulations can be difficult considering the time since the last consolidation. The official index that comes out with the *Canada Gazette Part II* is not wholly satisfactory, which has led to a private publisher supplementing it. In this comprehensive listing, with references to the *Consolidation 1978* and the *Canada Gazette*, regulations can be quickly located. It is updated monthly.

Electronic: The *Consolidated Regulations of Canada*, arranged in alphabetical order, are also available on the Internet at the Department of Justice site <*http://laws.justice.gc.ca*> and CANLII at <*www.canlii.org*>.

Provincial

This area is subject to periodic change and the current state of finding regulations and updating is well set out in MJ Sinclair, *Updating Statutes and Regulations for all Canadian Jurisdictions*, 4th ed, Canadian Law Information Council, 1995. However, because most researching – at least by Australian researchers – will be done on the net, use Ted Tjaden's "Doing

Legal Research in Canada – Canadian Primary Legal Resources" for an excellent table that sets out a lot of hyperlinks to Provincial legislatures, parliamentary debates, statutes, bills and **regulations**. This comprehensive table can be located at: <*www.llrx.com/features/ca_pri.htm*>

(c) Reports

Federal

Canada Supreme Court Reports (SCR) (1876+). (This has also been entitled Canada Law Reports, Supreme Court of Canada) This is the official report series and each case appears in both French and English versions. Since 1975 all cases are reported.

Canada Federal Court Reports (FC) (1971+). This set replaces the following set and began when the Federal Court was created, with Appeal and Trial Divisions. This is a selection of cases from both Divisions.

Exchequer Court Reports (ECR) (1875-1971). (This has also been entitled *Canada Law Reports, Exchequer Court*). This set covers an array of federal matters: patent, copyright, income tax appeals, etc, but ceased with the establishment of the Federal Court.

National Reporter (Maritime Law Book, 1974+). This is an unofficial series reporting all the Supreme Court and Federal Court of Appeal cases. Like all such report series it has the advantage of speed in production and is better indexed.

Federal Trial Reports (Maritime Law Book, 1986+). These report the cases of the Trial Division of the Federal Court.

Electronic: Currently the decisions of the Supreme Court of Canada, the Federal Court and the Tax Court are available on CanLII at <*www.canlii.org*>. There is a growing list of boards and tribunals now available as well but all of these databases are really limited to only the last few years. Thus, without the broad coverage that is freely offered in Australia and even the United States, to obtain a comprehensive selection of Canadian Federal court reports the researcher will need the commercial services of LexisNexis Canada's Quicklaw. Its Source Directory lists the extraordinary range of databases available. The principal rival electronic publisher – Westlaw*e*CARSWELL – has also an impressive collection including Supreme Court and Privy Council decisions back to 1867 and Federal Court decisions from the mid-1970s. All Carswell reports are available electronically as well.

Pan-Canada Report Series

Dominion Law Reports (Canada Law Book, 1912+). This contains a selection of cases from the Supreme Court, Federal Court of Appeal and of the provincial courts as well. It is probably one of the best known Canadian report series outside Canada and is highly respected.

Old Series (1912-1922, 70 volumes)
New Series (1923-1955, 70 volumes)
Second Series (1956-1968, 150 volumes)
Third Series (1969-1984, 150 volumes)
Fourth Series (1984+)

Indexes: there is a two volume index to the Third Series and index volumes to parts of the Fourth Series are being progressively released. To the Second Series there is a table of cases but no subject index.

Annotations: A excellent feature of this series is the annotation service to the cases within the series. This provides information on appeals from, and judicial consideration of, cases previously published in the various series. Made up of a number of permanent volumes and cumulative annual volumes for the Second, Third and Fourth series, this allows a researcher, having found the case using the index, to update it with ease.

Western Weekly Reports (Carswell, 1912+) (Superseded the *Western Law Reporter* (1905-1916)). This is a selection of cases from the Supreme Court, and Court of Appeal but includes leading cases of British Columbia, Alberta, Saskatchewan, Manitoba, the Yukon Territory, Northwest Territories and Nunavut.

Atlantic Provinces Reports (Maritime Law Book, 1975+) (Has taken the place of *Eastern Law Reporter* (1906-1914) and *Maritime Provinces Reports* (1929-1968)). This contains the decisions of New Brunswick, Nova Scotia, Newfoundland and Prince Edward Island, as previously reported in the three series covering those Provinces. It appears in bound volume only with no advance parts.

Provincial Reports

There are law report series for all the provinces. Many of these have only reappeared since the 1970s. There was a long period in the middle of this century when there did appear to be a rationalisation in provincial reporting. But it was short-lived. The current list is:

Alberta Reports (1977+) and *Alberta Law Reports*, (1976-1992) Second Series; Third Series (1992+)

British Columbia Law Reports (1976+)

Manitoba Reports, Second Series (1979+)

New Brunswick Reports, Second Series (1969+)

Newfoundland and Prince Edward Island Reports (1971+)

Nova Scotia Reports, Second Series (1970+)

Ontario Reports, Second Series (1974-1991) Third Series (1991+)

Quebec Appeal Cases/Causes en appel au Québec (1987+). A selection of the cases that may be of interest to persons outside of Quebec has been recently brought together and published as the *Quebec Common Law Cases* (Maritime Law Book, 1990+)

Saskatchewan Reports (1980+)

Northwest Territories Reports (1983+)

Yukon Reports (1987-1989)

There have been many sets of reports published over the years in the various colonies, territories and provinces that now make up the Dominion of Canada. There is a variety of information given in the researching guides but as Banks notes on p 23, the Sweet & Maxwell *Legal Bibliography of the British Commonwealth*, published in 1955, is still a good way to become familiar with the earlier series from these jurisdictions.

Electronic: Clearly the most comprehensive and freely accessible site for federal and provincial reports is CanLII (<*www.canlii.org*>). While not totally complete, it does allow access to the superior court decisions of all Canadian jurisdictions at least recently.

Commercial services are also available via LexisNexis' Quicklaw and Westlaw*e*CARSWELL. For the courts and various administrative tribunals of Quebec, SOQUIJ (Société québécoise d'information juridique) (*www.soquij.qc.ca*) also provides an online subscription service. For electronic reports covering the western provinces, see also Western Legal Publications, now affiliated with Canada Law Books.

3. Secondary sources

Digests

While a number of digests allow some of the Canadian cases to be located by subject, there is one service that stands head and shoulders above them all. This is the ***Canadian Abridgment Research System*** (Carswell). Because of the wide acceptance of this publication, and the fact that it can be found in so many Australian libraries, it is essential that the various parts should be thoroughly understood. It does, in fact, have three main components: the citator service, examined shortly; the literature index, examined below and the main component, being the digesting of the principal cases from the federal and provincial courts of Canada, arranged by subject. This component is examined directly below. However, if you are serious about your research of the *Canadian Abridgment*, the publishers have available for downloading *A Short Guide to the Canadian Abridgment in print and on WestlaweCARSWELL* currently at <*hwww.carswell.com/areasofinterest/law/print/abridgment.htm*>.

The Canadian Abridgment

At the end of 2007, Carswell completed the replacement of the Second Edition with the Third Edition. This has made life much simpler for users in both initially finding the right subject area and updating that information. At the core of the *Canadian Abridgment* is a series of volumes that contain digests of all Canadian cases – estimated by the publishers at 550,000 – arranged in over 50 subject areas and including "virtually every case reported in Canada back to 1803, and every case received from the courts since 1986, whether reported or unreported, with the exception of Québec civil law." (**LawSource** – The Full Picture)

Key & Research Guide and General Index

As with all Digests, be they the *Australian Digest* or *American Digest*, the finding of relevant topics within the service can be problematic. Subject indexes have their limitations. To this end the *Key & Research Guide* is an approach used both in Australia and Canada. Here, by the use of alphabetic topics and copious cross-referencing, the researcher has a far better chance of locating the area of law of interest. By going from the general to the particular (specific), the area can be pinpointed. In Australia reference is made to a [ ] number; in the US to a key number. But the *Canadian Abridgment* tends to use the topics and classification numbers themselves to group the numbered paragraphs of case digests.

The **General Index** can also be used to find information in the main volumes but reference there will always be to a specific volume and specific case numbers rather than classification number.

Updating this information

With all the main topic volumes so recently replaced, updating the case information found within each is now much simpler. For each volume there is an *Annual Supplement* which includes all new cases up until the December of the previous year. This is consolidated and replaced annually. Thus there is never more than one supplementary volume to each main volume.

To update since that supplementary volume, reference must be made to *Canadian Current Law – Case Digests*. This is a monthly publication and the subject titles are set out alphabetically in each. There are cumulations in the March, June, September and December issues to assist in finding all new cases.

Electronic form

The *Canadian Abridgment* is available online through Westlaw*e*CARSWELL's **Lawsource** as well as other Westlaw*e*CARSWELL services. Of particular advantage to using the electronic product is that searching for relevant cases can be much simpler. Thus, a researcher can:

Browse the Abridgment Key

Search the Abridgment Digest by key word

Linking from a decision on point to locate digests of other cases on the same issue.

The *Short Guide* noted earlier takes the researcher through a series of examples utilising these three approaches.

~~B~~-*The Canadian Abridgment*: Case and Statute Citations

One of the most valuable tools available to a researcher is to locate the subsequent history of a case, or a statute, in laster cases. Thus what good is a case authority if it has been doubted by a later court? This is where the citators come into their own – **in "noting up" a case**. And in much the same way a researcher must also know how a court interprets a particular statute or section of a statute.

Canadian Case Citations: contains the full history of all Canadian reported cases back to 1867 "plus judicial treatment of Canadian and foreign cases discussed in Canadian that fall within the following coverage:

- Comprehensive coverage of references in reported cases, 1977-
- Comprehensive coverage of references in unreported cases, 1986-
- Selective coverage of references in reported cases, 1867-"

Canadian Statute Citations/Rules Judicially Considered: "Includes judicial treatment of Canadian and foreign statutes, treaties and rules in Canadian decisions that fall within the following coverage:

- Comprehensive coverage of references in reported cases, 1977-
- Comprehensive coverage of references in unreported cases, 1986-
- Selective coverage of references in reported cases, 1867-"

Electronic form

To electronically note up a case, a researcher will use Westlaw *e*CARSWELL's KeyCite*Canada*, Non-Canadian cases, but referred to in Canadian cases, can also be noted up. Using similar techniques Key-Cite *Canada* allows a researcher to note up a statute, a regulation and a rule finding those cases where it has been the subject of judicial consideration. Once again the methods used are simply set out in the publisher's *Short Guide*.

The Canadian Abridgment: Index to Canadian Legal Literature (ICLL)

This is dealt with below under the heading "Journal Articles".

Encyclopaedias

As noted previously when dealing with encyclopaedias generally, they do provide the researcher with the ability to gain an overview, without the undercurrent of minutiae completely distracting and maybe even submerging them. Yet when detail is needed, the footnoting provides the necessary authorities and usually further avenues of research. *Halsbury's Laws of England, Corpus Juris Secundum* (US) and *American Jurisprudence* are good examples.

Canada has an encyclopaedia that provides this service, published in two editions (although it can happen that both editions are identical in some areas of law):

Canadian Encyclopedic Digest (Western, 3rd ed) (Carswell)

Canadian Encyclopedic Digest (Ontario, 3rd ed) (Carswell)

Canadian Encyclopedic Digest (Western, 3rd ed) (CED (West 3rd))

Scope: This publication has a broad coverage of Canadian law but gives special emphasis, through the use of footnotes, to the material that comes from the western provinces (Alberta, British Columbia, Manitoba and Saskatchewan), together with federal material. However, where relevant, material of other Canadian and overseas common law jurisdictions is also included.

Canadian Encyclopedic Digest (Ontario 3rd ed) (CED (Ont 3rd))

Scope: Once again there is a broad coverage of Canadian law but in this work the special emphasis is on the laws of Ontario, the most populous of the Canadian provinces. Like CED (West 3rd), this work also includes relevant footnoted material from other common law jurisdictions.

Content and Format of the CED: The content and format is that of an encyclopaedia and, by using the appropriate subject headings, the researcher will find the law systematically and logically organised via main headings, sub-headings and paragraphs. The text is narrative and there is cross-referencing to other Carswell publications, principally the *Canadian Abridgment*.

Finding Material in the CED: The problem always faced by persons using the encyclopaedia is that they tend not to know a great amount about the subject – because that is one of the main features of starting with an encyclopaedia – thus they do not always know where to start. The choice is always between a *Key*-type finding aid, or an *index*. In this set there is a separate volume named "Key" which provides a number of approaches to finding the relevant part. Principally, there is the setting out of the subject titles, sub-headings, etc, which allows immediate access to the subject's arrangement. By providing cross-references, this is the way the publishers would expect the material in the *Digest* to be located. There is also a Statute Key which allows access by statute name, and at the end of every topic, an index.

Updating: Unlike previous editions, the third is a looseleaf service and is contained in 41 binders. The updating occurs by annual, cumulative, releases for each topic. Coloured (yellow) pages are used to distinguish the updated information.

Electronic: The CED is kept up to date electronically via **LawSource** on Westlaw*e*CARSWELL.

Journal articles

Canadian journals, especially the English language legal journals, are indexed in a number of places already mentioned when dealing with journal articles generally, for example, the *Index to Legal Periodicals*. Some of the material from Quebec, in French, can also be found in *Index to*

Foreign Legal Periodicals. However, in 1986, an arrangement between the Canadian Association of Law Libraries, the Canadian Law Information Council and Carswell, the legal publishers, established *Index to Canadian Legal Literature* as the primary source of information for Canadian journal articles.

Index to Canadian Legal Literature (ICLL)

Marketed either separately or as a part of the *Canadian Abridgment*, or online, the ICLL has a coverage which is far greater than only legal periodicals. While it does index over 100 Canadian legal and legal-related periodicals, also included in its coverage are monographs, individual essays from edited collections, federal and provincial government publications and the publications of law faculties and legal research institutes. Material in both French and English is included.

Contents: It contains five sections: Subject Index, Author Index, Table of Cases, Table of Statutes and Book Review Index.

Note: Depending upon the form which is used, it is regularly updated. However, the researcher should be aware that as part of the *Canadian Abridgment*, Australian library catalogues may not show that the ICLL is held, while in fact it is available through the *Canadian Abridgment* service.

Electronic: Also available on Westlaw*e*CARSWELL and LexisNexis/ Quicklaw.

Law reform publications

The importance of law reform publications has been previously discussed at pp 134-136. Suffice it to note here that the law reform movement in Canada was, and is, just as strong as in Australia and there have flourished over the years a number of important law reform agencies.

Indeed, a product of the British Columbia Law Reform Commission is the *Law Reform Database*. This database is one of the most sophisticated ways of searching the vast mass of law reform materials. The latest version (5.4) contains over 7000 records. It allows the researcher to enter keywords and provides a variety of services including an implementation notation in the REMARK field for many of the records. This allows the researcher to determine exactly the name of the legislation that may have resulted from the law reform body's proposal. The database can be found at <*www.bcli.org*>.

4. Electronic legal research in Canada

Canada has been a leader in the computerisation of legal information and while there has been a history of duplication amongst the services there has been a recent process of rationalisation partly due to incorporation of Quicklaw into the LexisNexis global platform and the maturing of Canada Law Book online. As well as the established publishers the Canadian Legal Information Institute (CanLII) offers limited legislation and case resources.

At the present time, there are three major commercial services:

(a) LexisNexis Canada (incorporating Quicklaw)

(b) Westlaw*e*CARSWELL

(c) Canada Law Book

LexisNexis Canada

With the removal of Canada Law Book materials the strength of the LexisNexis offering has been boosted by the recently integrated Quicklaw content. LexisNexis includes provincial, territorial and Federal legislation; the QuickCITE case and statute annotators and a comprehensive case and case digest offering. There is also a considerable range of commentary materials.

WestlaweCARSWELL

CARSWELL has been a leading and respected Canadian publisher for many years and, with Thompson Corporation the owner of both West and CARSWELL, it was obvious that they would come together – sooner or later. It has come sooner – and through this union, CARSWELL publications now have an effective Internet base in Westlaw*e*CARSWELL.

In an analysis of the new service, Catherine Best, author of the Best Guide to Canadian Legal Research (see Additional Assistance below), has published a thorough analysis that should be read by anyone thinking of taking out a subscription. These are the views of a professional legal researcher and can be found at *<www.llrx.com/features/carswell.htm>*.

KeyCite is a comprehensive citator facility that allows a researcher to locate and update both Canadian statute and case references and is based upon the material within the *Canadian Abridgment Cases Judicially Considered* and *Canadian Abridgment Statutes Judicially Considered*. Long considered the leading citator of Canadian material because of both its breadth and long time coverage, this will prove essential to those librarians outside Canada who are reassessing their need for paper sources and relinquishing them in favour of electronic ones.

Canada Law Book

Canada Law Book reports used to be published on LexisNexis. However as of April 2008, Dominion Law Reports, Canadian Criminal Cases, and their other case resources including the All-Canada Weekly Summaries, Weekly Criminal Bulletin are no longer be available on LexisNexis. They are available on various Canada Law Book online interations. Canada Law Book has launched BestCase, which comprises the content that Canada Law Book used to have on Quicklaw including unreported decisions. BestCase will include PDF images of reports series. The service additionally provides extensive secondary source material, not only from Canada but other common law jurisdictions, that is also very useful.

Additional Assistance

For more information about electronic searching of Canadian material, see:

- Ted Tjaden, "Researching Canadian Law" at *<www.nyulawglobal.org/globalex/Canada1.htm>*
- Catherine Best, *Best Guide to Canadian Legal Research <http://legalresearch.org>* that has a special section on electronic researching.

5. The law of Quebec

In a sea of common law, the Province of Quebec stands out alone in Canada. Although not totally civil law, the public law of the province being derived from the common law, the private law of Quebec is based on French law, which in turn has its origins in Roman law.

The Civil Codes: The principal source of civil and commercial law for Quebec is contained in the *Civil Code of Lower Canada* adopted in 1865 to come into force on 1 August 1866. Patterned upon the French *Code civil* (Napoleonic Code of 1804), it is divided into books, titles and articles. When change is needed it is done by legislation of the Quebec Legislature. Because of the antiquity of many of the *Code's* provisions, a major revision was commissioned in 1955. A final report in 1978 containing a draft, together with commentaries, was presented to the government. The current *Civil Code* came into force in 1994 and is divided into 10 "books" constituting the general law concerning persons, family, succession, property, obligations, evidence, prescription, publication of rights and private international law.

The text of the Code is available through a number of private publishers in looseleaf format and with English translations. These include Kingsland Publications' *Civil Code of the Province of Quebec,* Wilson & Lafleur's *The Civil Codes* and *The Civil Codes: A Critical Edition*, published by Chambre des notaires du Québec under the direction of Paul-A Crepeau.

Electronic: The Civil Code of Quebec is available on the internet at <*www.bcli.org*> and <*www.justice.gouv.qc.ca/English/sujets/glossaire/code-civil-a.htm*>. For the context in which it operates, see the Government of Quebec's home page: "The Rule of Law" at <*www.gouv.qc.ca/portail/quebec/pgs/commun/gouv/societedroit/?lang=en*>.

Specific literature on changes to the Codes

JEC Brierly, "Quebec's Civil law codification viewed and reviewed" (1968) 14 *McGill LJ* 521

RA Macdonald, "Civil law – Quebec – the new draft Code in perspective" (1980) 58 *Can Bar Rev* 185

Legislation

Quebec legislation, as previously noted in considering provincial legislation, has been consolidated in the *Revised Statutes of Quebec 1977*. These are officially published in either the 10 volume hardcover set or in looseleaf format. The former are kept up to date via the annual volumes, the latter by official updates supplied twice a year.

Electronic: La Société Québécoise D'Information Juridique (SOQUIJ) was founded in 1976 with the purpose of making available the law of Quebec and for promoting legal research in Quebec. To this end, the legislation and case law can be found, in French, and by subscription at <*www.soquij.qc.ca*>. However, at Publications du Québec, located at <*www2.publicationsduquebec.gouv.qc.ca/home.php*>, the researcher can freely find Québec legislation, both statutes and regulations, in English together with a search facility.

Delegated legislation

Quebec delegated legislation, as previously noted in considering provincial delegated legislation, is contained in the *Revised Regulations of Quebec 1981*, in 10 volumes, with an 11th volume being an index. This is supplemented annually. As noted by in MacEllven, *Legal Research Handbook,* there is no statute on regulations in Quebec and so the common law rules apply in the use of delegated power. This statement is in keeping with the general rule that the common law is applicable in the area of public law generally unless otherwise negated.

Electronic: Publications du Québec, located at <*www2.publicationsdu quebec.gouv.qc.ca/home.php*> also includes regulations.

Case Law

It is in the area of case law that the researcher is likely to see the greatest variation between the civil and common law systems. In keeping with the idea that *stare decisis* does not exist in civil law, the role of the judiciary is to interpret and apply the written law: "… the code, as interpreted by the Courts, is the Supreme law".[9] Because of a number of factors, including the public/civil law dichotomy, the application of precedent in the traditional civil law areas of private law is such that the practice is remarkably close to that of the common law. This has been the subject of an important analysis by Wolfgang Friedmann, "Stare decisis at common law and under the code of Quebec" (1953) 31 *Can Bar Rev* 723.

Further material on Quebec legal materials

MA Banks, *Banks on Using a Law Library*, 6th ed, Carswell, 1994, Chapter 7: "Quebec Legal Materials", is excellent, as usual, in supplying the bibliographical details of the material needed to research the law of Quebec. This includes reports, digests and encyclopaedias, together with a good historical analysis.

DT MacEllven and MJ McGuire, *Legal Research Handbook*, 5th ed, Butterworths, 2004, Chapter 12: "Researching Quebec Law". This contains a well presented, bibliographically useful, analysis of Quebec law and how it works. This chapter also contains contacts for useful Quebec legal information.

GL Gall, *The Canadian Legal System*, 5th ed, Carswell, 2004, Chapter 8 (by Pearl Eliadis and revised by Frances Allard) introduces the reader to Quebec law with emphasis on the civil law/common law differences.

Internet: the home page of the Faculty of Law, University of Montreal, contains links to a wide variety of Quebec legal resources on the internet. It can be found at <*www.lexum.umontreal.ca/index_en.html*>.

---

9 Mignault, "The authority of decided cases" (1925) *Can Bar Rev* 1 at 14.

India

Key references

HC Jain, *Indian Legal Material: A Bibliographic Guide*, Tripathi and Oceana, 1970. While this work is not completely up to date, it is an essential publication for the full understanding of the complexities of some aspects of Indian legal materials, particularly in the regulatory area. The historic bibliographic material is still relevant.

For a good overview of the constitutional and legal structure of India, together with electronic sources where available, see V Ramakrishnan, "Guide to Indian Laws" January 2006, being an article based upon a previous LLRX feature by the author. This article can be found at: <*www.nyulawglobal.org/Globalex/India.htm*>

Outline

1 Indian Legal Environment

2 Court Structure

3 Indian Legal Materials

1. Indian legal environment

The modern state of India came into existence on 15 August 1947 when by the *Indian Independence Act* the nation was split into the Dominions of India and Pakistan. It was worked out by the last Viceroy, Earl Mountbatten, when it became clear that the two principal political/religious groups, the Muslim League led by Muhammad Ali Jinnah, who spoke for the vast majority of Moslems, and the Congress Party, led by Jawaharlal Nehru and made up principally of Hindus, could never agree to the creation of the new state. Even Mahatma Gandhi, who had been so involved and instrumental in achieving independence for India, could not bring the parties together and the partition came about.

The Indian Constitution

India set about the task of drafting a constitution. The Constituent Assembly, in existence before partition with the task of drafting a constitution, reassembled on 14 August 1947 as the sovereign Assembly for the Dominion of India and began the task anew. It was a mammoth exercise, and even when a draft was prepared there were over 8000 amendments moved, 2473 being debated in the Assembly. Three years later, on 26 November 1949, it was adopted as the Constitution of India and when it came into force on 26 January 1950, so did the Republic of India come into existence.

The Constituent Assembly Debates, in 12 volumes, is periodically reprinted by the Indian Parliament and is now available online at <*http://parliamentofindia.nic.in/ls/debates/debates.htm*>. There are also a number of general accounts, including B Rau, *India's Constitution in the Making*, 2nd ed, India Institute of Public Administration, 1963 and HR Kenna, *The Making of India's Constitution*, Eastern Book Co, 1982.

The Constitution is one of the longest documents of its type, with nearly 400 Articles and, unlike the Australian Constitution, it has been amended on 90 occasions since 1950.

Yet it is clear, both from an examination of the document, as well as from reading the *Debates of the Constituent Assembly*, that the United States Constitution as well as the Constitutions of Canada, Australia and Ireland, have all played some part in the shaping of the Indian Constitution. Yet, even so, it has gone further in some areas and deserves far more study and recognition outside India than it has been given in the past.

For immediate purposes it can only be noted that it has created a federal system, with a central government coupled with State governments.

The text of the Constitution can be found at <*http://indiacode.nic.in/coiweb/welcome.html*>.

On the 50th Anniversary of the Constitution, a National Commission to Review the Working of the Constitution was established. Its final report, issued on 31 March 2002, can be seen at <*http://lawmin.nic.in/ncrwc/final report.htm*>.

Central government

Central legislative power is vested in the Parliament, a bicameral institution which is made up of the House of the People (Lok Sabha) and the upper chamber which is designated the Council of State (Rajya Sabha). While in normal times there are many powers that are concurrently shared between the central and State governments, there is also provision in Arts 356 and 357 for the President to assume to him or herself all or any of the functions of a State in the case of an emergency leading to the failure of the machinery of the State. However, in the midst of what appears to be wide executive powers exercised by the

President and Council of Ministers in the Westminster tradition, the powers of the Supreme Court, exercising the judicial function, are there for review. It is not hard to see, after reading the Indian Constitution, the reason for the widespread interest and development of administrative law and the wealth of literature about judicial independence on and from the sub-continent.

State governments

The structure of most of the States is similar to that of the central government. In seven States there are bicameral legislatures, with a Governor, a Legislative Council (Vidhan Parishad) and a Legislative Assembly (Vidhan Sabha). In the other States, they are unicameral, with a Governor and Legislative Assembly.

2. Court structure

The Constitution created a Supreme Court at the apex of the Indian judicial system. While originally one chief justice and seven other judges were appointed, subsequent alterations now mean there are, since 1986, 26 judges. Its original jurisdiction is more limited than the Australian High Court and it has a wider appellate jurisdiction than the Supreme Court of the United States. Notwithstanding the approach taken by both the Australian and US Courts on advisory opinions, the power has been given to the Court in India and it has been exercised. It has been observed to have functioned more than satisfactorily and even been "creative in value".[10] In the matter of appointment to the Court, the Constitution requires a President who appoints them to consult with the Chief Justice and other Supreme Court and High Court judges when deemed necessary.

The State judiciary consists of a High Court as well as a variety of subordinate courts. There are 18 such courts and while each State has a high court, some are common to a number of States. Like the Supreme Court, the high court judicial appointment is also vested in the President, after consultation with the Chief Justice of the Supreme Court, the Governor and Chief Justice of that High Court. In the case of both High Court and Supreme Court appointments there has been much disquiet, and even litigation, when a number of contentious appointments have been made (or not made).

10 MP Jain, *Indian Constitutional Law*, 4th ed, NM Tripathi Private Ltd, at 146. This is a leading Indian text on the subject and now in its 5th edition, 2003.

For more about the Supreme Court, including the rules of court and details of the judges, see the homepage at <*http://supremecourtofindia. nic.in*>.

3. Indian legal material

(a) Federal legislation

Since 1951, Indian legislation has appeared as Part 2 of the *Gazette of India* and is bound each year as the *Acts of Parliament (year)*. It includes a table showing the effect of the legislation and also an index.

There have been numerous codifications over the years. The current series is the 10th and is being progressively published by the Ministry of Law and Justice, New Delhi.

There is also a number of private publications of this information: *AIR Manual: Civil and Criminal*, 5th ed, vols 1-45, 1989+, sets out all the Acts passed by the central government that are still in force. *Current Indian Statutes*, 1923+, Chandigarh, and *Current Central Legislation*, Lucknow, Eastern Book Co, merely set out the legislation in annual volumes. *Current Indian Statutes* does also contain the legislation of a number of States as well: Maharashtra, Gujarat, West Bengal, Bihar, Orissa, Madhya Pradesh and Rajasthan, as well as some of the regulations of the central government.

Civil Procedure Legislation

The Civil Court Manual (Central Acts), 12th ed, Madras Law Journal, 1986-2003. In 46 volumes.

Criminal Procedure Legislation

The Code of Criminal Procedure, 17th ed, Ratanlal & Dhirajlal, 2004.

Electronic: A valuable electronic resource is the **India Code (Indian Code Information System),** maintained by the Ministry of Law and Justice's Legislative Department, and contains a complete coverage of Central (Federal) legislation – "from 1836 onwards". Material can be retrieved using short title, Act number, date, Acts objectives or free text search. The database provides the full text of the Act. This can be found at: <*http://indiacode.nic.in*>

For convenience this is also available on **AsianLII** (Asian Legal Information Institute), launched in 2006, in a form that is identical to AustLII and with the same SINO search facility.

(b) Federal delegated legislation

This material is published in the *Gazette of India,* an official publication. It is divided into a number of Parts and Sections, with the following being relevant:

Part II Sec 3(i) has the General Statutory Rules (including orders, by-laws etc of a general character) issued by the Ministries of Government of India (other than Defence).

Part II Sec 3(ii) has Statutory Orders and notifications issued by the Ministries of Government of India (other than Defence).

Part II Sec 4 has Statutory Rules issued by Ministry of Defence.

Part III Sec 2 contains notifications and notes issued by the Patents Office, Calcutta.

Electronic: The India Code, it would appear, intends to place on the site the text of delegated legislation but it is so far limited to some regulations made under the Constitution and some electoral regulations.

(c) Indian Reports

Pre-1950

Law Reports: Moore's Indian Appeals, 1836-1872, 14 vols. Compiled by Edmund Moore, this series contains cases on appeal from the various early courts of India to the Privy Council.

Law Reports Indian Appeals, 1872 –1950, 79 vols. The judgments of the Privy Council on appeal from India.

Indian Cases, 1909-1947. This series is comprehensive and reports cases from all the High Courts of India and the Privy Council.

Federal Court Reports, 1939-1950, was the official set of reports for the Federal Court before the Supreme Court was created in 1950.

Supreme Court

Official: *Supreme Court Reports* (SCR), 1950+. Published under authority of the Court, it now consists of over 160 volumes.

Unofficial: *All India Reporter* (AIR (year) SC), 1950+.
Supreme Court Cases (SCC), 1969+ (Eastern Book Co). Also published in Criminal, Labour & Services and Taxation series.

Supreme Court Cases 1950-2006 is now available on CD-ROM as well.

Electronic: There are a number of services available to access Supreme Court decisions back to 1950:

Judis: Judgment Information Service <www.judis.nic.in>

AsianLII <www.asianlii.org> freely available

SC Judgments (http://scjudgments.com) (subscription necessary)

Supreme Court Caselaw <www.supremecourtcaselaw.com> (subscription necessary)

Indlaw.Com <www.indlaw.com> (subscription necessary)

High Courts (States)

Official: *Indian Law Reports* (ILR (state)). Although the authorised report series, this will seldom be found in the Australian collections.

Unofficial: *All India Reporter (*AIR), 1914+. This publication is one of the best known and complete series of India. In it are found the reported cases from the Supreme Court, as noted above, but also in the main series are decisions from all the High Courts and courts of the Union Territories. The various High Court decisions of each State are kept together and published within the series under the name of the State. The AIR has a journal section which gives references to journal articles

Because of the wide coverage, it has nearly 700 volumes in the total set. Although there is not any consolidated index of the material in this set, it is found in the AIR Digest series.

Electronic: There are some services available:

Judis: Judgment Information Service (www.judis.nic.in) (at the present time this does not cover all States but merely about half. These cannot be easily identified on Judic but are on:

AsianLII (*www.asianlii.org/*)

Indlaw.Com (www.indlaw.com) (subscription necessary)

(d) Digests

There is a wide selection of digests available from India. They can be national and comprehensive, national and subject specific, or State-based and comprehensive. For a complete current list it is best to approach the major publishers or booksellers for details. The Law Publishers, Allahabad, periodically make available pamphlets on Indian legal materials and one, "A Check List of Indian Law Reports and Digests", currently lists over 70 such digests. Another bookseller and agent, DK Agencies of New Delhi, also produces regularly "Recent Notable Indian Works on Law" which is also most valuable for seeing a broad cross-section of Indian primary and secondary material currently published.

National

AIR Fifty-Year Digest, 1901-1950, in 14 volumes

AIR Fifteen-Year Digest, 1951-1965, in 14 volumes

Quinquennial Digest, 1966-1970 in 5 volumes

Quinquennial Digest, 1971-1975, in 5 volumes

Quinquennial Digest, 1976-1980, in 5 volumes

Quinquennial Digest, 1981-1985, in 7 volumes

Fifteen Year Digest, 1985-1999, in 4 volumes

Yearly Digest, 1 volume per year (Vinod Publications, Dehli)

Supreme Court

AIR Supreme Court Millennium Digest, 1950-2000, in 7 volumes. This publication follows the format of the digest above.

Complete Digest of Supreme Court Cases, ed by Surendra Malik, Eastern Book Co, in 16 volumes. This foundation work, containing cases from 1950 has now been supplemented by:

Supreme Court Decennial Digest 1981-1990;

Supreme Court Quinquennial Digest 1991-1995;

Supreme Court Quinquennial Digest 1996-2000 (2007), and

Supreme Court Yearly Digest 2001+

Supreme Court Criminal Digest 1950-2006 (4 volumes) JK Soonavala, Butterworths/Wadhwa Nagpur, 2007.

(e) Encyclopaedia

With the entry of LexisNexis Butterworths India into legal publishing in India in 1997, one of their first ventures was the publication of *Halsbury's Laws of India*. To be completed in 45 looseleaf volumes, this venture is very near completion.

Indian secondary material

The secondary source that is produced for the Indian profession, scholar and students is vast. Few libraries in Australia will have more than a smattering of the texts and reference books. The public law areas, the Indian Penal Code and some private law areas are selectively collected but such material is limited to the major university law collections.

A great number of legal journals is also published. Many of these have legislative and case material occupying a fair proportion of each issue and they are of little use outside the jurisdiction. But there are some, for example, the *Journal of the Indian Law Institute, Annual Survey of Indian Law* and the *Indian Journal of International Law,* which should be in all major law collections.

Electronic access to Indian legal material

Access to Indian material via the internet is slowly growing in momentum, principally through a number of commercial ventures and official attitude changes. Thus, it is excellent that the legislation of the Central Government is now freely available. And the early reluctance to place judgments online, and make them freely available, has also recently been abandoned. Now there is a broad spectrum of Indian court material that can be easily accessed – and in a uniform format when located on the AsianLII site – that makes accessing now a regular feature of those who wish to keep up-to-date with legal developments from this important common law country.

Of continued relevance to those who quickly want to get an overview of Indian materials – and excellent links – see:

Library of Congress site at <*www.loc/law/help/india.html*> and the linked site: Guide to Law Online: India

India: A Legal Researching Guide kept current by the University of Wisconsin Law Library at <*http://library.law.wisc.edu/cgi-bin/wp2 html?indialaw.wpd*>

Chapter 7

Finding the Law in the United States of America

Outline

1. Basic Classification and Legal Environment
   - (a) Legislative Structure
   - (b) Court Structure
2. Primary Sources of Law and Legal Materials
   - (a) Federal
   - (b) Delegated Legislation
   - (c) Reports
3. State Law
   - (a) Legislation
   - (b) Delegated Legislation
   - (c) Reports
   - (d) Some Secondary Sources for Finding State Law
4. Principal Secondary Sources for American Law
   - (a) Legal Encyclopaedias
   - (b) National Digests
   - (c) Other Secondary Sources of American Law

Key references

RC Berring and E Edinger, *Finding the Law*, 12th ed, West, 2005.

M Cohen and K Olsen, *Legal Research in a Nutshell*, 9th ed, West, 2007.

MO Prince, H Bitner and S Bysiewicz, *Effective Legal Research*, 4th ed, Little, Brown, 1979.

Mersky and Dunn's Fundamentals of Legal Research, 8th ed, West, 2002.

KL Hall (ed), *The Oxford Companion to the Supreme Court of the United States* Oxford University Press, New York, 1992

KL Hall (ed), *The Oxford Guide to United States Supreme Court Decisions*, 2nd ed, Oxford University Press, New York, 2005.

Internet: With a wide array of choice, probably one of the best starting points for American Internet research is the Cornell Law School's Legal Information Institute (LII) at <*www.law.cornell.edu*>. But see also other major "first-call" sites like FindLaw (<*www.findlaw.com*>); Fedlaw (<*www.gsa.gov*>); Hieros Gamos (<*www.hg.org*>) and "Guide to Law Online", Library of Congress at <*www.loc.gov/law/public/law-guide.html*> for comprehensive legal resource links.

1. Basic classification and legal environment

Like all legal materials associated with the common law, American legal publications can be classified initially into primary sources of law and those secondary sources that are used to find the law. This basic division can further be refined by classifying the primary material into its component parts of legislation, delegated legislation and authoritative law reports. Secondary material can then be classified according to the law which it is aimed at locating: digests for cases, legislative indexes for Acts, etc.

American material is further complicated by the federal nature of their legal system, a system which has some basic differences from the Australian legal structure. While this federal division will be important in locating the law, there is less effect on secondary source material, although, as we shall see, when there are choices to be made as to which publication to use some are biased towards federal law and some have their orientation towards the States.

In order to facilitate an understanding of this material, set out below is a short examination of the American federal legal system.

(a) Legislative structure

Federal

By Art I, s 1, all legislative power granted by the Constitution was vested in "a Congress of the United States, which shall consist of a Senate and House of Representatives".

Like the Australian Constitution modelled upon it, the US Constitution grants only specific and enumerated powers to the Congress, allowing the State legislatures to exercise power in these matters as well as those not enumerated. The Constitution provides for the supremacy of federal law.

Presidential v Cabinet Form of Government

Unlike our own form of government where the executive arm is responsible to and able to control the activities of the legislative arm, the American presidential system does not formally have the same control. Whether the Presidential will is carried out will depend upon a number of factors, the most important being the political make-up of the two chambers. For our purposes, however, one of the most important ramifications of the American system is that the legislative output is not nearly as controlled or regimented as in the Westminster or cabinet form of government. Merely because prospective legislation, also called a Bill, is introduced into either the US Senate or the House of Representatives does not mean that it becomes law. While the same can be said of our own system, the very fact that the executive (government) must be in control of the lower chamber, means there is a far greater chance of the Bill being ultimately enacted. The Australian system, either at federal or State levels, also is dependent upon the vagaries of the upper chamber not being controlled by the government, but with that exception, the system is tightly controlled. However, for the President to get legislation enacted, he must first get a compliant Senator or member of the House of Representatives to introduce it into the Congress. Moreover, the legislators, all 535 of them, wish to have, and be seen to be having, a "slice of the action". The result is that the vast majority of Bills introduced into the Congress have little chance of being enacted. But at least by this process the legislator has the opportunity of marshalling support, and can be seen by the constituency to be looking after its interests.

One further ramification of the American system is that the Congressional terms are regulated. A Congress runs for two years – the same length of time as each Representatives' term – and is divided into two (annual) sessions. The Senators are elected for six years and are divided into three classes with a new class elected every two years. Every second Congressional election coincides with the Presidential election.

The Legislative Process

Once legislators decide to enact a law by introducing it into the Congress, they become the "**sponsor**" of that Bill. They will initially need to organise its drafting, to introduce it (where it is numbered in the order in which it is introduced) and then, in practically all cases, to marshal it through the chamber's appropriate **Committee**(s). After the most careful scrutiny by the Committee's members and staff, who usually have a high degree of expertise, and with witnesses called if clarification or information is needed, the committee will return the Bill to the chamber floor, with a report, either favourably or with suggested amendments. In most cases it will be a recommendation of one of these two types, as committee displeasure is usually dealt with by inactivity. This report is also numbered in the order in which it is filed. The **report** is an ideal place to find the purpose and scope of the Bill, explanations of the committee's amendments, proposed changes to the existing law and usually the text of communications with relevant government and agency witnesses consulted by the committee.

At this stage to get the matter considered by the chamber is the next problem. In the lower chamber, usually the chairman of the committee, together with the sponsor, appears before the House Rules Committee to request a special rule to get it considered. It might be noted that Bills from certain committees and general appropriation Bills are exempt or privileged from this step. In the House, the relevant member of the Rule Committee then raises in that chamber a rule which sets out the Bill and length of time that debate should ensue, and, if that passes, the Bill is ready for consideration by the House. Initially in a Committee of the Whole for preliminary consideration of the Bill, after reporting to the Speaker, the full House votes on the Bill, including any amendments.

After passage through both houses, a Bill will go to the President for his signature. If he should refuse and veto it, a vote of two thirds of both houses of Congress will override that veto.

Types of Legislation

American federal legislation is not uniformly of the same type. It can be divided into that which is permanent and public and where both are of general application, those that are private (ie, refer to a specific and named matter), those that relate to local law and, finally, temporary legislation. While the concept of the private law is observable in our own legislation, it is not nearly as prevalent as in the US. However, the texts of the private and temporary laws are published in the *Statutes at Large* ("Stat"), although the failure to include them in many secondary sources can make them difficult to find. Those public laws which are temporary and local are published in *Statutes at Large* but are also included in *US Code Congressional and Administrative News*.

The discussion of the legislative process above is that which relates to the general law. The procedures adopted for private Bills are similar although with important differences, one of which includes the fact that a person other than a member of the Congress can introduce such a Bill. The concept itself of the private Bill is recognised as the lawmaker's admission of fallibility, for they are generally used to address some particular problem which public laws either created or overlooked. In the case of the US, the principal areas where such Bills arise are private claims against the US, usually arising pursuant to Art I, s 8, cl 1, whereby "The Congress shall have power ... to pay the debts ... of the United States". This has been interpreted to include not only legal, but moral obligations as well: "The Nation ... owes a 'debt' to an individual when his claim grows out of general principles of right and justice" (*US v Realty Company* 163 US 427 (1895)).

Other areas include immigration and naturalisation, whereby private Bills obviate the existing provisions in cases of hardship, and claims against the government which do not fall within the Federal Tort Claim Act of August 2, 1946.

Electronic: CW Johnson, a member of the US House of Representatives, "How our Laws are Made" at <*www.loc.gov/home/lawsmade.toc.html*>.

State

While the origins of Australia and the United States are superficially similar, there are some profound constitutional differences. In Australia the six colonies accepted by popular vote the Constitution that had been drafted by colonialists and subsequently enacted by the Parliament at Westminster. The newly created Commonwealth of Australia was clearly also a colony and independence did not come until well into the 20th century. In the case of America, the 13 colonies had declared their independence in 1776 and it was as independent States that initially in 1781 they entered into a limited union, while specifically retaining their sovereignty. In 1789 it was not the people but the legislatures of the 13 States that adopted the Constitution that had been drafted at Philadelphia.

Notwithstanding these differences, the ultimate supremacy of the central national authority in both nations has gradually asserted itself to the point that in both federations it would be difficult to deny that there are any significant areas of State power that cannot be reached and virtually supplanted by the exertion of federal power if the national government so resolved. Yet it suits both national governments that there are large areas of commercial interest that still remain in the hands of the State governments. Therefore State law needs to be thoroughly understood.

There is a second important difference between the Australian States and the States of America. In Australia each State has a constitution which is little more than the legal authority for the creation of the legislative organs of government and certainly contains few fundamental legal restraints, power being vested in the Parliaments of the States in plenary form. However, in the United States we find in every State long, complicated Constitutions which have all been adopted by the people at some stage, and which import into the State law the concept of separation of powers reinforced by the full system of checks and balances.

State legislative process

The existence of 50 State legislatures makes generalisation difficult but there is great similarity between the legislative process and the way that the legislation is organised on publication. One point that is interesting to Australians is that while we have one State that has one chamber: Queensland, so the United States also has one State which is unicameral: Nebraska.

However, in selecting one State for review, California has been chosen principally because of the importance of the trade links between that State and Australia.

The legislature, situated in the California State Capitol, Sacramento, consists of the Senate and Assembly with the executive being headed by the Governor of the State.

Legislation is introduced in Bill form and may undergo several revisions before acceptance by both legislative chambers. Like the US Congress, in California committees are used at the intermediate stage to examine the reasons for the legislation and the community cost, and indeed a Bill may well need to be considered by a number of committees before final Assembly or Senate consideration. Once this is done it is presented to the Governor for signature. Like the President of the United States, the Governor of California may veto it by returning it with any objections to the house of its origin. Further and detailed provisions then apply before the Bill can become law.

The legislative process itself is of no real concern to the legal researcher. However, at various stages in the process, documentation has come into existence which can later be used in determining legislative intent. This has already been explained in Chapter 2 when discussing the use that is currently made of legislative histories, both in the various Australian jurisdictions through recent legislative changes, and in the United States. It is this documentation that makes up legislative intent together with any other material that may have been relevant in the preparation of the Bill before it reached the legislature. This, for example, may be a California Law Revision Commission Report that considered the proposal, a *Legislative Counsel's Digest*, similar to the

Explanatory Memorandum of Australian jurisdictions, or any other committee report that caused the Bill to come into existence.

Thus, it is important to understand the legislative process. For California, this is explained in some detail in DW Martin (ed), *Henke*'s *California Law Guide*, 6th ed, Butterworths, 2002, in a section entitled "The legislative process – records of action". Some of this material may well also show up if searching the annotations to the *West's Annotated Code*, or *Deering's California Codes*.

For California there is the additional source of the *Pacific Law Journal*, which since 1970 has a section "Review of Selected California Legislation". Many of the other journals that are published by universities in California carry relevant material which can also be found using the annotated legislative services or the indexes to the law journal.

The whole question of legislative intent, specifically relating to California, has been examined in two good articles:

White, "Sources of legislative intent in California" (1972) 3 *Pacific Law Journal* 63

Hurst, "The use of extrinsic aids in determining legislative intent in California: the need for standardised criteria", (1981) 12 *Pacific Law Journal* 189

Many of these same techniques can be successfully used in other jurisdictions to the same ends.

(b) Court structure

Federal

Pursuant to the Constitution of the United States, the judicial power is contained within ss 1 and 2 of Article III:

> Section 1. The judicial power of the United States shall be vested in one Supreme Court, and in such inferior courts as the Congress may from time to time ordain and establish. The judges of both the supreme and inferior courts, shall hold their office during good behaviour, and shall, at stated times, receive for their services a compensation which shall not be diminished during their continuance in office.
>
> Section 2. The judicial power shall extend to all cases, in law and equity, arising under this Constitution, the laws of the United States, and treaties made, or which shall be made, under their authority; to all cases affecting ambassadors, other public ministers, and consuls; to all cases of admiralty and maritime jurisdiction; to controversies to which the United States shall be a party; to controversies between two or more States; between a State and a citizen of another State; between citizens of different States; between citizens of the same State claiming land under grants of different

> States, and between a State or a citizen thereof, and foreign State, citizens, or subjects.
>
> In all cases affecting ambassadors, other public ministers and consuls, and those in which a State shall be a party, the supreme court shall have original jurisdiction. In all other cases before mentioned, the supreme court shall have appellate jurisdiction, both as to law and fact, with such exceptions, and under such regulations as the Congress shall make ...

Between the Constitution and various Acts enacted by the United States Congress, a federal court structure has been created consisting of the Supreme Court, 13 circuit courts of appeal and 56 district courts. These are considered in turn.

The Supreme Court

Authority of the Court

Pursuant to Art III, s 1 of the Constitution, the Supreme Court was created by the Judiciary Act of 24 September 1789 (1 Stat 73) and came into being on 2 February 1790.

Jurisdiction

The basic jurisdiction of the Supreme Court is set out in Art III, s 2, of the Constitution and, pursuant to that power, the appellate jurisdiction has been conferred by Congress with the extent and controls being found in 28 USCA 1251-1258, together with various other statutes. Yet it must be noted that while the Court has both an original and appellate jurisdiction, the latter is limited and should be distinguished from the general appellate jurisdiction of the High Court under the Australian Constitution. At the time of drafting, the Supreme Court of Canada was the model rather than the Supreme Court of the United States. Consequently whereas the Supreme Court of the US has a jurisdiction that only provides for appeals in matters arising under one of the enumerated classes set out in s 2 in which the "judicial power" is expressed to extend and in those areas where it does not extend, the court of last resort within the State is final. In Australia, by giving to the High Court a general appellate jurisdiction, that Court took its place at the apex of the whole judicial structure – federal and non-federal – for Australia and thus created not merely a *federal* court but also a *national* court.[1] This difference has to be kept in mind for it has considerable effect upon searching US case law and explains why so many of the American secondary sources are arranged in the way they are.

---

1 J Quick and RR Garran, *The Annotated Constitution of the Commonwealth of Australia* (1901) Legal Books, Sydney, 1996, p 737.

Personnel

The Court is comprised of the Chief Justice of the United States, and since 1948 (62 Stat 869; 28 USCA 1), eight Associate Justices. They are nominated by the President, subject to the advice and consent of the Senate (Art I, s 2) and hold office subject to Art III, s 1. It is assumed in the United States that this constitutional provision guarantees a Justice life tenure, subject only to the other provisions of that section. When Roosevelt's "court-packing" plan failed in 1937, whereby the President proposed that he be allowed to appoint a new member of the Supreme Court whenever a sitting justice reached the age of 70 years, a law was passed that provided that Justices may, *if they so desired,* retire from regular active service at the age of 70 years after serving for 10 years as a federal judge or at 65 after 15 years of service, continuing to receive their salary (28 USCA 371).

Courts of Appeal

History and Authority

The function of the Circuit Court of Appeal is to provide an intermediate appellate court between the district courts, hearing the trial, and the final appellate court, the Supreme Court. The authority for their establishment is contained in Art III, s 1, and they were created in 1891 (26 Stat 826; 28 USCA ch 3) to relieve the Supreme Court of considering all appeals from federal cases at first instance.

Before their establishment, Art III and the first Judiciary Act had indeed created three different types of federal courts: district courts, circuit courts and the Supreme Court, but had created only two types of judge: district judges and the justices of the Supreme Court. The district courts were trial courts and were presided over by one judge sitting alone. The circuit courts were presided over by one district court judge and two Supreme Court justices. While they had some appellate function, they were principally trial courts. Appeals would go to the Supreme Court from these, as well as from the district courts and State appellate courts in federal matters.

Problems led to a reorganisation in 1891. These changes were not absolute and final, for the older circuit courts continued until 1911 and appeals to the Supreme Court from these courts did not become discretionary until 1925.

The federal court system is basically regional. The original district courts were State-based as were the nine circuit courts of appeal covering certain State groupings. These have now been increased to 13, with one, the Federal Circuit, not being regional.

Jurisdiction

By the reorganisation legislation of 1891, these courts were empowered to review all final decisions and certain interlocutory decisions (see 28 USCA 1291-2) of district courts, except in those very few situations where legislation provides for direct review by the Supreme Court.

They are also empowered to review and enforce orders of many federal administrative bodies, and in these as well as those from the district courts, the decision is final except if they are subject to discretionary review or appeal in the Supreme Court.

Structure and Personnel

As already noted, the United States is geographically divided into 12 judicial circuits, including the District of Columbia as a circuit, together with one Federal Circuit, being a nationwide circuit defined by subject (see below).

Each of the Circuit Courts of Appeal has between 6 to 28 permanent circuit judgeships, 168 in all, depending upon the caseload. Like the Supreme Court justices, these judges hold office subject to Art III, s 1, of the Constitution.

The judge senior in commission who is under 65 years of age, has been in office for at least one year and has not previously been chief judge, serves as the chief judge of the court for a seven-year term.

Each Court normally hears cases in panels of three judges but can sit *en banc*. To each circuit a Supreme Court justice is assigned as circuit justice to deal with special and emergency petitions that may arise.

The Court of Appeal of the Federal Circuit

This Court was established under Art III, pursuant to the Federal Courts Improvement Act of 1982 (96 Stat 25; 28 USCA 41) as the successor of a number of special subject federal appellate courts. The jurisdiction of the Court is nationwide and includes appeals from the United States district and territorial courts in patents, trademarks and copyright cases; appeals from those courts in contract, internal revenue, and other cases where the US Government is a defendant; appeals from the final decisions of the US Claims Court; US Court of International Trade, and review of administrative rulings by the Patents and Trademarks Office, US International Trade Commission, Secretary of Commerce, agency boards of contract appeals and the Merit System Protection Board (associated with the protection of the rights of federal employees).

It presently has 12 judges and sits principally in Washington.

Indeed the creation of this subject-specialist Federal Circuit has renewed and given impetus to the debate that there should be greater subject specialisation in the federal court structure.

Stare Decisis and the Federal Circuits

Because of the existence of such a restricted right to take matters on appeal to the Supreme Court, relative to the number of appeals that could go on appeal, the 13 federal Courts of Appeal are in fact, if not in name, the court of last resort. Until a Supreme Court decision may determine a matter, there can well be considerable variation in the law found in various circuits. Outsiders, that is, persons who are not specifically searching for precedents for use in a particular circuit, should be aware of this fact, particularly when using the digests, encyclopaedias and journal articles. In such searching the importance of identifying the circuit in which a case was determined becomes evident in the way that the circuits take on the characteristics of a jurisdiction. The courts find themselves in a "complicated situation" in regard to *stare decisis*.[2] There are in fact three classes of decisions to consider: the decisions of the Supreme Court, their own circuit decisions and the decisions of other circuit courts. The present "tendency" in this matter is that while the Supreme Court and its own decisions are deemed authoritative and are interpreted broadly, decisions of other circuits are treated as no more than persuasive and interpreted narrowly.[3]

District Courts

History and Authority

The district courts are the trial courts of the general federal jurisdiction. Originally each State was a single federal district, but now there are up to four districts in some of the more populous States, constituting 91 districts in all. This includes districts covering the District of Columbia and the Commonwealth of Puerto Rico, a US Territory. Except for Puerto Rico, all judges hold their office pursuant to Art III of the Constitution, while that Court is established, and the judges hold their office, pursuant to the Territories power (Art IV, s 3, cl 2) and during good behaviour.

---

2 RA Posner, *The Federal Courts: Crisis and Reform*, Cambridge, Mass, Harvard UP, 1985, p 251. See also *The Federal Courts: Challenge and Reform*, Harvard UP, 1996, a second edition to the 1985 work.

3 Judge Richard Posner, Circuit Judge, US Court of Appeals for the Seventh Circuit, gives a lucid and interesting account of the problems faced by the federal courts in this and many other matters.

Jurisdiction

The jurisdiction of the District Courts is set out in 28 USCA ch 85, with the decisions of the courts being reviewable on appeal by the applicable US Court of Appeal, except in so far as injunctive orders of special three-judge district courts and certain decisions holding US legislation unconstitutional may be appealed directly to the Supreme Court (28 USCA 1252).

Personnel and Structure

At present, each district court has from two to 27 federal district judges. Trials are usually only handled by one judge but in some limited matters three can sit (28 USCA 2284). The appointment of the senior judge is similar to that of the courts of appeal, while there are over 550 permanent district court judges at the moment.

Other Federal Courts

The courts previously discussed constitute Art III courts, but there are others.

Temporary Emergency Court of Appeal: Constituted pursuant to the Economic Stabilization Act Amendment of 1971 (85 Stat 743) it has exclusive jurisdiction over all appeals from the district courts arising under economic stabilisation laws. It consists of eight circuit and district court judges designated by the Chief Justice. It has been operating since 1972 and sits principally in Washington DC.

United States Claims Court: established pursuant to 96 Stat 27; 28 USCA 171, it has been operational since 1982 and succeeds to the jurisdiction formerly exercised by the Court of Claims (see 28 USCA 1491-1508). *Jurisdiction*: includes disputes against the US founded either upon the Constitution, Act of Congress, regulation, or any express, or implied in fact, contract with the US government or for liquidated or unliquidated damages in cases not sounding in tort. As part of its jurisdiction over contract claims, the court has the authority, if the claim is filed before the contract is awarded, to grant a declaratory judgment and such equitable relief including but not limited to injunctive relief. *Personnel*: The court is composed of 16 judges appointed by the President and confirmed by the Senate for 15 years, one of whom is designated as the chief judge by the President.

United States Court of International Trade: This court was originally established as the Board of Unites States General Appraisers by an Act of June 10, 1890, to deal with actions arising under Tariff Acts. It was superseded by the United States Customs Court in 1926 and integrated into the federal legal structure in 1948 (28 USCA 1582). In 1956 (by 70 Stat 532; 28 USCA 251) it was established as a court of record under Art III of the Constitution, and by the Customs Court Act of 1980 (94 Stat 1727; 28 USCA 251) it was finally constituted in its present form.

Jurisdiction: This court has jurisdiction in any civil action against the US arising from federal laws governing import transactions, including classification and valuation cases, as well as authority to review certain agency determinations under the Trade Agreements Act of 1979 (93 Stat 144; 19 USCA 2501) involving anti-dumping and countervailing duty matters. In addition, it has exclusive jurisdiction to review determinations as to the eligibility of workers, firms and communities for adjustment assistance under the Trade Act of 1974 (88 Stat 1978; 19 USCA 2101). Civil actions to recover customs duties, to recover on a customs bond, or for certain civil penalties alleging fraud or negligence are also within the exclusive jurisdiction of the court.

It has all the powers in law and equity of a district court, and appeals are to the US Court of Appeals for the Federal Circuit.

Personnel: It is composed of a chief judge and eight judges, not more than five of whom may belong to any one political party. These judges are appointed by the President with the advice and consent of the Senate. The legislation also stipulates that the principal offices of the court shall be located in New York city.

Other Federal courts, not established under Art III of the Constitution, and not considered here, are the US Court of Military Appeal and the US Tax Court.

Federal Practice Books

Unlike the practice that has occurred in England whereby the courts initially prescribed their own procedures, briefly flirted with Parliamentary made rules pursuant to the *Common Law Procedure Act 1852*, but had control of the rule-making power since the *Judicature Act 1873*, the situation in the United States is not as clear. The question of exactly which organ of government has the power to make procedural rules is hampered by the fact that the Constitution is silent. After some debate, the weight of authority now is that Congress has the power to regulate federal practice and procedure, with the power to delegate to the courts power to make rules not inconsistent with the Constitution or Acts of the Congress.[4]

---

4 *Sibbach v Wilson & Co*, 312 US 1, 61 St Ct 422, 85 L Ed 479.

It was not until 1938 with the enactment of the *Federal Rules of Civil Procedure* that rules were standardised. Drafted by a committee and receiving the assent of the Court before enactment, the rules were well accepted. They did not seek to import radical approaches to procedure but rather were largely based upon the old equity rules, and the rules themselves set out that their purpose shall be "to secure the just, speedy, and inexpensive determination of every action".

Practice Book: The principal source of information about federal procedure is the multi-volumed work: CA Wright & AR Miller, *Federal Practice and Procedure,* published by West and kept up-to-date with annual pocket parts. This is gradually being replaced by Wright, Miller & Kane, a new second edition.

Procedural Reports: Unlike anything within our own jurisdiction are the *Federal Rules Decisions* (FRD). This is a set of law reports published by West Publishing which reports nothing but those decisions of federal courts that relate to procedural matters, but which also contain articles about the same subject. Thus within this (primary) source of law is (secondary) commentary.

Electronic: a valuable resource that has been made available by the *Law Library Research Xchange* (LLRX) is "Court Rules, Forms and Dockets" and which contains over 700 sources of State and Federal court rules, forms and dockets and, where available, details of filing online. It can be found at <*www.llrx.com/courtrules*>.

State

We have been dealing above with the federal court structure. In dealing with the States the same problem of generalisation is once again evident as all that can be done is endeavour to make such statements and then to isolate one jurisdiction.

Structure

As in the case of the legislative process, so it is in the judicial area as well that there is a wide variety in the structure of the various courts of the States. Most have followed the federal structure and have provided for a three-tier hierarchy but the names and additional special features can lead to confusion.

State Practice Books

Notwithstanding the diversity of courts in each of the States, a number of States have adopted the 1938 *Federal Rules of Civil Procedure* with only minor modification. So too has the 1963 *Civil Practice Law and Rules of New York* had an influence on other States. However, for a detailed list of those books and services which spell out the specific rules that apply to each court, see Frances Doyle, *Searching the Law: the States*, 4th ed, Transnational Pub, Dobbs Ferry, NY 2003.

Jurisdiction

Excepting where the federal jurisdiction is exclusive, including, inter alia, bankruptcy, patent and copyright, and antitrust, the jurisdiction of the State courts is concurrent with that of the federal courts. Where the jurisdiction is not thus restricted, it will extend to all persons without regard to their citizenship and to all subject matter.

However, where there is a federal element, and this might be because it involves federal law, or by reason of the "diversity of citizenship" (either involving a resident of another State or country, or even if totally a matter of State law there has been a breach of the constitutional guarantee of "due process"), there is a right of appeal to the higher federal appellate courts. If there is no federal element whatsoever, then the matter is finally determined by the highest State court.

You might note, however, that the law that is to apply may be different. Thus:

(i) If a State court is determining a matter of pure State interest, State law will apply and a federal court will be bound by that decision, excepting where the law conflicts with the federal law and then the Constitution's paramountcy clause (cf s 109 of the Australian Constitution) comes into play.

(ii) If the federal court is to decide questions of law because of their "diversity" jurisdiction, it will also be under State law.

(iii) If a matter of federal law can be brought under either State or federal law (concurrent jurisdiction), it will be decided under federal law.

(iv) If mixed, ie, involving State and federal law, the same principle applies. If the two are not in conflict, the US Supreme Court prefers to decide the case on the basis of State law and leave the federal question undecided.

2. Primary sources of law and legal materials

(a) Federal

Legislation

The legislation of the Congress is published in three separate ways, organised by the time it becomes publicly available:

(i) Slip Laws
(ii) Session Laws
(iii) Codes

Slip Laws

All federal legislation appears initially in a form known locally as the "slip law" form. This is comparable to our own "paper" copy which is usually available from the government publishers shortly after legislation is enacted. It includes not only public law but private as well. In order to obtain "slip law" quickly, some of the materials to consult include:

- *US Law Week* (Bureau of National Affairs)
- *Advance Sheets, United States Code Service* (Lawyers Cooperative)
- Subject specialist looseleaf services.

Session Laws

The legislation of Congress, initially issued as slip law, is bound annually and is called session law. Session laws are released both officially and unofficially.

Official: the *Statutes at Large*, as the officially published form of legislation, contain all the legislation enacted in each session. Reference to it is the most authoritative citation that you can use. However, there are three points to note: first, the *Statutes at Large* are very slow in publication; secondly, their use is limited in research because there is no quick reference to later amendments in this form; and thirdly, very few libraries in Australia bother to hold it in this form. It is far more usual for libraries which need to have reference to current US legislation to use the unofficial *US Code Congressional and Administrative News*.

Unofficial *United States Code Congressional and Administrative News* (USCCAN). Published by West Publishing, this in practice is one of the quickest ways of obtaining all the public laws that are enacted by the Congress, with pagination that reflects the official *Statutes at Large*. Contained within this publication is a range of services that are needed in researching federal law, including a selection of Congressional Committee reports and other items that are useful in determining the background to the legislation and that can be used in its interpretation. For these additional services, USCCAN is indispensable in a US law collection.

Electronic: Thomas (<*http://thomas.loc.gov*>), being the home page of the Library of Congress for legislative information, and GPO Access (<*www.gpoaccess.gov/index.html*>), a service of the US Government Printing Office, are the two principal sites for US Federal legislative and regulatory information. Thomas provides the status of Bills as they pass through the Congress, as well as summaries, sponsorship and the text of Bills. There is also the *Congressional Record* (cf Hansard), Congressional reports and links to other relevant documents and reports.

Codes

United States Code[5]

In 1875 the US authorities took the *Statutes at Large* (published since 1789) and incorporated them. This was then presented to Congress which formally re-enacted the legislation in the new form. Thus codified, they became substantive law. All the previous law as shown in the *Statutes at Large* was, in fact, repealed by this process.

There were inaccuracies in the new code and this was recognised in 1878 when they were corrected in a new incorporation which was not codified. This meant that the law shown in the 1878 edition of the code was only prima facie the law.

---

5 The citation of American federal legislation can be confusing because of the way in the US the word "Code" is used. There are three terms which can give trouble in this area. They are: *incorporated, consolidated* and *codified*. The first and second terms are interchangeable in most situations. Thus in 1937 and 1957, the legislation of NSW was *consolidated* into a number of volumes and published with indexes ("Green Statutes" and "Red Statutes"). These are usually referred to as consolidations and the legislation of the jurisdiction is published at a particular date with all the amendments included. Replacing this method of keeping NSW legislation up-to-date is the reprint method. Adopting the Victorian approach, NSW now periodically incorporates all amendments into principal Acts and then reprints them. While usually referred to as *reprints*, they can also be described as *incorporations. Codification,* on the other hand can mean either the work carried out for a consolidation, but where the end result goes back before the legislative body and is "re-dedicated" as an Act (whereby any errors made in the consolidation process become law), OR, it can mean the bringing together of all statute law and the common law principles and being synthesised, with the end product being presented to the legislature for its approval.

It should be noted that the Americans tend to refer to *consolidation* and *codification* (in the first sense) as *codifications,* and do not make the distinction that we do in Australia. Consequently in Australia, reference is made to *consolidations* (or *incorporation*) on the one hand and *codification* (in the second sense), on the other.

In 1926 the *United States Code* was published whereby all previous legislation was organised into 50 titles and published in four volumes. The Code is now prepared by the Office of Law Revision Counsel of the House of Representatives and a new edition is published every six years. The latest edition is a consolidation and codification "of all the general and permanent laws of the United States in force on January 26, 1994. By statutory authority this edition may be cited 'USC 1994 ed'." Supplements are published at the end of each session of the Congress.

Twenty-two of the 50 titles have been revised and enacted into positive law, and two have been eliminated after consolidation with other titles. Where that process has occurred, the correct citation is to the USC. If not, the correct citation is to the *Statutes at Large* followed by the USC reference. The titles so codified are set out in the preface of recent editions of the USCA. It also means that courts receive these titles as proof of those laws. Eventually all titles should be so revised and enacted into positive law.

Organisation of the Code: As previously stated, the Code is divided into 50 topics reflecting the major divisions of federal law, called "Titles", and then further subdivided into "sections", which are designated in citations by the symbol "§".

Updating: While subject to a new revision every six years, a cumulative supplement is published annually during the period between editions and these are used in conjunction with the principal volume.

Electronic: There are a number of places where the US Code can be found on the Internet but the hyper-text US Code maintained by Cornell Law School's Legal Information Institute (*<www.law.cornell.edu/uscode>*)is surely one of the best. It allows searching in six different ways, including headings, titles, popular names and a specific section of a title.

United States Code in Annotated Form

It was previously noted that few Australian libraries subscribe to the *Statutes at Large*. The same comment applies to the official *United States Code*. Most libraries prefer to subscribe to those services privately published which provide more than the mere text of federal legislation. The services listed below provide not only the text but include additional information principally relating to judicial interpretation:

United States Code Annotated (USCA) – published by West

United States Code Service (USCS) – published by Lawyers Cooperative

Federal Code Annotated (FCA) – published by Bobbs-Merill

All have their distinctive and saleable features, mostly associated with cross-referencing to other publications in the publisher's stable. Thus, the USCA has extensive cross-referencing to the West's *US Code Congressional and Administrative News*. In order to demonstrate the value of the annotation services generally, the *United States Code Annotated* will be specifically examined. But many of the features contained in the USCA are also in the USCS and FCA.

United States Code Annotated. While it must be understood to be an unofficial Code, it is usually cited in preference to the official version. There are no real problems created because the format is exactly the same – the same titles and sections, including the Constitution, but with an advantage over the official Code because of the extensive cross-referencing to other relevant publication under headings like "Legislative History". Finally, and most importantly from the point of view of the researcher, there are extensive case annotations to the legislation. Occasionally this practically reaches the point of absurdity. Thus, within the Constitutional volumes, particularly where the first, second and third amendments are set out, the legislative text in a volume of nearly 900 pages is barely more than a dozen lines, with the rest of the book given over to case annotations. The 14th Amendment has generated over 5000 pages of case digests. However, to assist the researcher, the case annotations are organised into a coherent scheme and provide a tremendous research resource upon this topic.

Updating: This unofficial set is not subject to the same timetable as the official set and new volumes are released by the publishers as amendments make it necessary. In the interim, a new pocket part is released annually, in step with the Congressional sessions, which keeps the volume up to date. Set out clearly on the front of each pocket part is the Congressional number and session covered by that part. To update from that point, all that is necessary is to find amendments to the Code in the latest USCCAN, via Table 3.

Indexes. Some of the most valuable parts of the unofficial Codes are the subject indexes. The nine volume *General Index* of the USCA provides an extraordinarily useful introduction to federal legislation. Although for Australian researchers it may take a little time to get used to the terminology, once this is mastered the law is quickly revealed in the USCA. It is produced in softcover and replaced every few years to keep it up-to-date. For each Congressional session since the date of the softcover General Indexes see the subject index in the latest issue of USCCAN.

Electronic: The USCA can be searched on Westlaw. This allows the researcher to find not only the text of the Code but also to find and view

Example from *US Code Congressional and Administrative News*

PUBLIC LAW 100–386 [S. 2385]; August 10, 1988

COMMUNITY AND MIGRANT HEALTH CENTERS AMENDMENTS OF 1988

For Legislative History of Act, see Report for P.L. 100–386 in U.S.C.C. & A.N. Legislative History Section.

An Act to amend the Public Health Service Act to revise and extend the programs establishing migrant health centers and community health centers.

Be it enacted by the Senate and House of Representatives of the United States of America in Congress assembled,

Community and Migrant Health Centers Amendments of 1988.
42 USC 201 note.

SECTION 1. SHORT TITLE, REFERENCE TO ACT.

(a) SHORT TITLE.—This Act may be cited as the "Community and Migrant Health Centers Amendments of 1988".

(b) REFERENCE.—Whenever in this Act an amendment or repeal is expressed in terms of an amendment to, or repeal of, a section or other provision, the reference shall be considered to be made to a section or other provision of the Public Health Service Act.

SEC. 2. MIGRANT HEALTH CENTERS.

(a) ADDITION OF PATIENT CASE MANAGEMENT SERVICES TO LIST OF PROVIDED SERVICES.—Section 329(a)(1) (42 U.S.C. 254b(a)(1)) is amended—

(1) by striking "and " at the end of subparagraph (F) and inserting "and" at the end of subparagraph (G); and

(2) by inserting after subparagraph (G) the following new subparagraph:

"(H) patient case management services (including outreach, counseling, referral, and follow-up services),".

(b) ADDITION OF APPROPRIATE HEALTH NEEDS TO LIST OF SUPPLEMENTAL HEALTH SERVICES.—Section 329(a)(7) (42 U.S.C. 254b(a)(7)) is amended—

(1) by striking "and " at the end of subparagraph (K);

[illegible]

...information ... respect to ... determination.

(d) REQUIREMENT OF FEES CONSISTENT WITH LOCALLY PREVAILING RATES.—Section 329(f)(3)(F)(i) (42 U.S.C. 254b(f)(3)(F)(i)) is amended—

(1) by inserting after "provision of its services" the following: "consistent with locally prevailing rates or charges and"; and

(2) by inserting "has prepared" after "operation and".

102 STAT. 919

summaries of those cases which interpret a section of the Code. Other related Westlaw databases include USC Legislative History (LH) and the Code of Federal Regulations (CFR).

Citation of Federal Legislation

For the reasons set out above, principally because of the various ways the legislation is published, there can be difficulties in choosing the most correct citation. Extracted below is a piece of legislation from the *US Code Congressional and Administrative News*:

Note a number of points about this extract:

1. This is a Public Law, being the 386th enacted in the 100th Congress. In fact, it was the 2385th Bill introduced in the Senate, and the enactment occurred when the President signed the Bill into law on the date shown.
2. Like our own legislation, there is a short title or popular name, with reference to the principal Act.
3. The sidenote indicates the short title, together with the location of the Act in the USC (or USCA) if deemed necessary. To be included it must be of "public, general and permanent interest". Thus Appropriation Acts will seldom be included.
4. The official citation is also shown, in this case being 102 Stat 919.

Note that there are, consequently, four (if not five) ways that this Act can be cited. This number may also increase if the Act is given a common or popular title because of the work done in initiating and marshalling the Bill through Congress. This may be a reference to a single name: the *Sherman Act*, or to a number of names: the *Miller-Tyding Act*. The one that is used depends upon the circumstances of the occasion of the citation.

Example of Citations

Public Law	Pub L No 96-272
United States Statutes at Large	94 Stat 500 (1988)
Unites States Code Congressional and Administrative News	(1988) US Code Cong & Admin News (99 Stat) 116
United States Code	42 USC § 602 (1994)
United States Code Annotated	42 USCA § 602 (West 1989)

Popular Names or Short Titles

The subject matter of the legislation and/or the names of those people who have been instrumental in introducing and marshalling it through Congress will usually be given to the legislation. Or the naming can occur informally but still be quite widespread. Notwithstanding how it occurred, it will occasionally be necessary to utilise one of the popular names tables to find the official citation. Such Tables can be found in:

- Shepard's *Acts and Cases by Popular Names – Federal and State*
- The General Index of the USCA
- The General Index of the US Code
- The *US Code Congressional and Administrative News,* for the current session of Congress.
- "US Code Table of Popular Names" at *<www4.law.cornell.edu/uscode/topn>.*

Example

Find the *Sherman Act* in a library that has the USCA. In this case one would also have to know that the *Sherman Act* was legislation dealing with anti-trust because there have been various Sherman Acts enacted over the years. By using the Common Names Tables in the last volume of the General Index, the reference can be found:

Sherley Amendment (Food and Drugs)
Aug. 23, 1912, ch. 352, 37 Stat. 416
Mar. 3, 1913, ch. 117, 37 Stat. 732

Sherman Act
Nov. 16, 1990, Pub.L. 101–588, § 4, 104 Stat. 2880 (Title 15, §§ 1 to 3)

Sherman Act (Purchase of Silver)
July 14, 1890, ch. 708, 26 Stat. 289

Sherman Anti-Trust Act (Trusts)
July 2, 1890, ch. 647, 26 Stat. 209 (Title 15, §§ 1–7)
Aug. 17, 1937, ch. 690, title VII, 50 Stat. 693 (Title 15, § 1)

The Constitution

Because of the federal nature of the American legal and political system, constitutional law is extremely important. In the legal sphere, because of the federal appellate jurisdiction of the Supreme Court, it is probably more so than in Australia. Consequently, one is frequently needing to consult aspects of constitutional law. One publication in this area which has no equal in our own system is:

Finding US Legislation Using the USCA

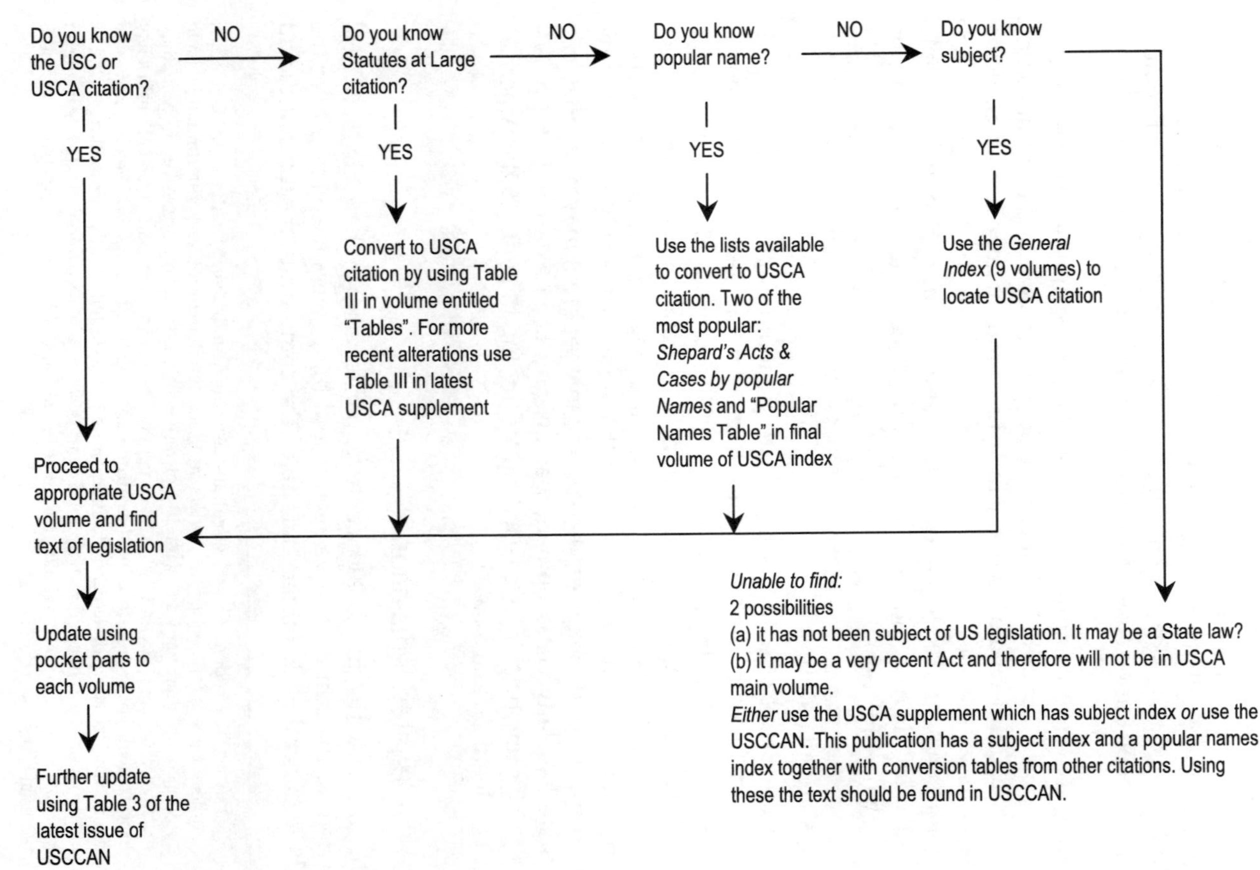
Do you know the USC or USCA citation?
YES
Proceed to appropriate USCA volume and find text of legislation
Update using pocket parts to each volume
Further update using Table 3 of the latest issue of USCCAN
NO
Do you know Statutes at Large citation?
YES
Convert to USCA citation by using Table III in volume entitled "Tables". For more recent alterations use Table III in latest USCA supplement
NO
Do you know popular name?
YES
Use the lists available to convert to USCA citation. Two of the most popular: Shepard's Acts & Cases by popular Names and "Popular Names Table" in final volume of USCA index
NO
Do you know subject?
YES
Use the General Index (9 volumes) to locate USCA citation
Unable to find:
2 possibilities
(a) it has not been subject of US legislation. It may be a State law?
(b) it may be a very recent Act and therefore will not be in USCA main volume.
Either use the USCA supplement which has subject index or use the USCCAN. This publication has a subject index and a popular names index together with conversion tables from other citations. Using these the text should be found in USCCAN.

The Constitution of the United States of America: Analysis and Interpretation (Washington, DC, Library of Congress)

This publication came into being because of a Joint Resolution of the Congress and, because of the authority associated with the work, is always an excellent place to start any sort of legal analysis of the Constitution. It has also been placed on the Internet together with a number of other important constitutional documents at: *<www.gpoaccess.gov/constitution/index html>*.

For the most comprehensive annotated Constitution, see *Constitution of the United States Annotated in the USCA*, published by West Publishing. This is a multi-volume work which has brought together all principal cases under the various sections and clauses of the Constitution, and amendments. It has the additional feature of being annually supplemented and is now indexed in the main subject index of the USCA (this being a new feature).

Legislative History

The importance of the legislative history should not be underestimated.[6] In Australia with the recent enactment by the federal Parliament of s 15AB of the *Acts Interpretation Act 1901* (see 58-62) the use within our jurisdiction of an approach to statutory interpretation that has always been available in America means that we are now in a better position to appreciate the methods used to find this information and the use that the court makes of it. Some of the specific material that may be available in a State legislative environment has already been examined at pp 194-196. The same principles of use, and of finding it, apply to the American federal legal system as well.

(b) Delegated legislation

The dramatic rise in the 20th century, particularly in the early New Deal period, of the administrative agency and the powers it exercises over the whole general and commercial life of the community meant that the ad

6 RA Posner, The Federal Courts: Crisis and Reform, Cambridge, Mass, Harvard UP, p 339: "Almost three years of reading briefs in cases involving statutory interpretation have convinced me that many lawyers do not research legislative history as carefully as they research case law . . . I would guess that not one lawyer in a thousand has real proficiency in it. He will not pick it up in his law firm, and he will not learn – not well anyway – by doing. The mastery of research techniques is not as intellectually stimulating as other elements of law school education, but library science is a recognised field of learning in first-class universities; it would not demean our law schools to adapt some of these materials for a law school course"!

hoc method of publishing administrative orders and regulations that had existed up until that time, had to be regularised. One of the great benefits to a government of delegating the law-making authority, pursuant to legislation, is that the making of such law, if within the bounds of the authority, is easy because it does not require the formality of the Congressional or Parliamentary procedures. However, that ease of law making can also get out of hand in the dissemination of the law. The turning point in the US was the case of *Panama Refining Co v Ryan* 293 US 388 (1935) when a prosecution reached the Supreme Court notwithstanding that the regulation, the basis of the prosecution, had been revoked. The Supreme Court was not amused and an embarrassed Attorney General proceeded to institute a scheme of publication centred upon the *Federal Register*.

In order to control delegated legislation, controls were placed upon the general rule-making powers of the federal administrative agencies. The two most important are contained in the Federal Register Act, 44 USC § 15 (1934) and the Administrative Procedure Act, 5 USC §§ 551-576 (1946). Federal agencies must publish a "Notice of Proposed Rule-making" in order that interested parties may advance their own views. The notice includes a suggested rule. Once the decision as to the form of the rule is made, at least 30 days before the rule taking effect, it must be published in the *Federal Register*, together with information as to reasons for any changes, made during the consultation period, from the original suggested rule.

The *Federal Register* commenced in March 1936 and is published Monday to Friday, excluding federal public holidays. For any administrative ruling or regulation of general applicability, issued by the executive or other independent agencies, to have legal effect it must appear in the *Federal Register* (1 CFR 1 1, 1984). Consequently, even though it started in 1936, it now has many hundreds of volumes, and 40-50,000 pages are added annually.

Each issue of the *Federal Register* contains a table of contents arranged by agency name and any rules, proposed rules, and notices of the agency, followed by a table of changes in regulations (List of Sections Affected) arranged by Code of Federal Regulations citation. The last issue of the month contains a cumulative list of sections affected.

Federal Register Index: a cumulative monthly publication which provides rules made under the name of the agency. Because of inadequate subject cross referencing, it is not easily used without specific agency name information. The January-December issue serves as the annual index to the *Federal Register*.

Electronic: Few Australian libraries have the *Federal Register* and electronic access is free and by far the easiest way, especially as it can also be searched using key-words from vol 59, 1994. It can be found at <*www. gpoaccess.gov/fr/index.html*>.

See also "Federal Web Locator", maintained by the Center for Information Law and Policy. Created as a one-stop shop for all Federal government information including links to all federal government agencies (the source of the material in the *Federal Register*), it can be found at <*www. infoctr.edu/fwl*>.

The Code of Federal Regulations: The *Federal Register* is analogous to the *Statutes at Large* insofar as it quickly became unwieldy and needed further supplementation. This was supplied, in 1937, in the form of the *Code of Federal Regulations* (CFR), a subject-based grouping of 50 volumes which follows very roughly the subject approach of the *US Code*.

It is kept up-to-date with perpetual rotating revision by the issuing of new volumes during the year:

Titles 1-16 as of 1 January

Titles 17-27 as of 1 April

Titles 28-41 as of 1 July

Titles 42-50 as of 1 October.

These volumes are further updated by the monthly, cumulative *CFR Parts Affected* and that part of the cumulative *List of CSR Sections Affected* in the daily *Federal Register*.

CFR Index and Finding Aids

In most cases of researching the regulations the initial approach will be made with a regulation citation already known. The task then is to ensure that it is still correct. Where there is a need to locate a regulation via a subject approach, the *CSR Index and Finding Guide* is reasonably useful. Published annually, it does allow limited searching by subject. However, the greatest use for it is the "Parallel Table of Statutory Authorities and Rules" which provides the cross-referencing of rules and regulations made under the legislation. Thus, by searching this table using a USC citation, reference is made to the CSR made pursuant to it.

The most comprehensive subject index is the *Index to the Code of Federal Regulations*, published annually in four volumes by the Congressional Information Service.

Updating Electronically

Australian researchers should be aware that searching for such regulations in local law collections can be unrewarding because of the lack of currency of most collections. While there are some libraries that have microfiche sets of the *Federal Register* or the *Code of Federal Regulations*, few are up-to-date, and certainly very few get the (daily) *Federal Register*. The Code is now freely available, and searchable, from a number of sources, including *<www.gpoaccess.gov/cfr/index.html>*. The CFR volumes are online concurrently with the release of the paper edition. When revised CFR volumes are added, the previous edition remains in *GPO Access* and can be searched. There are different ways to access the information. The entire CFR database can be searched covering all 50 titles including the most recent volumes. Alternately, if the researcher knows the CFR citation (title and section), this can be specifically retrieved. This can be done for most recent or historic volumes. Alternately, the search can be limited to specific titles. Finally there is a special facility called the LSA Service (**L**ist of CFR **S**ections **A**ffected) which allows recent changes to be located since the last updated title.

Example of Citations

Federal Register	22 Fed Reg 267 (1990)
Code of Federal Regulations	44 CFR § 22.182 (1990)

(c) Reports

From the material set out in the previous part, the hierarchy of federal courts was explained: the Supreme Court, the Circuit Courts of Appeal and the District Court. This division is reflected in the reports.

Supreme Court

There is a number of sets of reports of these decisions:

US Reports ("US")

US Supreme Court Reports, Lawyers' Edition (published by Lawyers Cooperative) ("US L Ed" or "US L Ed 2d")

Supreme Court Reporter (Published by West Pub) ("Sup Ct" or "S Ct")

United States Law Week (Bureau of Nat Affs)

CCH-United States Supreme Court Bulletin (CCH)

US Reports

These are the official reports of the US Supreme Court, and as such their citation takes precedence over all others. They have been published since 1789, although until 1874 it was under the reporter's name:

Dallas	1 – 4 Dall	(1 – 4 US)
Cranch	1 – 9 Cranch	(5 – 13 US)
Wheaton	1 – 12 Wheat	(14 – 25 US)
Peters	1 – 16 Pet	(26 – 41 US)
Howard	1 – 24 How	(42 – 65 US)
Black	1 – 2 Black	(66 – 67 US)
Wallace	1 – 23 Wall	(68 – 90 US)

Since vol 91 (1875) it has been known as the *US Reports* and all previous volumes have been renumbered (see material in parenthesis above). The way such early cases are now cited is:

Durant v Essex Co, 74 US (7 Wall) 107 (1869)

The *US Reports* are initially published in slip form which is later replaced by preliminary sheets which in turn are replaced by bound volumes. There are approximately three to four bound volumes each year. Each case has a headnote and indexes are prepared by government officials.

***US Supreme Court Reports*, Lawyers Ed (Lawyers Cooperative)**

This set of reports is an unofficial publication containing the decisions of the Court. Insofar as the cases are the same as the official set, the spine of this set carries the "US Report" citation as well as its own. It does have, however, a number of individual features:

(i) there is a selection of the summaries of briefs submitted to the court by the attorneys involved;

(ii) the headnote or case summary varies from the official set;

(iii) as part of the "annotated" series, these reports also contain annotations, ie, an appraisal of the relevance of the case written by a commentator (more will be said of this service when examining the *American Law Reports*);

(iv) there is a subject index at the end of each volume;

(v) there are extensive cross-references to other Lawyers Cooperative publications dealing with the same subject matter at the beginning of each case; and

(vi) there are pocket parts, supplied each year to each volume, which:

(a) provide a *Citator Service* whereby later Supreme Court decisions which have made significant references to decisions in the volume are noted;
(b) provides a *Later Case Service* which allows the annotations to be supplemented by later case references; and
(c) provides *Corrections* – showing final correction from the authorised reports mainly made by the Justices, after the Lawyers Edition was published.

Supreme Court Reporter (West Publishing)

This series commenced in 1882 and consequently vols 1-105 US are not included. Like the other unofficial sets, they have their own headnotes and this set cross-references extensively to the other West Publications.

Electronic

It used to be an imperative to have access to airmailed editions of publications like *US Law Week* to quickly obtain copies of recent Supreme Court decisions. The Internet has now changed that dramatically.

Since 11 May 1990, US Supreme Court decisions are available online as part of Project Hermes. By using <*www.law.cornell.edu*>, the researcher can access almost all decisions back to 1990, hypertexted and with excellent indexes.

In addition there are a number of historic collections available free of charge. First, Cornell's ILL has collected 631 historically important decisions (currently up to 2002) and put them both on their LII site and on a CD-ROM for sale at a relatively cheap price. Secondly, a project of the US Air Force has involved putting Supreme Court decisions into electronic form covering the period 1937-1975. With 7407 decisions, they are available at <*http: //www.fedworld.gov/supcourt/index.htm*>.

Finally, the researcher can now visit the home page of the Supreme Court. Unveiled only in April 2000 at <*www.supremecourtus.gov*>, the delay in getting the site established was to invite comment and some background material: see "The Supreme Court enters the Internet Age: the Court and technology" by Roy M Mersky and Kumar Percy, feature for the *Law Library Research Xchange* (LLRX) at <*www.llrx.com/features/supremect.htm*>.

Court Briefs

It is a feature of the *Commonwealth Law Reports* to include, before the judgment of the Court, a précis of the argument of counsel. This is extremely beneficial in many cases for it allows the researcher to determine the full scope of an unsuccessful argument, a fact not always apparent from the judgment. In the Supreme Court counsel does not have unlimited time to argue. They have precisely 30 minutes (although extensions are given by the Bench on occasions). There, the principal method of getting their argument across is by using the written brief. Recently a publication has become available which publishes in full all material submitted to the court before the case. Although it is, as yet, only for selected cases, these will certainly be the most important of the cases in that area. This set is called *Landmark Briefs and Arguments of the Supreme Court of the US*.

Electronic

The transcripts of US Supreme Court oral arguments are now available on Westlaw since the 1990-91. LexisNexis has the briefs filed for Supreme Court cases since October 1979.

Another development is *The Oyez Project* of the Northwestern University. Many hundreds of hours on tape of judges and advocates associated with some of the leading constitutional law cases have been brought together and are accessible to the researcher. The necessary software to hear this material is also freely available. Indeed, so popular is the material that Northwestern University Press have released a CD-ROM entitled *The Supreme Court's Greatest Hits,* consisting, in Version 2.0, of 62 leading cases. This site is at <*www.oyez.org*>.

Circuit Courts of Appeal

Unlike the Supreme Court, the choice of reports covering this intermediate court level is not nearly as great. There are basically only two: one being published by West Publishing and the other by Lawyers Cooperative.

West

Federal Cases (1789-1880)

Federal Reporter

1st Series 1-300 (1880-1924)

2nd Series 1-999 (1924-1993)

3rd Series 1- (1993+)

Note: There has been a jurisdictional change over this period of time:

1880-1931 *Federal Reporter* included the Circuit Courts of Appeal, US Court of Customs & Patent Appeals, US Emergency Court of Appeal, and selected District Court decisions.

1932+ As above excluding the District Court.

Lawyers Cooperative

American Law Reports Federal (1966+)

This is part of the Annotated Report series and in a way is similar to the companion volumes of the *American Law Reports* which covers State decisions. This set is selective in its coverage ("the leading decisions") and only provides annotations where the publishers feel it would lead to a greater understanding of the decision. This is dealt with in a more complete fashion in the next section.

Example: Citation of Circuit Court Decisions

There are many areas of law where there are differences in approach between various Circuit Courts. Certainly the matter could be settled by a ruling of the Supreme Court but until that occurs there is the possibility of conflict. An example is in the area of disclosure of "soft" information in an insider trading action. The Second, Third and Sixth Circuits have all taken different attitudes. Thus *Gerstle v Gamble-Skogmo, Inc* 478 F 2d 1281 (2d Cir 1973) held that asset appraisal did not have to be disclosed in a merger context. In *Starkman v Marathon Oil Co* 772 F 2d 231 (6th Cir 1985), *cert den* 475 US 1015 (1986), it was held that soft information must be disclosed if it is as certain as hard facts. Yet the Third Circuit in *Flynn v Bass Bros Enters* 744 F 2d 978 (3rd Cir 1984) espoused the adoption of a case-by-case approach to the determination of this question. It is essential that the Circuit Court be inserted if the true scope of this difference is to be understood. It also helps American researchers as they look for authorities that will determine the issue in their own jurisdiction. The fact that the Supreme Court in *Starkman* refused certiorari to review the decision (*certiorari denied*) also tells us a little more about the problem as well.

District Courts

Federal Supplement (1932+), (West Pub)

As noted above, the District Court cases were dropped from the *Federal Reporter* in 1932, when this publication commenced. For a period it included other federal courts, including the Court of Claims, until 1960 when it returned to the *Federal Reporter*. Its contents now tend to be restricted to District Court cases.

Example: Citation of District Court Decisions

In most States there was only one District Court – serving as a court of first instances in Federal matters. With 90 Courts now, there are many of the larger States that have two, three or even four Courts. The identification usually adopts geographic points: Northern, Southern, etc. (New York and Texas), or Eastern, Middle and Western (Pennsylvania, North Carolina), followed by the State abbreviation. Thus *US v Crawford* 815 F Supp (E D Va 1993), or *Consumer Gas and Oil v Farmland Industries* 815 F Supp (D Colo 1992).

Other Federal Courts

Various federal courts can be found in a number of the West Publications, including *Federal Reporter, Federal Supplement* and *Federal Rules Decisions*. However, these are certainly not complete.

Official reports are available now for all of the principal federal courts. They include:

Court of Claims
Court of Customs and Patent Appeals
Customs Courts
Emergency Court of Appeals
Court of Military Appeals
Tax Court of the United States.

Electronic

LexisNexis and Westlaw in various directories.

3. State Law

(a) Legislation

In many respects the legislation of the various States of the United States is similar to the federal body, although there are differences in nomenclature and in procedures. There is also, like Quebec in Canada, one State within the United States that is an exception to the general rule that all

States have a legal system based on the common law. That is Louisiana, the State law of which is based upon the civil law.

With rare exceptions, few of these Codes are located in Australian collections and one of the easier ways of finding State legislation is via LEXIS. They are also available on Westlaw, while many are also available on the Internet at <*www.findlaw.com/casecode/codes.html*>. Before going online, it may be useful to check if the legislative provisions are not within one of the looseleaf specialist services that may be located in the region. Thus the *CCH Blue Sky Reporter*,[7] which deals comprehensively with the sale of securities and is a matter of State law, brings together the laws and regulations of all 50 States, the District of Columbia, Guam and Puerto Rico. In the area of taxation, corporations, family and insurance law such services can be found.

Restatements of the Law

In 1923 the American Law Institute was founded after concern by many jurists that the development of the common law in the United States was growing far too uncertain and, in some areas, unduly complex. "It was feared that the increasing mass of unorganised judicial opinions threatened to break down the system of articulated and developing case law".[8] It was to assist in solving this problem that the Institute undertook to produce a clear and precise restatement of the existing common law that would have "authority greater than that now accorded to any legal treaties, an authority more nearly on a par with that accorded the decisions of the courts". *Report of the Committee on the Establishment …American Law Institute*, 1923. Thus the *Restatements of the Law* came into being.

Over the years there has been a subtle change in the use of the *Restatements*. Initially it was seen by many as a codification of the common law. To this end the first series of Restatements omitted report citations. Since 1952, the second series have made reference to reports and will, when required, indicate new trends in the common law together with what they consider the rule should be. In the second series, the *Restatements* for agency, contracts, conflict of laws, foreign relations law, judgments, property, landlord and tenant, tort and trusts have been released. They are extensively referred to in the courts and are well indexed: the first series with a one-volume index to all *Restatements*, the

7 The Blue Sky legislation is now a commonly accepted term for this type of legislation. It came about because such legislation aims to prevent "speculative schemes which have no more basis than so many feet of blue sky": *Hall v Geiger & Jones Co* 242 US 539 (1917).

8 Lewis, "History of the American Law Institute and the First Restatement of the Law" in *ALI Restatements in the Courts* (1945), p 1.

second series volumes each with their own index, and they can be Shepardised.[9] They are available on CD-ROM and online from Westlaw (at REST – followed by title) and LEXIS (at RESTAT).

National Conference of Commissioners on Uniform State Law

The same movement for reform in the early 1900s that resulted in the Restatement, had already led in 1912 to the establishment of the National Conference of Commissioners on Uniform State Laws. The aim is to "promote uniformity in State laws where uniformity is deemed desirable and practicable".

The Conference meets once a year and has approved over 200 Acts. There are different names for these: the Conference will designate an Act a *Uniform Act* when it has a reasonable possibility of ultimate enactment in a substantial number of jurisdictions. Acts which tend to be in subject areas without wide interstate application, and thus without the same pressure for uniformity, are usually referred to as *Model Acts*.

Occasionally the American Law Institute and the National Conference will come together in the production of an Act. An example is the most important Uniform Commercial Code. For a way that the UCC works as a legal authority, and the use that can be made of it by Australian researchers, see Justice LJ Priestley, "A Guide to a Comparison of Australian and United States Contract Law" (1989) 12 *UNSWLJ* 4.

Lists of Model and Uniform Acts:[10] The annual Handbook of the National Conference of Commissioners on Uniform State Laws lists all Acts, as well as those States that have adopted them together with the date.

Uniform Laws Annotated: Published by West Publishing, all the Uniform Laws have been published in a format which provides annotated commentary and annual pocket supplementation.

Electronic: The *Uniform Laws Annotated* is available on Westlaw. LexisNexis has the *Uniform Commercial Code,* both text and commentaries available. Researchers on the Internet should go to Cornell's *Legal Information Institute* (LII) at < *www.law.cornell.edu/ucc*>.

---

9 See pp 109-111.

10 The concept of the model code and uniform law causes a great deal of confusion. In response to a request to de-mystify the model codes and Acts, a panel of librarians responded through the "Questions & Answers" column of (1992) 84 *Law Library Journal* 215 at 218, providing a wealth of material in their answer.

(b) Delegated legislation

Like the use that is made of regulations at the federal level, so with the States. Because of the diversity of publications, only the *California Code of Regulations* will be dealt with here. Many of the same procedures, however, are followed in other States.

California Code of Regulations

California has the system, provided by law (California Administrative Procedures Act, §§ 11340-11356) that the making or altering of delegated legislation requires initial public notification. A "Notice of Proposed Action" is published in the *California Regulatory Notice Register*. At least 45 days are required for hearings or comments, after which the regulation is reviewed by the Office of Administrative Law to ensure procedural compliance. Once approved it is printed in the *California Code of Regulations* (before 1988 known as the *California Administrative Code*).

The *California Code of Regulations* consists of 60 looseleaf volumes, arranged into 26 numbered titles. The way of finding regulations is either by subject, or pursuant to part of the legislative Code. Both are examined below.

Subject: The Code itself does not have an index and, while the 26 titles can be used with the various chapter headings, it is easier to use the privately produced *Comprehensive Index to the Administrative Code* published by University Microfilms International. An annual, cumulative publication updated with advance sheets, it provides a good index via subject matter.

Parallel Code/Regulation Tables: The *Comprehensive Index* provides both a "Regulation to Statute Table" as well as "Statutes to Regulation Table", thus allowing ready reference to most researchers' needs.

Electronic: As at the beginning of 2004, there is little regulatory material on the net, outside the Federal Code. There are some Administrative Codes on LexisNexis, including California's.

(c) Reports

In many States, legislation has provided for the reports of certain cases within their appellate court structure to be officially published. These then are "official" and can be equated within the Australian "authorised" reports. They are not of primary concern for few are found in Australian law collections. They must always be kept in mind because the practice is followed in America of citing the official citation before all others.

However, there are other series of reports of State decisions which, because of their widespread distribution, are of considerable interest. There are two:

The *National Reporter System* (West Publishing), and

The *Annotated Reports* (Lawyers Cooperative).

The National Reporter System (also known as the Region Reporter)

Other West publications in the federal area have been examined: *Federal Reporter*, *Federal Supplement* and *Federal Rules Decisions*, but it is the State reports which make up the National Reporter System. The aim of the publishers is *to report all decisions of all appellate courts of the States*. This is done by publishing those reports in series that group States of similar geographical and economic conditions, with the result that there are nine sections to the system: seven geographical or regional sections plus two supplements covering New York and California. The regions of the National Reporter System are:

Atlantic (A) (1886+)

Connecticut, Delaware, Maine, Maryland, New Hampshire, New Jersey, Pennsylvania, Rhode Island and Vermont.

North Eastern Reporter (NE) (1885+)

Illinois, Indiana, Massachusetts, New York and Ohio.

North Western Reporter (NW) (1879+)

Iowa, Michigan, Minnesota, Nebraska, North Dakota, South Dakota and Wisconsin.

Pacific Reporter (P) (1884+)

Arizona, California, Colorado, Hawaii, Idaho, Kansas, Montana, Nevada, New Mexico, Oklahoma, Oregon, Utah, Washington and Wyoming.

South Eastern Reporter (SE) (1887+)

Georgia, North Carolina, South Carolina, Virginia and West Virginia.

South Western Reporter (SW) (1887+)

Arkansas, Kentucky, Missouri, Tennessee and Texas.

Southern Reporter (S) (1887+)

Alabama, Florida, Louisiana and Mississippi.

California Reporter (Cal Rptr) (1960+)

New York Supplement (NYS) (1888+)

Special Feature of the National Reporter System

The National Reporter Blue Book and State White Books: These publications provide parallel citations – from the (official) State Report to the National Reporter System in the *Blue Book*, while the *White Book* provides the State Report citation from the (unofficial) National Reporter System citation.

Annotated Reports

The Reports in this set are:

Trinity Series (1760-1911)

American Decisions

American Reports

American State Reports

American and English Annotated Cases (1906-1911)

American Annotated Cases (1912-1918)

Lawyers Reports, Annotated (1885-1918)

American Law Reports,

1st series, vols 1-175 (1918-1947)

2nd series, vols 1-100 (1948-1965)

3rd series, vols 1-100 (1965-1980)

4th series, vols 1-90 (1980-1991)

5th series, vols 1- 120 (1992-2004)

6th series, vols 1- (2005+)

Like the National Reporter System, there is also a federal component:

American Law Reports, Federal Series

1st series, vols 1-200 (1969-2005)

2nd series, vols 1- (2005+)

That is where the similarity between the two series ends. They approach reporting from different perspectives. The National Reporter System aims to publish *all cases* from the State appellate structure, while the Annotated Reports contain only the *most important* of the State cases.

The second major difference is the inclusion of the selected annotations, a feature that has previously been mentioned in regard to this publisher's *Supreme Court Reports, Lawyers' Edition* but will be explained here. The concept of the annotation is completely unknown in the report series of Australia or Great Britain. The idea that within the primary sources of law, the law report, one should be able to find a legal analysis of the case, written usually by an academic, and placing the case in its historic or conceptual context, is something which we find difficult to accept. The use that is made of these, particularly by students in the United States, however, cannot be underestimated. It allows a reader quickly to grasp the principal points of a decision. The publishers supply indexes to allow the researcher to find cases by name or subject in the annotations and any changes to the material in the supplement. If a new annotation supersedes an older annotation, this is shown in the pocket parts that are filed at the end of each volume of the law reports in the series.

Principal Problems

A problem inherent in such a series as the Annotated Reports must be the selectivity of cases chosen for inclusion. By only choosing the most important cases, usually decided shortly after the case is handed down, we find many important cases overlooked, and students will have to be prepared to use the alternate, and much more comprehensive, collection of cases in the National Reporter System.

Another problem is the "stable" mentality of the publishers. At the beginning of each annotation is extensive cross-referencing to other Lawyers Cooperative publications. There is usually one exception to this rule because West's "key numbers", without the symbol, are also shown.

The way these two leading publishers promoted their own publications at the expense of competitors in this fashion now seems a little ironic insofar as they are now both owned by the Thompson Company and we may well see rationalisation in the future.

(d) Some Secondary Sources for Finding State Law

State Practice Books: One of the most helpful of recent publications in finding State legal materials by subject is FR Doyle, *Searching the Law – the States, a selective bibliography of State practice materials in the 50 States*, 4th ed, Dobbs Ferry, NY, Transnational, 2003. This is a select bibliography of State practice in all States This can be supplemented by the periodic publication of State practice material in the Law Library Journal. States covered so far include New York, Michigan, Texas, Pennsylvania, California, New Jersey, Arizona, Arkansas, Alabama, New Mexico, Montana, Utah, Idaho, Oregon, Colorado, Delaware, Wisconsin, Connecticut and Nevada. See (1999) 91 *Law Lib J* 313 for a list of the articles and publication details. Until recently, these reviews of State material appeared regularly in the Journal. That has not been the case over the past few years.

State Court Practice

While West provides annual State court rules for Alabama, Alaska, Arizona, California, Louisiana, Maine, Montana, New Jersey, Pennsylvania, South Carolina, Tennessee and Washington, Lawyers Cooperative supplements these by a variety of general and limited rules for many of the other States. For more complete details see the recent article by Reiginger and Lemmon, "Sources of rules of State Courts" 82 *Law Library Journal*, 761-776 (1990).

Additional references to State law can be found in State legal encyclopaedias, listed below.

Electronic: a valuable resource that has been made available by the *Law Library Research Xchange* (LLRX) is "Court Rules, Forms and Dockets" containing over 700 sources of State (and Federal) court rules, forms and dockets and where available, details of filing online. It can be found at: *<www.llrx.com/courtrules>*.

4. Principal Secondary Sources for American Law

(a) Legal encyclopaedias

National

The starting point for so much research has to be the legal encyclopaedia. While the Australian researcher has traditionally sought assistance in *Halsbury's Laws of England*, and more recently with *Halsbury's Laws of Australia*, and the *Laws of Australia*, research of American law can be considerably shortened by recourse to *Corpus Juris Secundum* (West Publishing) and *American Jurisprudence* (Lawyers Cooperative). Both publications are found in most university and principal court collections and provide a comprehensive statement of the law, alphabetically arranged by subject title, and by using the pocket parts, can be brought reasonably up to date.

When using these encyclopaedias the researcher should be particularly aware of the publisher. Both rely extensively on cross-referencing to other publications to direct the researcher to other sources of additional or related materials. However, the references tend to be to their own or

Example from *Corpus Juris Secundum*

§ 16. Imposition of Conditions

A trial court in releasing an accused on bail may impose conditions which, under the facts and circumstances of the particular case, are reasonably necessary to assure the appearance of the accused as required.

Research Note

Revocation or modification of an order admitting accused to bail is discussed infra §§ 62, 63. Breach or performance of condition of bond, undertaking, or recognizance is discussed infra § 140 et seq.

Library References

Bail ⇐42.5.

A trial court in releasing accused on bail may impose conditions which, under the facts and circumstances of the particular case, are reasonably necessary to assure the appearance of accused as required.[49] The conditions of release are intrusted to the sound discretion of the trial court.[50] Hence, the authority to impose conditions can only be exercised for a legally permissible purpose,[51] and the court may impose only such conditions as reasonably relate to providing assurance that accused will appear at trial.[52]

In deciding what conditions to impose, the trial court may consider accused's respect for the law, including evidence of past criminal record.[53] The conditions for release of those who are obvious bail risks may be much more stringent than those set for persons who are not.[54]

Modification.

When so authorized by law, a higher judicial authority may modify the conditions imposed by a lower authority.[55]

§ 17. Waiver of Forfeiture of Right

A right to be admitted to bail may be waived or forfeited.

Library References

Bail ⇐42.

Accused in a state prosecution may waive[56] or forfeit[57] his right to bail, as where he fails to pursue diligently his right to bail,[58] or where he engages in a felonious criminal activity while out on bail,[59] or where he voluntarily waives a prelim-

49. Ala.—Shabazz v. State, Cr.App., 440 So.2d 1200.

Colo.—Hafelfinger v. District Court In and For Eighth Judicial Dist., 674 P.2d 375.

D.C.—Matter of Rosen, App., 470 A.2d 292.

Fla.—Carter v. Carson, App., 370 So.2d 1241.

Ind.—State ex rel. Williams v. Ryan, 490 N.E.2d 1113.

Ill.—People v. Ealy, 365 N.E.2d 149, 7 Ill.Dec. 854, 49 Ill.App.3d 922.

N.J.—State v. Casavina, 394 A.2d 142, 163 N.J.Super. 27.

Or.—Collins v. Foster, 698 P.2d 953, 299 Or. 90.

R.I.—Mello v. Superior Court, 370 A.2d 1262, 117 R.I. 578.

Vt.—State v. Brown, 396 A.2d 134, 136 Vt. 561.

Wyo.—Application of Allied Fidelity Ins. Co., 664 P.2d 1322.

Abstinence from alcohol

Where defendant had alcohol problem, it was appropriate for trial court, in exercise of its discretion, to require that defendant neither use, possess, nor consume alcohol during period of "security release agreement," since abuse of alcohol could result in forgetfulness or irresponsibility which, in turn, might result in defendant's failure to appear at trial.

Or.—Sexson v. Merten, 631 P.2d 1367, 291 Or. 441.

Good behavior

Trial court may impose conditions of good behavior upon grant of pretrial release to defendant.

Fla.—Harp v. Hinckley, App. 4 Dist., 410 So.2d 619.

Va.—Heacock v. Commonwealth, 321 S.E.2d 645, 228 Va. 235.

Placement on probation

Trial court had authority to place defendant, as condition of release upon posting of secured appearance bond, in custody of probation office and require him to report weekly to specified person at designated time.

N.C.—State v. Cooley, 274 S.E.2d 274, 50 N.C.App. 544, review denied 280 S.E.2d 442, 302 N.C. 631.

50. Minn.—State v. Rogers, App., 392 N.W.2d 11.

Wyo.—Application of Allied Fidelity Ins. Co., 664 P.2d 1322.

51. Fla.—Olinton v. Wille, App. 4 Dist., 457 So.2d 563.

Or.—Cooper v. Burks, 702 P.2d 1107, 299 Or. 449.

Imposition of curfew

Imposition of curfew as condition of release of petitioner who had been charged with loitering for purpose of engaging in prostitution and who was released upon $25 bail, for ostensible purpose of preventive detention was for legally impermissible purpose and was therefore invalid.

N.Y.—People ex rel. Shaw v. Lombard, 408 N.Y.S.2d 664, 95 Misc.2d 664.

52. Fla.—Carter v. Carson, App., 370 So.2d 1241.

Primary issue

In setting conditions of release, primary issue, is whether detainee will appear for subsequent court proceedings

Cal.—People v. Barbarick, 4 Dist., 214 Cal.Rptr. 322, 168 C.A.3d 731, review denied.

Participation in health programs

Requiring defendants to involuntarily participate in governmental health programs is too tenuously related to assurance of defendant's later appearance at trial to provide trial courts with authority to impose such condition in "security release agreements."

Or.—Sexson v. Merten, 631 P.2d 1367, 291 Or. 441.

53. Fla.—Harp v. Hinckley, App. 4 Dist., 410 So.2d 619.

54. Fla.—Harp v. Hinckley, App. 4 Dist., 410 So.2d 619.

55. D.C.—Clotterbuck v. U.S., App., 459 A.2d 134.

56. Ky.—Gray v. McAtee, 25 S.W.2d 65, 233 Ky. 97.

57. Tenn.—Wallace v. State, 245 S.W.2d 192, 193 Tenn. 182.

58. Mont.—State v. Beach, 705 P.2d 94.

59. Ala.—Shabazz v. State, Cr.App., 440 So.2d 1200.

31

Example from *American Jurisprudence*

§ 77. —Seriousness of offense; penalty.

In setting the amount of bail, the principal factor considered, to the determination of which most other factors are directed, is the probability of the appearance of the accused, or of his flight to avoid punishment.[62] Hence, the possible penalty that may be imposed is a major factor to be considered in determining the amount of bail.[63] And the severity of the penalty, of course, generally depends on the seriousness of the crime with which the defendant is charged. Therefore, the seriousness of the offense is a valid consideration.[64]

Since crimes of the same class often differ greatly in their character, different provisions as to bail may be made in different cases, even though the offenses are of the same class.[65]

Bail is reasonable if, in view of the nature of the offense and the penalty which the law attaches to it, it seems no more than sufficient to secure the attendance of the accused.[66]

§ 78. —Character and previous behavior of the defendant.

A major factor in determining the amount of bail in a current matter is the character and former criminal record of the defendant.[67] It has been held,

item of abiiity of accused to give bail is omitted.

Factors to be considered in determining the reasonableness of bail are: the seriousness of the offense and the penalty for conviction; evidence of the character and reputation of accused along with any criminal record; and evidence bearing on the probability or lack thereof of accused's appearance for trial. Abbott v Columbus, 32 Ohio Misc 152, 61 Ohio Ops 2d 268, 289 NE2d 589.

In murder prosecution, $75,000 bail was excessive where, from examination of record before court, it appeared that petitioner was certainly unable to make bail by himself, that attempts of others to post bond for him had been rejected by sheriff, evidence of his guilt was circumstantial, and likelihood of his jumping bail seemed minimal. Ex parte Redline (Tex Crim) 529 SW2d 68.

See also the Bail Reform Act of 1966, 18 USCS § 3146(b), prescribing factors to be considered in imposing conditions of release of defendant on his personal recognizance pending trial, and 18 USCS § 3148 (release in capital cases or after conviction).

61. Gusick v Boies, 72 **Ariz** 309, 234 P2d 430; State ex rel. Corella v Miles, 303 **Mo** 648, 262 SW 364.

62. People ex rel. Sammons v Snow, 340 **Ill** 464, 173 NE 8, 72 ALR 798.

See also the Bail Reform Act of 1966, 18 USCS §§ 3146(b), 3148, as to conditions to be considered in setting bail, discussed in §§ 28, 32, supra.

Annotation: 96 L Ed 16.

63. Moore v Aderhold (CA10 Kan) 108 F2d 729; People ex rel. Sammons v Snow, 340 **Ill** 464, 173 NE 8, 72 ALR 798; State v Mastrian, 266 **Minn** 58, 122 NW2d 621, cert den 375 US 942, 11 L Ed 2d 274, 84 S Ct 349; Application of Kennedy, 169 **Neb** 586, 100 NW2d 550; Ex parte Malley, 50 **Nev** 248, 256 P 512, 53 ALR 395.

Bail of $125,000 for the offense of exercising control of personal property valued at more than $200 and less than $10,000 without the owner's consent and with the intent to deprive the owner of the property was not excessive where accused had two prior felony convictions and, if convicted, the punishment would be life imprisonment. Ex parte Runo (Tex Crim) 535 SW2d 188.

64. People ex rel. Sammons v Snow, 340 **Ill** 464, 173 NE 8, 72 ALR 798; Ex parte Malley, 50 **Nev** 248, 256 P 512, 53 ALR 395; People ex rel. Rubenstein v Warden of City Prison, 279 App Div 47, 107 NYS2d 948; Petition of McNair, 324 **Pa** 48, 187 A 498, 106 ALR 1373; Ex parte Glass, 81 **W Va** 111, 93 SE 1036.

Annotation: 49 ALR2d 1238; 96 L Ed 18.

65. Green v Petit, 222 **Ind** 467, 54 NE2d 281.

66. People ex rel. Sammons v Snow, 340 **Ill** 464, 173 NE 8, 72 ALR 798; Ex parte Malley, 50 **Nev** 248, 256 P 512, 53 ALR 395.

67. Jones v Grimes, 219 **Ga** 585, 134 SE2d 790; People v Officer, 10 **Ill** 2d 203, 139 NE2d 773; People ex rel. Sammons v Snow, 340 **Ill**

related publications only. Consequently the inexperienced researcher may fail to follow all leads unless this is recognised.

See sample pages for both encyclopaedias on the following pages. *Note* particularly the references in the footnotes to *Corpus Juris*. This is a reference to the original edition and where the footnote references are still relevant in that publication they have not been reproduced in the second edition. This can be a difficulty because it is in few Australian law collections. Volumes are kept up to date by cumulative pocket parts.

Differences between Corpus Juris Secundum and American Jurisprudence

When would a researcher use one over the other? What are the differences? There is not a huge amount, although from the pages extracted it should be apparent that the references to other publications differ significantly. This can lead to the suggestion that *Corpus Juris Secundum* is probably the preferable starting point if the research involves State law matters, and *American Jurisprudence* in federal matters.

State

A number of the more populous States also have general legal encyclopaedias:

California Jurisprudence 3d (Bancroft-Whitney) (**Westlaw**)

Summary of California Law (Witkin) (**Westlaw**) (**LexisNexis**)

Colorado Law Annotated 2d (Lawyers Cooperative)

Florida Jurisprudence 2d (Lawyers Cooperative) (**Westlaw**) (**LexisNexis**)

Georgia Jurisprudence (**Westlaw**)

Illinois Law and Practice (**Westlaw**)

Illinois Jurisprudence (**LexisNexis**)

Illinois Law and Practice (**Westlaw**)

Indiana Law Encyclopedia (West) (**Westlaw**)

Kentucky Jurisprudence (Lawyers Cooperative)

Louisiana Civil Law Treatise (20 vols) (**Westlaw**)

Maryland Law Encyclopedia (**Westlaw**)

Massachusetts Practice (**Westlaw**)

Michigan Law and Practice Encyclopedia (**LexisNexis**)

Minnesota Practice (**Westlaw**)

Encyclopedia of Mississippi Law (West)

New Hampshire Practice (**LexisNexis**)

New Jersey Practice (**Westlaw**)

New York Jurisprudence 2d (Lawyers Cooperative) (**Westlaw**) (**LexisNexis**)

Strong's North Carolina Index 4th (**Westlaw**)

Ohio Jurisprudence 3d (**Westlaw**) (**LexisNexis**)

Pennsylvania Law Encyclopedia (**LexisNexis**)

Pennsylvania Jurisprudence (**Westlaw**)

South Carolina Jurisprudence (**Westlaw**)

Tennessee Jurisprudence (**LexisNexis**)

Texas Jurisprudence 3d (Lawyers Cooperative) (**Westlaw**) (**LexisNexis**)

Michie's Jurisprudence of Virginia and West Virginia (**LexisNexis**)

(b) National Digests

American Digest System

To find the most comprehensive collection of American cases upon a subject, the starting point is the *American Digest System*, published by West.

Unlike the *Australian Digest*, which is published in editions, and whereby the addition of new cases and subtraction of obsolete or overruled cases means that only the latest edition is searched, there are no editions with the American case finder.

The American Digest System is made up of:

Century Digest	1658-1896	50 volumes
First Decennial	1897-1906	25 volumes
Second Decennial	1907-1916	24 volumes
Third Decennial	1916-1926	29 volumes
Fourth Decennial	1926-1936	34 volumes
Fifth Decennial	1936-1946	49 volumes
Sixth Decennial	1946-1956	36 volumes
Seventh Decennial	1956-1966	38 volumes
Eighth Decennial	1966-1976	50 volumes
Ninth Decennial (Pt 1)	1976-1981	38 volumes
Ninth Decennial (Pt 2)	1981-1986	48 volumes
Tenth Decennial (Pt 1)	1986-1991	44 volumes

Tenth Decennial (Pt 2)	1991-1996	64 volumes
Eleventh Decennial (Pt 1)	1996-2001	64 volumes
Eleventh Decennial (Pt 2)	2001-2004	62 volumes
Eleventh Decennial (Pt 3)	2004-2007	60 volumes
General Digest 11th Series	2007	
General Digest 12th Series	2008 to date	

It will be noted that the ten-year coverage was replaced with two series in the Tenth Decennial, and three series with the Eleventh Decennial. Such is the magnitude of American case law.

In order to find cases on a particular subject matter it is necessary to initially determine the key number classification (see below) and then proceed to the various volumes (individually) in the General Digest, followed by the relevant (single) volume within the various three series of the Eleventh Decennial, the two series of the Tenth Decennial and so on, working your way back as far as you wish to go.

Key Number Classification

In the publication of a digest of cases, the main problem faced by the publisher is to arrange the cases in a logical order, grouping like cases together, thus allowing easy reference to them and at the same time allowing new cases to be found that will ultimately find their way into the same group. In the *Australian Digest Service* this is the concept of the "*[ ] number*". In the *American Digest System*, they have employed the "key number", whereby a small key is followed by a number. When grouped with a title name, that number indicates that it is a reference to the area of law within the American Digest Service. It can be found throughout all West Publication books and serials. Consequently it provides the researcher with an immediate source of cases upon the same topic.

Additional Special Features

Descriptive Word Index: Described in promotional material as the "starting point of research", this index does allow a specialised topic to be located within the considerable list of general topics digested. "It indexes the facts as well as the law of the cases covered by this digest, and is an indispensable guide to cases dealing with similar facts and legal principles". (p iii, *Ninth Decennial Digest*, Part 2)

Table of Cases: This table is more than merely allowing a digest of a case to be found when the plaintiff's name is known. It does provide a complete set of alternate citations to the case.

United States Supreme Court Digest, Lawyers' Edition

This series allows the researcher to find US Supreme Court decisions by subject. For Australian researchers, that is usually all they need. Because the number of cases is so much less than the number of cases in the *American Digest*, important material can quickly be found.

Other parts of the service include the *Rules* volumes (17-22) which include the Supreme Court Rules, Appellate Procedure Rules, Civil Procedure Rules, Criminal Procedure Rules and the Federal Rules of Evidence.

The table of cases is useful because many of the determinations of the Supreme Court *without reasons* have been excluded, leaving an uncluttered list of those cases which have been reported with opinions.

(c) Other Secondary Sources of American Law

There are many other secondary sources that can be used to find American law. They include, inter alia, law texts and journal articles. Aspects of these have already been dealt with generally in the chapter on secondary sources. However, there is a number of specific places to search for American text and reference books.

One of the most important is *Law Books in Print,* 8th ed, Glanville, 1997. This is a six-volume work which provides a wide coverage of material used in the United States.

There are also two books published by Transnational Publishers that have as their aim the simplification of legal research and the finding of US materials:

Frank S Bae, Edward J Bander, FR Doyle, Joel Fishman, and Paul Richert, *Searching the Law,* 3rd ed, Dobbs Ferry, NY, Transnational, 2005. This is an alphabetical arrangement of US legal terms and law topics and which provides extensive bibliographic references where appropriate. Under a heading like "Medico-legal" there are nearly four pages of bibliographic information, broken down into various types of publications – general texts, dictionaries and relevant journals, under a variety of headings, such as genetics, malpractice and mental retardation. An examination under "Forms" gives a full treatment of the general and specific form books that exist in the United States.

FR Doyle, *Searching the Law: the States*, 4th ed, Dobbs Ferry, NY Transnational Pub, 2003. Under the heading of each State, the major legal texts and practice books of the jurisdiction are listed under subject headings. This has proved invaluable to this author when needing information from the family law practice books from three States.

Chapter 8

International Law

Outline

1 What is International Law?

2 What is the Relationship of International Law to Domestic (or National) Law?

3 Sources of International Law

  (a) Treaties

  (b) Custom

  (c) International Law Reports and Arbitrations

4 Specific Areas of International Law

  (a) Protecting Rights and the Environment in a World of Sovereign States

  (b) International Trade Law and Commercial Arbitrations

1. What is international law?

The answer to this question, at the end of the 20th century, will be vastly different from that which would have been given at the beginning. Even as late as 1940[1] the definition would have simply identified the subject as a "body of rules governing the relations between states". However, after the dramatic events of the Second World War there are other "subjects" of international law. Now usually referred to as "non-typical subjects" or "objects", they include the international organisations, be they inter-governmental or supranational, that now play such an important role generally in peace-keeping, trade, etc, or specifically, in the areas of telecommunications, postal or meteorological services.

Also recognised are the groups of "people" who may, because of aspirations of self-determination, claim special assistance from the international community through law. This particular extension has been

1 GH Hackworth, *Digest of International Law*, vol 1, p 1 (1940).

assisted by the part played by the international community, particularly the United Nations, in the whole decolonisation movement.

Finally, there is the individual. This has been the most dramatic extension of international law. No longer is the individual to be seen as needing protection as a member of a minority group or the like, but rather as needing protection as *an individual human being*. Such protection has taken the form of rights contained in many of the most important human rights conventions. These include the Optional Protocol to the International Covenant on Civil and Political Rights 1966, the Convention on Racial Discrimination, 1965 and the Convention on Torture, whereby individual nationals may submit "communications" about violations of terms of the treaty by national governments to various committees, including the Human Rights Committee of the United Nations. Coupled with this development is the obligation now being recognised which places on the large industrial enterprises, including transnational corporations (TNCs), in the field of global environmental protection. Thus in 1989, the General Assembly of the United Nations noted that such bodies "conduct activities in sectors that have an impact on the environment and, to that extent, have specific responsibilities and that, in this context, efforts need to be encouraged and mobilised to protect and enhance the environment in all countries" (Resolution 44/228, sect I, para 10).

The "new" definition indicates these changes. An example, taken from the introductory paragraph of a popular student text, Michael Akehurst, *A Modern Introduction to International Law* (1968), p 1, reads:

> International law (otherwise known as public international law or law of nations) is the system of law which governs relations between states. At one time states were the only bodies which had rights and duties under international law, but nowadays international organisations, companies and individuals also sometimes have rights and duties under international law: however, it is still true to say that international law is primarily concerned with states.

2. What is the relationship of international law to domestic (or national) law?

The recent expansion of the Australian Parliament's powers pursuant to the High Court's interpretation of the external affairs head of power (s 51(xxix) Constitution) has resulted in an increased profile of international law within the general legal framework of Australia. Since the 1920s the Australian Government has been committing Australia to international obligations by the signing of treaties, but only recently has it been recognised that power is vested in the Australian Parliament to legislate to implement those obligations nationally. There is now considerable interest about the place of international law in Australia as a regulator of behaviour, and courts increasingly are being asked to look at international law as a guide to establishing basic international standards of conduct within Australia. This is particularly evident in the area of human rights.[2] However, as yet, it is difficult for such norms to be incorporated into our law without legislative sanction.

Australia has inherited, both via the common law and responsible government, the legal regime that recognises that the executive arm of government has the right to conduct the international affairs of the nation with virtually no interference from the courts. However if, arising from those dealings, rights and obligations fall upon Australian citizens or residents, the parliament is the only body that can establish such law. And in Australia that will also be subject to judicial review if enacted by the national parliament. This situation is quite clear when it is a treaty that has created the right or obligation.[3]

In such cases there are various forms the legislation can take: legislation may be enacted with no special reference to the treaty but simply embodying its terms. As it looks like any other piece of legislation the connection with the treaty may only be known by consulting extrinsic material associated with the enactment; for example, the Second Reading debate speech made by the Minister introducing the bill, or the explanatory memorandum. Another way of legislating with respect to the treaty is to incorporate the treaty in the Act, usually in the form of a schedule, and give it the force of law. In such a case the court can rely on Articles 31 and 32 of the *Vienna Convention on Treaties* to interpret the treaty.[4]

2 Kirby, "The role of the judge in advancing human rights by reference to international human rights norms" (1988) 62 *ALJ* 514.

3 In recent years, particularly since *Minister for Immigration and Ethnic Affairs v Teoh* (1995) 183 CLR 273, commentators have noted that a treaty can have *indirect* affect upon domestic law notwithstanding that it may not have been legislated into local law. See particularly Chapter 6 of the Report of the Senate Legal and Constitutional References Committee, *Trick or Treaty? Commonwealth power to make and implement treaties*, November 1995, AGPS, but also available on the internet: *<www.austlii.edu.au/au/other/dfat>*.

4 Section 15AB of the *Acts Interpretation Act 1901* and Gibbs CJ in the *Tasmanian Dam Case* (1983) 158 CLR 1 at 93 where he expounded upon the use of *travaux preparatoires* (preparatory works or legislative history).

The question as to whether international customary law is part of domestic law cannot be stated so simply. There are two quite separate lines of opinion and as yet no clear Australian authority.[5]

In the United States the situation is different because the Constitution has provided specifically (Art 2, s 2(2)) that a President is to submit a treaty to the Senate for its advice and consent with respect to ratification. Because the legislature is involved in the making of the international obligation, it is appropriate that the treaty should then become, without further legislative intervention, the "supreme law of the land". This is the situation when it comes within the terms of the Constitution. The treaty is said to be self-executing. If not self-executing, legislation will be necessary for it to become binding.

3. Sources of international law

The determination of *what is the law of nations* is one of the most important, and controversial, questions in international law.[6] *What is* international law will depend very much upon the sources chosen to find it. Unlike our domestic law, where legislation and the cases provide the source of law with reasonable certainty, there is in international law not only greater uncertainty as to the law, but even as to the source of international law. The nearest we can come to such an authority for sources is Art 38(1) Statute of the Permanent Court of International Justice (1920) which states:

> The Court, whose function is to decide in accordance with international law such disputes as are submitted to it, shall apply:
> (a) international conventions, whether general or particular, establishing rules expressly recognised by the contesting states;
> (b) international custom, as evidence of a general practice accepted as law
> (c) the general principles of law recognised by civilised nations;
> (d) ... judicial decisions and the teachings of the most highly qualified.

Thus it is necessary to examine:

---

5 See Burmester "Is international law part of Australian law?" *Australian Law News*, July, 1989, pp 29-32.

6 An excellent analysis of the problem is set out in van GJH Hoof *Rethinking the Sources of International Law*, Deventer, Kluwer Law, 1983. A related aspect of the problem of "finding" international law is to confuse the substantive issue of "what is" international law from the documentary evidence of where it can be found. This work is only concerned with the latter issue.

Treaties – published in various forms: general, national, historic and specific

Custom – found in state practices and digests

Law Reports – including Digests

Writings of "the most highly qualified".

(a) Treaties

This subject is governed by its own treaty: *The Vienna Convention on the Law of Treaties* (1969) which is generally considered to be the codification of the law of treaties as a whole. The key points are the need for the Treaty to be in *writing* and for it to be *registered* with the United Nations Secretariat. By Art 18 of the Covenant of the League of Nations registration was required for validation. When Art 102 of the Charter of the United Nations replaced Art 18, unregistered treaties were not to be invalid but could not be invoked before any organ of the United Nations, including the International Court of Justice. Article 80 of the Vienna Convention also provides for registration under Art 102. These provisions have created a depository within the League of Nations and United Nations of all treaties since 1920.

Electronic: For an excellent overview of treaties and where they can be found, see Jill McC Watson, "ASIL Guide to Electronic Resources for International Law: Treaties", at <*www.asil.org/resource/treaty1.htm*>.

General Collections

The *Consolidated Treaty Series* (edited by Clive Parry) (1648-1920). This is an excellent source reference and is well supplemented by good indexes: an *Index-Guide to Treaties*; a *General Chronological List*, a *Special Chronology 1648-1920*, and a *Party Index*

League of Nations Treaty Series: publication of Treaties and International Engagements registered with the Secretariat of the League of Nations, 1920-1946. (4834 treaties in 205 vols). This also is well indexed.

United Nations Treaty Series: Treaties and International Agreements registered or filed and recorded with the Secretariat of the United Nations, 1946+ (2100 vols+, and being published at about 40 per year, but many years behind in publication). They are only published in UNTS when they enter into force. Thus the International Covenant on Civil and Political Rights was initially signed in 1966, entered into force in 1976 and was finally published in UNTS in

1983. United Nations Treaty Information System (UNTIS). This was a system created in 1975 to provide online search facilities that would allow speedy access to a reasonably broad spectrum of treaty information.

International Legal Materials (American Society of International Law). A monthly publication which provides, quickly, primary source international legal materials. The format is photo-offset which facilitates the speed of publication. The contents, however, are restricted to the more important treaties, legislation, arbitrations and case reports.

Electronic: A major advance in the past few years has been the placement of the United Nations treaty collection on the Internet at <*http://untreaty.un.org*>. Anticipated as being one of the truly great resources of international law, it is disappointing that access to this great collection is limited now to subscription. However, if you can afford the annual subscription (US$500 pa for non-profit organisations including universities) you can gain access to 13 databases including:

- *Status of Multilateral Treaties deposited with the Secretary-General*
- *United Nations Treaties Series* (UNTS)
- *League of Nations Treaty Series* (5 July 1920 – 3 October 1944)
- *Text of Recently Deposited Multilateral Treaties*
- *Monthly Statement of Treaties and International Agreements*
- *United Nations Treaty Series Cumulative Index*
- *Titles in the UN Official Languages*

Multiple search criteria, including date, participants, subject terms, popular names, registration number and key-word, are available to search the UNTS.

There is also a United Nations Treaty Series Cumulative Index on line (also for a fee).

For more information about the project of putting this material on the Internet, see Palitha Kohona, "The United Nations Treaty Collection on the Internet: developments and challenges" (2002) 30 *International Journal of Legal Information* 379.

Apart from this definitive collection, there are still a number of collections that can be freely accessed. These include:

- *Australian Treaties Library* on AustLII at <*www.austlii.edu.au*>
- *Fletcher Multilaterals Project* at <*http://fletcher.tufts.edu/multilaterals. html*>

The former allows all treaties that Australia has signed to be accessed, by date or key-word searching, while the latter groups a number of the more important treaties by subject. The subject areas are comprehensive and include areas like "marine and coastal"; "atmosphere and space" and "cultural protection".

Historic Collections

Collection of International Concessions and Related Instruments 595AD-1512. Compiled by Peter Fischer

Major Peace Treaties of Modern History 1648-1967

MO Hudson, *International Legislation*, 1919-1945. These are supplemented by a contemporary collection

JAS Grenville and B Wasserstein, *The Major International Treaties since 1945: a History and Guide with Texts*, Methuen, 1987

There are many others. See *List of Treaty Collections*, UN, 1956 (UN doc ST/LEG 5, 1955) where over 700 general and national treaty collections are listed.

National Collections

Australia

Department of Foreign Affairs, Treaties Series, 1948+ "*Australian Treaty Series*". Treaties entered into by the Australian Government are either signed, ratified or acceded to, depending upon the terms of the treaty. A complete list of these, to 31 December 1999, is set out in *Australian Treaty List*, issued by the Department of Foreign Affairs in the Australian Treaty Series, 1999 No 38. See Electronic below for annual and monthly updates.

Electronic: Under an agreement between the Department of Foreign Affairs and Trade and AustLII, the full text of treaties to which Australia is a party, together with other important materials relating to treaties produced by DFAT, have been placed on the AustLII site. This database, the ***Australian Treaties Library***, may be browsed or searched and is located at <*http: //www.austlii.edu.au/au/other/dfat*>.

United Kingdom

Hertslet's Commercial Treaties, vols 1-19 (1840-1895) Butterworths; vols 20-30 (1898-1925) HMSO

British and Foreign State Papers, 1812-1968, HMSO

United Kingdom Treaty Series, 1892+ HMSO

A treaty is published here with a treaty number as well as having a command paper number. "General Index to the Treaty Series". The latest covers the period 1977-1979, published in 1983 and states that it is to be the last.

These publications are relevant to Australia because in some instances early treaties entered into by Britain have continued in force after Federation, and these collections are the source of the document.

United States

Treaties and Other International Agreements of the US, 1776-1949 (ed by CE Bevan) in 13 volumes:

Vols 1-4 – multilateral treaties, in chronological order

Vols 5-12 – bilateral treaties, alphabetical by name of other party

Vol 13 – general index by subject and country

Treaties and other International Acts Series (TIAS) (1945+) The official version is issued initially in pamphlet form in this series.

United States Treaties and other International Agreements (UST) (1950+)

As well as being published in *Statutes at Large*, the treaty is formally published in this series and becomes the official text for court purposes.

Treaties and International Agreements Online (Oceana Publications) has over 11,500 treaties and international agreements, and contains all treaties and international agreements ratified by the US, major treaties in the process of ratification and all tax treaties (even those to which the US is not a party). Using either keyword or specific field searching by country, subject, parallel citation, treaty name or date or place of signing, it is certainly comprehensive. Subscription prices are based on the size and type of institution.

United States treaties are also available on the commercial sites LexisNexis and Westlaw. The former has the full text of all treaties that the US is, or has been, a party to, from 1776. The latter commences only in 1979.

Up-dating United States Treaties

Consolidated Treaties and International Agreements (CTIA), Oceana 4 releases a year, provides the text of all treaties and agreements signed by US since 1990. Also released in electronic form as part of TIARA CD-ROM.

Heins's United States Treaties and other international agreements (William S Hein Co). A current microfiche service provided within eight weeks of the release of the instrument by the Department of State.

Unperfected Treaties

Unperfected Treaties of the United States of America, 1776-1976 in 9 vols plus index (Oceana). This is a valuable work notwithstanding that it contains the text and annotations of treaties that may never have come into force. This is because it is never too late for either the legislature or the executive to change their minds. An excellent example is the *Geneva Protocol for the Prohibition of the Use in War of Asphyxiating, Poisonous or other Gases, and of Bacteriological Methods of Warfare of 1925*, which was finally ratified in 1975. The study of such material can thus reveal a great deal in any analysis of foreign relations or diplomatic history of the United States. The introduction to this work contains a succinct but comprehensive examination of the treaty procedures followed in the United States, together with information on the finding of source documentation associated with the ratification process.

Specialised Collections (examples only)

Investment Laws of the World

International Crimes: Digest/Index of International Instruments, 1815-1985

International Human Rights Instruments: a compilation of treaties, instruments and declarations of especial interest to the United States, RB Lillich, 1983.

Indexes to Treaties

International

Multilateral Treaties: index and current status. Edited by MJ Bowman and DJ Harris, University of Nottingham Treaty Centre, Butterworths, 1984, and updated by "bi-annual cumulative supplements" (The Treaty Centre, 2004). This publication should be particularly noted. The Treaty Centre was established in 1983 and with the publication of this work, and cumulative supplements, it has provided a quick and easy way of obtaining status information about treaties.

Multilateral Treaty Calendar 1648-1995, edited by Christian L Wiktor, Kluwer (English/French). This is quickly establishing itself as the leading print index of multilateral treaties mainly because of its extensive time coverage.

Multilateral Treaties Deposited with the Secretary General (UN) is useful because it has status details as well as reservations, although it is part of the subscription services of the UN.

National Indexes

Australia

Australian Treaty List, Australian Treaties Series, No 38, 1999 (electronically available on the *Australian Treaties Library* at <*www.austlii.edu.au/au/other/dfat/treaty_list/TL-introduction.html*>).

The *Australian Treaty List* is a list of all treaties to which Australia is a party or which have affected Australia. It replaces lists previously issued in 1955, 1970 and 1989 and is current to 31 December 1999. Monthly updates are available from the *Australian Treaties Library*: <*www.austlii.edu.au/au/other/dfat/monthly_updates*>.

The *List* is in two Parts.

- Part I: Bilateral Treaty List, and
- Part II: Multilateral Treaty List

There is a comprehensive introduction which should be consulted. Of particular interest is the scope of the new *List*. Most national lists include a summary of treaties to which a country is currently a party (usually known as a "treaties in force" list) or to which the country is, or has been, a party ("historic" list). Previous lists have been of the latter type. However, the current *List* reflects a change "flowing from the consultative process and the system of Parliamentary reporting introduced in the 1996 treaty reforms ...[and] a more expansive approach was needed". Thus, the *List* now provides, where confidentiality of unsigned texts is not an issue (basically multilateral treaties), references to prospective treaties to which the Australian Government is considering becoming a party. "Also [a]s enquiries often relate to well-known multilateral treaties to which Australia has never been a party, entries have been made for those in which most interest is shown" (Introduction).

Up-Dating the Australian Treaty List

The Australian Treaty List has been available in this format on the Internet since 1997, where it is updated annually. Monthly updates since the last annual update are set out on the site.

Selected Documents on International Affairs

Each year, since 1966, the Department has published *Selected Documents on International Affairs*. It generally contains the texts of multilateral treaties and conventions drawn up at conferences in which Australia participated during a particular year, but which did not enter into force for Australia during that year or which have not otherwise been published in the Australian Treaty Series (for example, amendments to certain existing treaties).

The texts are listed chronologically in an index to the *Australian Treaty List*. If a treaty appearing in *Select Documents* enters into force for Australia at a later date and is published in the Australian Treaty Series, the text will thereafter be found in the latter series on the net within Australian Treaties Library at <*www.austlii.edu.au/au/other/dfat*>.

"Treaty Terminology and Implementation Procedures"

This is a feature of the "Introduction" to the *Australian Treaty List* and provides a comprehensive glossary of terms used in the making and implementing of treaties. This is ideal for the novice researcher.

Australia and International Treaty Making Information Kit

This is an education–information kit put together by the Department of Foreign Affairs and Trade "in the interests of improving the understanding of Australia's participation in the treaty process". It sets out not only the practical side of treaty making in a federation but the text of major policy documents and review of the process. Finally, there is an extensive collection of web sites which hold treaty information. Like the glossary above, this is also ideal for the novice researcher but goes far beyond their needs as well. It is also in the *Australian Treaties Library* at <*www.austlii.edu. au/au/other/dfat*>.

Britain

An Index to British Treaties 1101-1988. Edited by C Parry and C Hopkins, HMSO 4 volumes.

Year Book of International Law contains a list of multilateral treaties entered into each year by the United Kingdom.

United States

Treaties in Force: a list of treaties and other international agreements of the United States. Published annually by the US Department of State since 1929. This information is updated in the monthly US Department of State Bulletin.

Treaties Index Online (Oceana Publications) allows for the searching of treaty by given fields, including country, subject, parallel citation, treaty name or date or place of signing. This is also a subscription service but researchers should be aware that there is a free Treaty Index available that allows a researcher, after registration, to search US treaties by name, country, year signed or subject.

United States Treaty Index (15 vols) I Kavass (ed), WS Hein Co. A comprehensive source for US treaty information, with subject, chronological, and country indexes. Supplemented by *Current Treaty Index.*

Current Treaty Index, I Kavass and A Sprudzs (eds) (looseleaf) WS Hein Co. Lists current treaties and agreements published in TIAS.

Papua New Guinea

"Papua New Guinea Treaty References" Appendix 1 in *A Guide to Legal Research in Papua New Guinea* by Heather Creech, Law Book Co, 1990.

Other countries

Three electronic resources that can be used to locate the treaties of a wide range of countries are: Jill McC Watson, "ASIL Guide to Electronic Resources for International Law: Treaties", at *<www.asil.org/ resource/ treaty1.htm>*; Stefanie Weigmann, "Researching Non-US Treaties" on LLRX at *<www.llrx.com/features/non_ustreaty.htm>* and Mark Engsberg, "An Introduction to Sources for Treaty Research", at *<www.nyulawglobal. org/Globalex/Treaty_Research.htm>*.

Annotated Treaty List

A comprehensive list of treaties, arranged according to date of signature and which have been subsequently cited or judicially referred to in cases reported in the *Annual Digest* or *International Law Reports*, Vols 1-125.

(b) Custom[7]

This is a difficult area in which to determine law, notwithstanding the prominence given to the source in Art 38. However, that there must be an international legal regime outside of treaty law is surely evident insofar as treaties cannot bind non-treaty states. But where should the international community look for that *law*? At the time Art 38 was drafted the world was decidedly Eurocentric. It was reasonable to look to what was being said and done by the major players in the world community at that time. By determining "State practice" (*repetitio factis*), the court could then assume that the State would be juridically bound (*opinio juris*). Flowing from the specific findings came general international legal precepts. While a state would not be bound if consistently opposed to such a rule, new states coming into existence would be bound by such rules if established and recognised generally.

But the homogeneity of that period of this century has vanished with the rise of the superpowers and the flood of new states that have entered the international arena because of both decolonisation and the effects of war.

> Hence the present crisis in customary international law: a broad social consensus no longer upholds long-established rules, which nevertheless continue to be accepted by certain States while others contest them hotly; at the same time, and for the same reasons, new forms of social consensus are emerging only with enormous difficulty.[8]

But during this period reliance has continued to be placed upon custom by both the Permanent Court of International Justice and the International Court of Justice.

The documentary source material needed to establish such state practice, however, can be difficult to locate. Notwithstanding a tentative lead by the United Nations in 1949 with the publication of *Ways and Means of making the evidence of customary international law more readily available*, and further support from the Council of Europe with the publication of a *Model Plan for the classification of documents concerning State practice in the field of public international law*, 1968, there are still few nations that have applied the methodology standards put forward.

---

7 Material in this area abounds and can be quickly located with a simple keyword search of recent journals via LegalTrac. However, an excellent discussion of the role and relevance of custom in international law is in Chapter 7, by Luigi Condorelli, in M Bedjaoui *International Law: Achievements and Prospects* (UNESCO, Paris, 1991) pp 179-211.

8 Condorelli, p 181.

One of the exceptions in this area is the United States of America. Commencing in the late 19th century, the US Department of State began publishing the practice or digest of international law, in a style and format that has quickly been emulated by other nations.

The idea behind their publication is to set out the national practice of the United States of America by including such documents that illustrate government belief and practice. In such publications can be found documents of diplomatic practice, case law and doctrine, either from international or domestic courts or tribunals, domestic legislation and agreements, all of which reflect the international views of the State.

United States

Digest of the Published Opinions of Attorneys-General and of the Leading Decisions of the Federal Courts, with reference to International Law, Treaties and Kindred Subjects. This was edited by John Cadwalader and published in 1877.

A Digest of the International Law of the United States, Taken from the Documents issued by Presidents and Secretaries of State, and from decisions of Federal Courts and Opinions of Attorneys-General. This was edited by Francis Warton and published in 1886.

A Digest of International Law, edited by John Bassett Moore, 1906.

Digest of International Law (1906-1939), edited by Green Hackworth, 1940-1944.

Digest of International Law (1940-1960), edited by Marjorie Whiteman, 1963-1973.

Digest of United States Practice in International Law. Compiled by the US Department of State, 1973+. This is an annual publication, and is updated by a section entitled "Contemporary practice of the US relating to international law" in *American Journal of International Law*, issued quarterly.

United Kingdom

A British Digest of International Law, compiled principally from the archives of the Foreign Office. The aim of this publication was to comprehensively bring together archival material, both published and non-published for the period 1860-1914 and 1914-1960. The projected 10 volumes for Phase One were never completed. Published only were vol 2b, *Territory*, vols 5 and 6, *The Individual in International Law* and vols 7 and 8, *Organs of State*.

Year Book of International Law. This annual publication contains a permanent section: "United Kingdom materials on International Law", together with a list of the multilateral treaties entered into, and national legislation enacted, during that year.

France

AC Kiss, *Repertoire de la practique française en matière de droit international public,* Paris, French Centre National de la Rechercher Scientifique, 1962-72 (6 vols). Covering the period from the French Revolution until the early 1960s, this is a collection of material that has been previously published in various forms and places.

Switzerland

Repertoire suisse de droit international public: documentation concernant la bratique de la confederation en matière de droit international public, 1914-1939. Basel, Helbing & Lichtenhahn, 1975+ in 4 volumes.

Netherlands

HF Van Panhuys, *International law in the Netherlands.* Published under the auspices of the TMC Asser Institute, Sijthoff & Noordhoff, 1978-80, in 3 volumes.

Australia

Australian Yearbook of International Law, a survey of current problems of public and private international law with a section on Australian practice in international law. Faculty of Law, Australian National University, 1970+. With the development of the Australian practice component of the Yearbook over the last decade, it is an even more valuable addition to Australian international law resources.

Law Council News, a monthly which contains a section on international law.

Others (examples only)

Japan

"Japan's assimilation of Western international law" in 69 *Proceedings of the American Society of International Law,* pp 63-87 (1975).

S Oda and H Owada, *The Practice of Japan in International Law, 1961-1970*, University of Tokyo Press, 1982

The Japanese Journal of International Law, International Law Association, Faculty of Law, University of Tokyo. This contains "Annual Review of Japanese Practice in International Law".

China, India etc

JA Cohen, *China's Practice of International Law: Some Case Studies*. Harvard, 1972.

JS Bains, *India's International Disputes: A Legal Study*. Asia Publishing House, 1962.

JC McKenna, *Diplomatic Protest in Foreign Policy: Analysis and Case Studies*. Loyola UP, 1962. This contains a number of US case studies.

These last examples show that where there are no established and comprehensive studies on state practice, articles can be used, either specifically or generally. In the example of Japan, the researcher can use a monograph and supplement that by later articles and annual reviews. For very recent material concerning the state practice of all nations, consult *Keesing's Contemporary Archives*.

A recent study in this area – *Sources of State Practice in International Law*, Ralph Gaebler and Maria Smolka-Day (eds) ((looseleaf) Transnational Publishers, 2002) – examines and documents state practice in Austria, Belgium, Canada, Denmark, Finland, France, Germany, Norway, Russia, Sweden, Switzerland, the United Kingdom and the United States.

Electronic Sources: See Silke Sahl, Customary International Law, State Practice and Pronouncements of States regarding International Law, a guide published by Globalex at <*www.nyulawglobal.org/Globalex/Customary_International_Law.htm*>.

(c) International Law Reports and Arbitrations

General

International Law Reports, 1919+ (vols 1-19 were known as *Annual Digest and Reports of Public International Law Cases*). This is a publication which is found in many of the larger libraries but which is consistently neglected as a source of case decisions. From what has been written, it will be clear that state practice includes the decisions of municipal courts. These will be found in the national series but, in so many instances, will not be available in Australian libraries. Consequently, when a set like this brings together, in English, the important international law decisions, it must be valuable for the researching of international law. An example will show the scope: in a recent volume (vol 122) there were decisions from the European Court of Human Rights, International Criminal Tribunal for the Former Yugoslavia, NAFTA Arbitration under the UNCITRAL Rules, Hong Kong Administrative Region, and English, Scottish and American decisions.

Also available to assist in finding relevant material are: *Consolidate Index* in 2 volumes: 1-35, 36-125; *Consolidated Table of Treaties* covering volumes 1-125, including indexes by party and subject; and *Consolidated Table of Cases* covering volumes 1-125.

International Tribunals

Permanent Court of International Justice

Details of the instruments creating the Court, commonly called the *World Court*, rules of the Court and personnel, are set out in the beginning of volume 1 of Hudson's *World Court Reports*, referred to below. This Court heard 65 cases and delivered 32 judgments and 27 advisory opinions.

Official Publications of the Court

Series A (1922-1930), Nos 1-24 Collection of Judgments

Series B (1922-1930), Nos 1-18 Collection of Advisory Opinions

Series A/B (1931-1946) Judgments, Orders and Advisory Opinions

Series D (1922-1946) Acts and Documents concerning the Organisation of the Court

Series E (1925-1946) Annual Reports

Series F General Indexes.

Unofficial Publication of Judgments and Advisory Opinions

World Court Reports: a collection of the judgments, orders and opinions of the Permanent Court of International Justice, ed by MO Hudson, 1922-1946. International Law Reports, 1919+.

International Court of Justice

Official Publications of the Court

Reports of Judgments, Advisory Opinions and Orders, 1947/48+.

Pleadings, Oral Arguments, and Documents, 1948+. These are irregularly published and include the documents filed by the parties in the case as well as a transcript of argument.

International Court of Justice Yearbook, 1946/7+. Prepared by the Registry of the Court.

Acts and Documents concerning the Court, No 1, 1946+.

Bibliography of the International Court of Justice, No 1, 1964/5+.

Unofficial Publication of Judgments and Advisory Opinions

International Law Reports, 1919+ (see index volume for list, by name and tribunal).

International Legal Materials (current).

Electronic: The home page of the International Court of Justice contains details of the Court, its judges and judgments. This site can be found at: <*www.icj-cij.org*>.

For a comprehensive bibliographic guide to the court, see *Germain's International Court of Justice Research Guide*, a chapter from Germain's Transnational Law Research, Transnational, (looseleaf) at <*http://library.lawschool.cornell.edu/WhatWeDo/ResearchGuides/ICJ.cfm*>.

International Arbitrations[9]

An important source of customary international law is found within the determinations of international arbitrations. Here, a solution to an international dispute is sought by formal submission (*compromiso*) of the dispute to a third party, acceptable to the disputants, and who by means of contentious proceedings will determine the issue by the rendering of an award.

Because of the need for flexibility in this area there is a great deal of variation in the establishing of an arbitration, but three models stand apart: the first is the Hague Conventions of 1899 and 1907,[10] the second is the General Act for the Pacific Settlements of International Disputes,[11]

9 Commercial arbitrations: both with respect to the collections of rules and awards, is dealt with separately specifically under the heading of "International trade law and commercial arbitrations", pp 222-232.

10 The text can be found at 187 *Consolidated Treat Series* (Parry) 221 (1899) and 205 *Consolidated Treaty Series* 233 (1907). They are also included, with extensive commentary in JB Scott, *The Reports of the Hague Conferences of 1899 and 1907*, Oxford, 1917, and the two are compared, paragraph by paragraph, in G Wetter, *The International Arbitral Process*, Oceana, 1979, vol V, p 187.

11 The text can be found in MO Hudson, *International legislation: a collection of multipartite international instruments of general interest*, Oceana, 1971, vol IV, p 2529.

adopted by the League of Nations on 26 August 1928, and the third is the United Nations Model on Arbitral Procedure.[12]

Finding Arbitration Awards[13]

AM Stuyt, *Survey of International Arbitrations, 1794-1970*, 2nd ed, Sijthoff, 1972.

JB Scott, *The Hague Court Reports*, 1st Series 1916, 2nd Series 1932.

Reports of International Arbitral Awards, UN, 1948+. This set acknowledges the earlier awards in Scott, and concentrates on collecting post-World War I awards.

International Law Reports, 1919. The index volume lists these awards under the name of the tribunals, parties name and key words.

International Legal Materials (current).

National Court Decisions concerning International Law

American International Law Cases, compiled by F Deak, and F Ruddy & B Reams

– 1783-1968 (Vols 1 – 20)

– 1969-1978 (Vols 21 – 28)

– 1979-1986, 1986-1988 (Vols 1-14, 2nd Series) This series has had *International Trade* cases added to the classification for the first time.

– 1988-1989, Vol 15+ 2nd Series)

Index by subject, plaintiff and defendant (looseleaf)

These volumes are arranged by series and within the various series the cases are arranged according to a broad and traditional international law classification. The researcher must be aware of the classification, set out in the first volume in each series, before searching for specific cases under that heading in each series.

---

12 Report of the International Law Commission, Official Records of the General Assembly, Eighth Session, Supplement No 9, Document A/2456 pp 9-11; and reproduced in Wetter, vol v, pp 228-231. There is an excellent detailed commentary put out by the UN on the Draft: A/CN4/92, April 1955.

13 A Permanent Court of Arbitration was established under the Hague Convention of 1899, later updated in 1907. While not a permanent tribunal, it was rather a panel of arbitrators serviced by International Bureau at The Hague. It was important before the First World War, but with its last arbitration in 1932 it is still in existence but dormant. It still plays a part, however, in the nomination of candidates to the International Court of Justice, pursuant to Art 4, para 1 of the ICJ Statute.

British International Law Cases: a collection of decisions of courts in the British Isles on points of international law, compiled by C Parry, Stevens and Oceana, 1964-73. 9 volumes. The aim with this collection was to supplement the International Law Reports, both by providing British cases before 1919, the starting point of the latter, as well as bringing together other cases decided in national courts, including Privy Council cases on appeal from overseas territories of the British Crown. While these cases relate to international law, they have specifically excluded prize cases and cases relating to war and neutrality from this set.

The cases in volumes 1 – 6 are arranged in a traditional international law classification, with cases ranging from 17th century to the mid-20th century. Volumes 7, 8 and 9 provide supplementary cases from 1951–1970. There is a consolidated index to the whole series in volume 9.

Commonwealth International Law Cases compiled by C Parry and JA Hopkins, in 13 volumes, Oceana, 1974-85.

This series extends the work of the *British International Law Cases* to "British courts overseas" (Preface), omitting in most instances those cases which had been included in the *International Law Reports*. The compilers acknowledge that because of the limited extraterritorial capacity of some of the legislatures of the colonies covered by this series, "[n]uggets of pure international gold are not expected to lie undiscovered". Nevertheless there is much of value and of interest.

Case Digests

E Hambro, *Case Law of the International Court*, Sijthoff, 1952+

Care must be taken using this publication. Contained within vol I are extracts from the majority judgments, advisory opinions and orders of the Permanent Court of International Justice and the International Court of Justice. These have been extracted not for the purpose of *stare decisis,* which applied to neither the PCIJ nor the ICJ, "but even in those countries whose legal systems do not accept this principle one may see the effect of precedent on the formation and development of the law" (Introduction p v).

Vol II updates the first volume to include the same type of decisions for the period 1952-1958. However, vol III went back and extracted the dissenting and individual opinions for 1947-1958. Subsequent volumes include both majority and dissenting opinions: vol IV covers 1959-1963, including a bibliography (1918-1964; vol V 1964-1966; vol VI 1967-1970; vol VII 1971-1972 and vol VIII 1973-1974.

K Marek, *Digest of Decisions of the International Court*, Martinus Nijhoff
Vol 1 is a summary of the decisions of the PCIJ, while vol 2, in two parts, summarises decisions of the ICJ. The last case digested is an advisory opinion of 12 July 1973.

Electronic: As noted previously, there are only basically summaries of decisions of the International Court of Justice on its home page. See also the *World Court Digest* maintained by the Max Planck Institute for Comparative Public Law and International Law's *Virtual Institute* at *<www.virtual-institute.de/en/wcd/wcd.cfm>*. Here can be found digests of Court decisions under headings arranged by legal principle.

Writings of the "Most Highly Qualified"

Encyclopaedias

Encyclopedia of Public International Law, North-Holland, 1981+.

Encyclopedic Dictionary of International Law, Oceana, 1986.

Catalogues

Catalogue of International Law, Oceana, 1972 (4 vols)

This material was incorporated into:

Law Catalogue of the University of Cambridge Squires Library, Oceana, 1973 (14 vols).

Catalogue of International Law and Relations, Harvard Law School Library, 1965-7.

Dictionary Catalogue of the Columbia University Law Library, 1967 (28 vols); Supplement to 1972 (7 vols).

For older materials, researchers can consult the British Library, *General Catalogue of Printed Books*, available in compact edition up to 1955, and the supplements 1956-65, 1966-70, 1971-75. All these are in book or CD-ROM form. The supplement 1976-1985 is on microfiche. Also available, online, is Kinetica, providing access to the national database of material held in Australian libraries. This allows the user to search the holdings of all major Australian libraries.

Researching Guides and Bibliographies

Guide to International Legal Research, 2006 ed, George Washington University Law School International Law Review, LexisNexis.

Elizabeth Beyerly, *Public International Law: a Guide to Information Sources*, London, Mansell, 1991. Although written pre-Internet, it still is extremely useful.

Electronic: Over the past few years there has been a proliferation of guides to researching on the internet, most coming out of university law libraries and all quite good. A Google search using key words will quickly bring them to the fore. However, in the international law area there are two guides that are pre-eminent:

- *ASIL Guide to Electronic Resources for International Law* compiled by Marci Hoffman and Jill Watson at <*www.asil.org/resource/ Home.htm*>. Produced under the auspices of the American Society of International Law (ASIL), this Guide contains a number of specialist areas, including human rights, criminal, commercial arbitration, economic, environmental, intellectual property and private international law.
- *International Law Guides*, Comparative and International Law Center, LLRX, at <*www.llrx.com/international_law.html*>. The site has such a wealth of information for the international law researcher it is difficult even to start to list its coverage, but suffice it to note that it is encyclopaedic. It has the added benefit of being constantly maintained.

Article Indexes

Public international Law: a current bibliography of articles (1975+). Published twice yearly under the auspices of the Max-Plank Institute for Comparative and International Law.

In addition to the specialised index above, the traditional indexes used for finding law articles are also relevant. These include:

LegalTrac/Legal Resource Index (1980+) (Butterworths Online, LexisNexis, Westlaw)

Index to Legal Periodicals (1886, 1926) (LexisNexis and Westlaw)

Index to Periodicals Relating to Law (1958) (Glanville)

Index to Foreign Legal Periodicals and Collections of Essays (1958) (AALI)

These indexes must be used with some circumspection. There are many excellent international law secondary sources that will not normally be picked up without care being exercised by the researcher. Thus one of the most useful sources is the *Recueil des Cours, Academie de Droit International de la Haye*, with many articles published in English. It is not indexed in *Index To Legal Periodicals*, and while it is indexed in *Index to Foreign Legal Periodicals*, that only covers the period since 1960, while the *Recueil* commenced in 1923. There are also problems with collections of essays published in honour of an individual (*festschriften, melanges*, etc). Only the *Index to Foreign Legal Periodicals* will index these.

International Law Texts

D Raistrick, Lawyers' Law Books: a Practical Index to Legal Literature, 3rd ed, Bowker Saur, 1997.

Carnegie Endowment for International Peace, *Classics of International Law* (microfilm), Trans-Media. This is a collection of classics in international law, based on state practice, and taken from first or early editions. "The masterpieces of Grotius are the centrepoint of the series, with the works of his leading predecessors and successors also included. Each volume contains an introduction describing the author's place in history, a photographic reproduction of the original text, and an English translation with explanatory note". This list is set out in full in the first edition of this work.

4. Specific areas of international law

(a) Protecting rights and the environment in a world of sovereign states

Unlike the domestic law of Victoria or Australia where, unless specifically exempted, everybody must comply with that law, this is not the case with international law. At the beginning of this chapter the definition of international law was shown to have expanded, at least to some degree, to encompass individuals and corporations. What we will now see is that the areas of human rights and protection of the environment have played major roles in that movement. However, what is also clear is that while individuals and corporations may come within the coverage of international law, they can also gain its protection. In order to understand the tremendous development in these areas, together with some of the factors that will inhibit further quick development, it would be wise to examine just how international law developed. Why was it that the nation dominated our international legal regime?

The answer lies in the origins of international law in Europe, whereby the European concept of "sovereignty" has tended to dominate the way we traditionally view international law and the rights and responsibilities which flow from it. At the core of the ideal is the belief that the world will only maintain an international peace if all national states respect the national integrity, or sovereignty, of all other nations. When a nation is recognised by other nations as being independent, and thus sovereign, it can then take its place equally with all other nations on the world stage.

But as a necessary corollary, the nation has the ability to exercise its independent will in that international community. Unless it attempts to break fundamental international law recognised as sacrosanct by all nations – for example the concept of self-determination has been raised to the status of an imperative legal principle (*jus cogens*) – nations are able to exercise their independence within the world community. They will of course be subject to agreements and obligations that they have undertaken (*pacta sunt servanda*) but otherwise their status as an equal member of the world community is assured.

This traditional view has come in for much criticism and this criticism is growing as the international law expands to include topics like the protection of human rights and of the environment. It is centred upon the notion that the present situation is somewhat akin to dining *à la carte*, insofar as a nation is in a position to pick and choose the obligations it supports. Thus a nation may or may not enter into a treaty that would commit it to reduce greenhouse gasses, or protect internationally recognised environmentally sensitive areas.

Against this view is one that would promote the supremacy of international legal order over national sovereignty. This changing attitude is apparent when one examines world community attitudes between the Stockholm Conference in 1972 and the Rio Conference in 1992. Yet even so, if you look in the preamble of most of the recent treaties in the environmental area, there will appear, usually at the insistence of those nations still supporting the sovereignty view, a reaffirmation of the traditional sovereignty doctrine. An example is the *Convention on Biological Diversity*. In the Preamble, the third and fourth paragraphs read:

> The Contracting Parties ...
>
> Affirm that the conservation of biological diversity is a common concern of humankind;
>
> Reaffirm that States have sovereign rights over their own biological resources.

Researching Strategies

From this overview, any researcher who wishes to undertake research in the international fields of the environment or human rights will see that a great deal of work will have to be done in two areas. The first is to find the various sources of law establishing these rights – usually associated with treaties. Having found the full text of the treaty, it is then necessary to turn to the second task – to analyse its effect. This is usually associated with secondary source material, ie articles and texts written by experts in the fields. In international law, it may also include the decisions of the courts.

Looking initially at finding primary material, the modern electronic facilities now make this task much easier than in the past. When world leaders come together in mega-conferences to examine environmental issues, or establish a world criminal court, the organisers have already spent years on planning. This means that there is already extensive documentation in existence and the extensive texts will usually already have been written and informally agreed upon. In many of these conferences, the written material including the text will already be available and the researchers' interest is associated with the attitude of the larger countries and the attitude that they bring.

Because of the existence of this material, in nearly all large recent conferences, the web site of the conference has been in existence for months before the conference and persons can keep track of what is happening by daily, even hourly, updates. Speeches are placed on the web within minutes of their being given and, once finished, this material remains as part of the record of the conference. For the researcher, this is extremely valuable.

Case study: Rome Statute of the International Criminal Court

In December 1989, in response to a request from Trinidad and Tobago, the General Assembly of the United Nations asked the *International Law Commission* to resume work – first initiated in the early 1950s – on the establishment of an international criminal court. In 1994, the ILC presented a draft statute and the General Assembly established the *Ad Hoc Committee on the Establishment of an International Criminal Court*. It met twice in 1995 and, after the General Assembly considered its report, the *Preparatory Committee on the Establishment of an International Criminal Court* was created to prepare a draft text to be submitted to a full diplomatic conference. The Preparatory Committee completed its draft in early 1998. At its 52nd session, the General Assembly decided to convene the

United Nations Diplomatic Conference of Plenipotentiaries of an International Criminal Court. It was this conference which met in Rome between 15 June and 17 July 1998 and which finally accepted the recommendations to establish the Court.

Much of the work of these various bodies, including the text of the final statute and material drafted since the Conference, can still be found on the Conference home page located at: <*www.un.org/icc/index.html*>.

How would you know that such a home page exists? How would a researcher locate other relevant material? The links given from the UN Conference home page are not extensive and other assistance is needed.

EISIL: Electronic Information System for International Law

One of the most valuable resources now available for the international law researcher is the **EISIL** site at <*www.eisil.org*>. Developed by the American Society of International Law (ASIL), with support from the Andrew W Mellon Foundation, its function is clear from the published goal of the Society:

ASIL's goal is to ensure, through EISIL, that web searchers can easily locate the highest quality primary materials, authoritative web sites and helpful research guides to international law on the Internet. To this end, EISIL has been designed as an open database of authenticated primary and other materials across the breadth of international law, which until now have been scattered in libraries, archives and specialized web sites.

One of the best features of the site is the ease with which the researcher is lead to the information. If a novice, there is a simple downloadable guide: *Using EISIL to Find and Understand International Law on the Web*, but the homepage clearly sets out the principal parameters for researching international law:

- General International law – Basic Sources, Historic Materials, Treaty Collections …
- States & Groups of States – Basic Sources, The State & Its Organs, Statehood …
- International Organizations – Basic Sources, United Nations, European Union …
- Individuals & Groups – Basic Sources, Social & Political Issues, Ethnic Groups, Minorities & Indigenous Peoples …

- International Air, Space & Water – Air & Aviation, Space, Antarctica & the Arctic …
- International Environmental Law – Basic Sources, Natural Disasters, Transboundary Cooperation …
- International Economic Law – Basic Sources, GATT/WTO System, International Trade Law ...
- International Human Rights – Basic Sources, Self-Determination, Prevention of Discrimination …
- International Criminal Law – Basic Sources, War Crimes & Crimes Against Humanity, Including Genocide, Terrorism …
- Communications & Transport – Communications & Information, Transport …
- Use of Force – Basic Sources, Collective Security, Law of Armed Conflict …
- International Dispute Settlement – Basic Sources, Arbitration, Mediation & Conciliation, Transnational Litigation …
- Private International Law – Basic Sources, Trade & Commerce, Finance & Banking …

While the creation of EISIL has greatly assisted in disseminating international law through the many, and ever increasing, electronic sites, it is not always easily to find exactly what one is needing. To this end the 'research guides' which have become such a part of the new electronic age has not been forgotten.

Thus there is, in addition to EISIL, the continued availability of the:

ASIL Guide to Electronic Resources for International Law

Divided into 11 principal subject areas (or chapters), this electronic research guide (referred to informally in its own literature as ERG, has been specifically created to allow researcher to find their own way through the literature. To this end there is a great deal of narrative discussion about the materials, including their use in international law research, within the ERGs. As itself notes:

> The chapter format of the ERG is designed to be used by students, teachers, practitioners and researchers as a self-guided tour of relevant, quality, up-to-date online resources covering important areas of international law. The ERG also serves as a ready-made teaching tool at graduate and undergraduate levels.

In addition to the Introduction to the *Guide*, currently those 11 chapters consist of:

- European Union
- Human Rights
- International Commercial Arbitration
- International Criminal Law
- International Economic Law
- International Environmental law
- International Intellectual Property Law
- International Organizations
- Private International Law
- Treaties, and
- United Nations

Importance

The major importance about the creation of EISIL is that we now have a comprehensive site that is constantly being updated not only by the resources of ASIL but a broad sweep of specialist librarians. It has meant that the sites that we traditionally looked for this type of information – principally the Law Library Research Xchange (LLRX) at <*www.llrx. com*> is not as important in the researching of international law as it once was. When a search is made of its Features archive, the material once there is not being replaced. That does not detract from the extraordinary role the LLRX stills plays in many other areas of legal research but not in the public international law area.

Nor will it stop others from entering the field and developing their own special collections. For many years Australia had the benefit of Francis Auburn's *Public International Law* site. While it is still available at <*http://law2.biz.uwa.edu.au/intlaw*> and has over 900 links to internet sites, it was last modified in 2001 and does suffer from that. It has, however, an Australian flavour and emphasis that is refreshing and the immense amount of work such people put into this type of endeavour ought to be recognized and encouraged more. It does mean that the benefits of the EISIL and *ASIL Guide* site should never be underestimated.

In the collection of material on international environmental law, there are quite a few electronic journals available (certainly in comparison with other areas of law and probably because of the subject matter). These are not listed on the links page in that format. To find a comprehensive collection, it is necessary to return to the *ASIL Guide to Electronic Resources for International Law: International Environmental Law* by Anne Burnett. There, the author lists 15 e-journals on the topic of international environmental law that provide full text retrieval at no charge.

Turning now to secondary material. The example just given is the exception that proves the rule. While there is much material located in the guides mentioned above that is secondary, in most cases they do not have the depth of analysis that is required to undertake a thorough research task. This is because so much of the secondary material is found in commercial publications, be they the traditional text or the journal. Except for the limited range of electronic journals that currently exist (in fields outside environmental and IT), the researcher will inevitably end up in the library (or using a commercial electronic service) to retrieve relevant second source material. At this point, reference should be made to how this material is located in the previous pages of this text.

(b) International Trade Law and Commercial Arbitrations

International Trade Law (the 20th century Lex Mercatoria?)

The distinction between private international law and public international law, usually recognisably different in most situations, may become blurred when international trade law is the subject. While in establishing an arbitration clause the parties can agree on the choice of law that will be used in the determination of any dispute that may arise, there is increasing pressure to adopt a modern version of the *lex mercatoria* or law merchant.

International Commercial Arbitration

In a social setting, the arbitral process is conceptually one of the easiest things to understand. At its heart is the private settlement of private disputes. Even in a commercial setting the concept loses none of its simplicity, and it is understandable that the trader wishes to expedite any dispute that may arise at the least cost to either party. But involved in the private settlement is the acceptance by both parties that if the dispute cannot be settled between themselves, a third party, the arbitrator, will determine the issue. Not by compromise but by making a decision.

When it is spelt out in this way, it can also be seen that there is to be an interaction between the arbitral process and the legal system. That is not to say that the common law has always recognised the arbitral process. It has not. There was a time in the late medieval period when

English law came close to ignoring arbitration. But with the need in commerce to be able to handle affairs in the way best suited to those involved in it, the common law settled on a role which would allow the legal rules to protect the parties, both in matters of procedure and substance, and would enforce the product of the arbitral process if not voluntarily complied with.

However, when the international component of arbitration is taken into account, the need for legal recognition becomes even more apparent and the complexity of the process is compounded.[14] Which legal system, in an international dispute, provides the legal rules that determines and enforces the agreement to arbitrate? The laws of which jurisdiction must be involved in the establishment of the arbitral process? Further, laws of which jurisdiction must be applied by the arbitral body to determine the issue before it? And, necessarily, there is still the problem of the choice of law in the recognition and enforcement of the award, the product of the arbitration, if a party refuses to comply. Consequently, the modern arbitral process has lost the original simplicity and has become far more institutionalised. Yet, at its core, three basic elements still exist: the agreement by the parties to arbitrate, the determination or decision rather than compromise, and the public enforcement of an ostensibly private agreement. This is no better to be seen than in the area of international commercial arbitration.

International Conventions[15]

In order to facilitate international trade, and thus overcome many of the problems associated with international commercial litigation, the United Nations, through its Commission on International Trade Law (UNCITRAL), has progressively enhanced international commercial dispute resolution via international acceptance of commercial arbitration. Commencing with the *Convention on the Recognition and Enforcement of Foreign Arbitral Awards* (New York 1958), followed by the UNCITRAL Arbitration Rules (1976) for use in *ad hoc* arbitrations, these were

---

14 A Redfern & M Hunter, *Law and Practice of International Commercial Arbitration*, Student ed, Sweet & Maxwell, 2003, at pp 11-19 spell out the semantic problems in this area even with such (simple) words as "international" and "commercial". Great care must be taken to understand many words and concepts which may take on other meanings when they have cross-jurisdictional use.

15 A number of specific international and regional treaties are set out below. The place where the text can be found has been footnoted. However, these are not exhaustive. It is set out in this way so that the researcher can get an idea where this type of material can be found. As more looseleaf services enter the field, and as they become more specialised, so more will be located in those sources.

complemented in 1985 by the UNCITRAL Model Law. The aim of the Model Law is to provide for, in as many nations as possible, a national or domestic legislative regime that will enhance and facilitate international dispute-settling in this form by *harmonising* national law.

Sources of domestic legislation

It is clear from what has been noted above, that it will be necessary to be aware, in many instances, of the domestic provisions that have been made in the judicial control and enforcement of arbitral awards. This is one area where the publishers have been busy and have brought much of it together. In both *World Arbitration Reporter* and Schmitthoff's *International Commercial Arbitration*, the legislation of the major trading jurisdictions can be found.

Australia and International Commercial Arbitration

There has been a recognition in Australia of the separation of domestic and international commercial arbitration. While the States have relevant commercial arbitration Acts, which provide substantive law governing the topic, the Commonwealth has legislated to implement a model law which provides a legal framework for the conduct of international arbitrations and which is in line with most of our major trading partners.

The original legislation, the *Arbitration (Foreign Awards and Agreements) Act 1974* (Cth), implemented the terms of the New York Convention 1958 by establishing rules governing the recognition and enforcement in Australia of international arbitral awards and agreements. In 1989, the Commonwealth went further and adopted the Model Law of UNCITRAL on international commercial arbitration after it had been accepted by the UN Commission on International Trade Law (UNCITRAL) on 21 June 1985.

That amending Act, the *International Arbitration Amendment Act 1989*, by s 4, also altered the name of the earlier Act to the *International Arbitration Act 1974*.

In 1990, by the *ICSID Implementation Act 1990*, the 1974 Act was further amended to establish a mechanism for the settlement by conciliation and arbitration of investment disputes between a state party to the Convention, or any agency of it, and investors from other States also party to it. The jurisdiction of the ICSID extends to any legal dispute arising directly out of an investment but both parties must agree to the centre's jurisdiction. However, once agreeing, neither party can withdraw unilaterally.

Value to Australia

As noted by the Attorney-General in his Second Reading Speech in the House of Representatives, 3 November 1988, *Hansard*, p 2400, and again on 22 August 1990, *Hansard*, p 1310, the implementation of the UNCITRAL Model Law, complementary as it is with the UNCITRAL arbitration rules, and ratification of the ICSID Convention, means that it should assist Australia's efforts to establish itself as a centre for international commercial arbitration. Both Melbourne and Sydney having facilities (Australian Centre for International Commercial Arbitration and the Australian Commercial Disputes Centre) for the conduct of international arbitrations.

The Principal International Commercial Arbitration Institutions

- The American Arbitration Association (AAA)
- The London Court of Arbitration (LCA)
- The International Centre for the Settlement of Investment Disputes (ICSID)
- The Court of Arbitration of the International Chamber of Commerce (ICC)
- The Arbitration Institute of the Stockholm Chamber of Commerce (SCC Institute)

The organisation, structure, contact points and rules of the major international commercial arbitration institutions are set out in a number of places. The three principal looseleaf services contain this information, together with many more. The relative size, jurisdiction, subject matter and special nature of the rules will all have a part to play in deciding which rules should be chosen for inclusion in any particular contract.

There has been some recent analysis and criticism of the various rules, and the looseleaf services, either in their commentary or in the bibliographic references that are included, should facilitate the finding of such comments. However, there has also been some comparative work undertaken in:

M Blessing, "The major Western and Soviet arbitration rules: a comparison of the Rules of UNCITRAL, UNCITRAL Model Law, LCIA, ICC, AAA and the rules of the USSR Chamber of Commerce and Industry" (1989) 6 *Journal of International Arbitration* 7.

M Jacob, *International Commercial Arbitration in Australia: Law and Practice*, para 4.440+. There is a detailed analysis under six headings, offering assistance to Australian drafters.

Jean M Wenger, *Update to International Commercial Arbitration: Locating the Resources, found at: <www.llrx.com/features/arbitration2.htm>*, under the heading "A Administering Institutions" lists both international institutions followed by the majority of national institutions associated with commercial arbitration.

Literature of International Commercial Arbitration

Arbitral Awards

While the arbitral award in the public international law area has a history and tradition of being published, providing the very nourishment for the growth of international law, the commercial arbitration area does not. In fact, this is a major reason why arbitration is so attractive to the commercial sector. Yet the award does have some value, both to the arbitrators and the parties.

In a detailed discussion,[16] Thomas E Carbonneau argued that reasoned awards, the awards accompanied by a written opinion based on law, "are an appropriate and useful instrument for fulfilling the normative potential of transnational arbitration and satisfying the 'aspiration towards a new type of law'. Reasoned awards could serve as a means of assessing the arbitrators' ability to assure the parties of a principled decisional basis. Furthermore, reasoned awards could act as a non-binding persuasive authority, gradually defining the basic substantive tenets of an international law merchant."

Carbonneau acknowledges that the historic lack of reasons has indeed come from England, where the court had the power to review on questions of law. Thus, the reasons were not included. This was subsequently accepted in the US. The position had been different in France but by the late 1800s it adopted the views of the major players in the field. In more recent times, there is an increasing trend to require reasons.

Thus Art 32(3) of the UNCITRAL Arbitration Rules, provides:

> (3) The arbitral tribunal shall state the reasons upon which the award is based unless the parties have agreed that no reasons shall be given.

The commentary in the *World Arbitration Reporter*[17] notes on this point that the award is not a public document and need not be made public, although it may if both parties agree. The commentary continues:

16 "Rendering arbitral awards with reasons: the elaboration of a common law of international transactions" (1985) 23 *Columbia Journal of Transnational Law* 579 at 583.

17 Binder 3, p 3166.

> The parties may give their consent to the publication on the condition that their names or other particulars be omitted. If consent of both parties cannot be obtained, the arbitrators should at least try, when questions of general interest are dealt with in the award, to obtain the parties' approval to the publication of an extract that does not reveal the identity of the parties (see Sanders, Commentary on the UNCITRAL Arbitration Rules, 2 *YB Com Arb* 209 (1977)). Publication of arbitral awards made under the UNCITRAL Rules could significantly contribute to the development of the Rules and add to their acceptability.

Finally there is the question of reasons being incorporated into the published award. Although not widespread, this has been done in the area of maritime arbitration awards for some time.[18]

Sources of Awards

(i) General

The remaining binders to be supplied in the *World Arbitration Reporter* are set aside for the reporting of awards and agreements. As yet they are not available. Until they are complete, the International Council for Commercial Arbitration, *Yearbook: Commercial Arbitration,* discussed later, is probably the best source, particularly when used with the *Yearbook Key 1990*. Using the *Yearbook Key* and subsequent *Yearbooks,* the researcher has an excellent subject approach to available arbitral awards.

Electronic: In mid-2003, Westlaw created a new collection of over 70 databases in the area of international commercial arbitration. These contain most aspects of international arbitration centred upon the various national centres and international organisations, but include, where possible, determinations. Of particular importance in this regard is *Mealey's International Arbitration Reports,* 1993 +. The coverage on Lexis-Nexis is not as great as that of its competitor.

(ii) Maritime

As noted above, there is a tradition of publishing maritime awards. One of the principal services is the *Award Service,* published by the Society of Maritime Arbitrators, New York. Each volume contains approximately

---

18 This tradition is noted by Carbonneau, at 587, and examined in some detail in K Tashiro, "Quest for a rational and proper method for the publication of arbitral awards" (1992) *Journal of International Arbitration* 97. In that article it is noted that the Japan Shipping Exchange Inc (JSE) has been publishing awards for more than 65 years. That tradition is followed by the Tokyo Maritime Arbitration Commission (TOMAC) and for two reasons. First, publication will secure rational and trustworthy proceedings, and secondly, it establishes proper and adequate commercial usage and custom to be followed.

20-25 full awards. From Japan, the *Bulletin of the Japan Shipping Exchange, Inc*, publishes awards, coming out annually, and is in English. The *Award Book on Tokyo Maritime Arbitration* is in Japanese only.

Looseleaf Services

International

World Arbitration Reporter (Smit & Pechota (eds), Parker School of Foreign and Comparative Law, Columbia University (multi-volume, looseleaf, Juris Publishing)

This is an ambitious publishing programme being undertaken by the Parker School of Foreign and Comparative Law to provide up-to-date information from around the world on commercial arbitration. The source material itself: international conventions and agreements, national legislation, details of international and national arbitration institutions and their rules, court decisions and arbitral awards, together with secondary source material relating to international arbitration is being brought together in a highly systematic and organised way. Published in conjunction with *Smit's Guides to International Arbitration* (11-volume set, Juris Publishing).

Clive Schmitthoff, *International Commercial Arbitration,* Oceana Publications, 1975+. This is to be a multi-volume set which is made up of: International Commercial Arbitration, (4 vols); International Chamber of Commerce Arbitration (2 vols); Commercial Arbitration Law in Asia and the Pacific (i vol); Reference and Finding Tools (1 vol).

MS Jacobs, *International Commercial Arbitration in Australia: Law and Practice,* looseleaf, LBC. In two binders. Published only in 1992, this is a major commentary upon the subject with special reference to Australian conditions. Set out are the text of the *International Arbitration Act 1974,* previously known as the *Arbitration (Foreign Awards and Agreements) Act 1974,* and the two important amendments: *International Arbitration Amendment Act 1988* (Cth), which adopted the United Nations Commission on International Trade Law (UNCITRAL) Model Law and the *ICSID Implementation Act 1990,* which implemented part of the International Centre for Settlement of Investment Disputes (ICSID) Convention 1965. There is also extensive commentary upon the international conventions, Australian court jurisdiction, enforcement, recognition procedures for foreign arbitral awards and principles of awarding costs. Also included are the major arbitral institutions of the world together with contact numbers.

The second binder contains rules and precedents of the various international arbitration institutions, together with other relevant Commonwealth and State legislation.

Principal Journals

This is only a selection of the principal journals in English. A far more detailed list of journals in a number of languages, together with publishing details, frequency and cost, is contained in each issue of the *Yearbook: Commercial Arbitration*, published by the International Council for Commercial Arbitration. These are arranged by country of production.

American Review of International Arbitration, vol 1, 1990+. Published quarterly by Juris Publications, under the auspices of the Parker School of Foreign and Comparative Law, Columbia University, NY.

Arbitration, vol 20, 1954+. Published quarterly by the journal of the Chartered Institute of Arbitrators, London. (Previously known as the *Arbitration Journal*)

Arbitration International, vol 1, 1985+. Published quarterly by Graham & Trotman, London.

Arbitration Journal, vol 1, 1937+. Published quarterly by the American Arbitration Association.

The Arbitrator, vol 1, 1981+. Published quarterly by the Institute of Arbitrators Australia.

Canadian Arbitration Journal. Published annually by the Arbitrator's Institute of Canada, Inc.

ICA Arbitration Quarterly Published quarterly by the Indian Council of Arbitration.

ICSID Review – Foreign Investment Law Journal, vol 1, 1986+. Published bi-annually by the Centre.

International Arbitration Reports, vol 1, 1986+. Published by Mealey Publications, Inc. Wayne PA.

Japan Commercial Arbitration Quarterly Published by the Japan Commercial Arbitration Association.

Journal of International Arbitration, vol 1, 1984+. Published quarterly by Werner Publishing, Geneva.

Resolution of Commercial Disputes Vol 1, 1987+. Published quarterly by the Australian Commercial Disputes Centre.

Yearbook

Yearbook: Commercial Arbitration, vol 1, 1976+. Published for the International Council for Commercial Arbitration by Kluwer.

This publication is extremely valuable for the wealth of material it contains:

Part 1: **National Reports.** Since vol XIII (1988), this part of the *Yearbook* has been transferred to a separate ICCA publication entitled *International Handbook on Commercial Arbitration*. This is looseleaf. In that publication, alphabetically arranged by country, text and commentary on national law can be found. Periodically the *Yearbook* will contain new, selective, National Reports. In vol XXVII (2002) of the *Yearbook*, the table of contents of the *Handbook* is set out.

Part II, A: **Arbitral Awards.** The *Yearbook* publishes a selection of awards with all references that might identify the parties removed unless already fully published, or when later court action puts the name into the public domain.

There is an index at the end which groups the cases in that issue by subject. This is used in conjunction with the Index of Arbitral Awards vols I (1995) – XV (1990); vols XVI (1991) – XX (1995) and the annual volumes since, for a complete index of awards since 1975. The full text of arbitral awards published in vols I–XXV (1976-2000) is available on subscription from the publisher.

Part II, B: **Court Decisions on Arbitration**. The decisions here exclude the material in Part V, but otherwise there is a broad selection of cases both previously published and unpublished.

Part II, C: **Court Decisions Applying the UNCITRAL Model Law.** Abstracts of cases from *Case Law on UNCITRAL Texts* (CLOUT) are set out by country. Part of the "User Guide" is also extracted.

Part III, A: **Arbitration Rules**. Set out here are new Arbitration Rules, both text and commentary where appropriate.

Part III, B: **Iran-US Claims Tribunal**. Set out in vol XXVIIa is an introduction, survey of the awards and decisions, as well as the text of the awards and decisions.

Part IV: **Recent Developments in Arbitration Law and Practice**. Here there is a selection, principally by jurisdiction, of recent changes.

Volume XXIVa has information on Belgium, Costa Rica, Ireland, Latvia, Macao, Sweden, Taiwan and Venezuela.

Part V, A: **Court Decisions on the New York Convention 1958.** With the excerpts provided in the latest vol XXVII (42), it brings to a total of 1002 decisions from 49 nations that have been included in the Yearbook since 1976. These cases are indexed in each volume and periodically consolidated.

Part V, B: **Court Decisions on the European Convention 1961**.

Part V, C: **Court Decisions on the Washington (ICSID) Convention 1965.**

Part V, D: **Court Decisions on the Panama Convention 1975**.

Part VI: **Articles on Arbitration**. Occasionally articles will be published in the Yearbook

Part VII: **Bibliography**: (i) general, (ii) by country and (iii) journals, with publishing details, on arbitration.

Electronic form

Reference

Jean M Wenger, "International Commercial Arbitration: locating the resources", prepared for, and published by, *Law Library Research Xchange* (LLRX) at <*www.llrx.com/features/arbitration2. htm*>.

Lyonette Louis-Jacques, "International Commercial Arbitration: resources in Print and Electronic Format", at <*www.lib.uchicago. edu/~llou/intlarb.html*>.

Charlotte L Bynum's Research Guide: *International Commercial Arbitration*, Cornell University Law Library at <*http://library. lawschool.cornell.edu/WhatWeDo/ResearchGuides/Intl-Commercial-Arbitration.cfm*>.

The internet is particularly valuable, as we have seen previously, in disseminating information. It is speedy in that it allows specific information to be quickly isolated and retrieved. For this reason, it is ideal for primary sources. For the same reasons, it is less good for secondary material where evaluation may be involved and the material is not as specific. Keeping this in mind, there are certain benefits in using the Internet.

It is worthwhile comparing the first two electronic guides mentioned above because they provide material from two different directions.

The **LLRX guide** consists of:

I. Introduction
A. Primers
B. MetaResources

II. Treaties
Treaty Compilations

III. Arbitral Institutions
A. Administering Institutions
    1. International Institutions
    2. National Institutions
    Compilations of Arbitral Institutions
B. Arbitrators
C. Cooperative Agreements between Arbitral Institutions

IV. Arbitration Rules
Arbitration Rules Compilations

V. National Law
National Law Compilations

VI. Drafting Arbitration Clauses – Model Clauses

VII. Decisions/Awards

VIII. Specialized Arbitration
A. Intellectual Property
B. Maritime
C. Sports

IX. Locating Literature and Resources
A. Online library catalogues
B. Bibliographies
C. Journal/Periodicals
    1. Search and identification
        (a) Subscription services
        (b) Web-based finding tools
    2. Specialized Journals
    3. Selected free-based web articles

X.Associations

Practical emphasis: There is an emphasis here on the practical side of international commercial arbitration. There is extensive reference to paper material, the author acknowledging that both are needed to adequately cover the material. The paper resources tend to be under the "Primer" heading, the electronic under the heading "MetaResources". However, the practical side of the guide is obvious when one examines "Arbitral Institutions". The author has listed, and linked, all of the international and national arbitration institutions, allowing the researcher to quickly isolate and search each in turn. Even under the Heading "Arbitrators", the author has attempted to link as many sources where arbitrators may be identified. In much the same way links have been created to all of the Arbitral rules and arbitral rules compilations. Finally, the last of this practical side can be seen with the linking to the model clauses under the heading "Drafting Arbitration Clauses". Of course, the references to decisions and awards is also there serving both the practical audience as well as the academic researcher.

Louis-Jacques's guide consists of:

- Bibliographies, Research Guides, and Background Sources
- Major Treatises, Casebooks, Practice Guides, and Looseleaf Services on International Arbitration
- Arbitration Journals and Newsletters
- Journal Indexes
- Arbitration Rules, Statutes, Model Laws, and Conventions
- Arbitration Reports
- Legal Databases
- Arbitration Courts and Organizations
- Internet Resources: Websites
- Internet Resources: Electronic Discussion Groups (Listservs)

Scholarly emphasis: as a counterpoint to the practical side of the guide above, this guide sets out to provide the researcher with as much primary and secondary material as possible, with emphasis on the monograph and the journal article. Providing extensive and complete bibliographical details, this list also has a substantial amount of secondary source material gleaned from e-journals and the like.

Of particular use is the information that is brought together from the commercial legal databases of LexisNexis and Westlaw. Here, the various material that is available from those sources is also shown. While acknowledging that they are commercial services, many of the larger university libraries do have access to these services making the material easily accessible.

There is one final aspect of this guide which makes it particularly useful. Under the final heading, "Internet Resources: Electronic Discussion Groups (Listservs)", can be found a number of discussion lists that encourage the discussion of international commercial arbitration matters. Any person – either academic or practitioner – with an interest in the area would find that the ability to receive information from like-minded persons can make the discovery of resources so much easier. It also comes as no surprise that this guide contains this list information because the author is internationally known for the maintenance of guides of these Listservs covering the whole spectrum of legal information.

Chapter 9

The Legal Materials of the European Union

Outline

1 European Institutions
   (a) The Council of Europe
   (b) The European Union
2 EU Institutions
   (a) European Commission
   (b) The European Council
   (c) Council of the European Union ("Council of Ministers")
   (d) European Parliament
   (e) Court of Justice of the European Communities
3 Community's Legal System
4 Community Documentation
   (a) Primary
   (b) Secondary
   (c) Third Source: External Treaties
   (d) Court of Justice of the European Communities
5 Secondary Source Materials
   (a) Researching Guides
   (b) Current Awareness Publications
   (c) Legal Journals Specialising in Community Law
   (d) Legal Encyclopaedias
   (e) European Union Databases

1. European institutions

Superimposed upon the political map of Europe is a number of bodies now having a tremendous impact upon the rest of the world – either socially or in trade matters. Two that are of considerable interest to Australia are:

(a) The Council of Europe

The Treaty establishing the Council of Europe was signed in London on 5 May 1949, after intense pressure by European leaders, including Winston Churchill, to resist any pressure that may be caused by an expanding USSR.

Article 1 of the Statute (Treaty) states:

> The aim of the Council of Europe is to achieve a greater unity between the members for the purpose of safeguarding and realising the ideals and principles which are common heritage and facilitating their economic and social progress.

While the ideals of "closer unity" and "closer association" were much less than the "union" and "unity" that had been agreed upon in 1948 by the Hague Declaration, it was to be a start which in some respects will culminate when the single market of Europe comes into effect.

While the list of subjects within the competence of the Council is extensive, they are basically those associated with Economics, Social, Cultural, Scientific, Legal and Human Rights. And it is the last topic that has done the most to lift the profile of the Council. The European Convention on Human Rights came into force in 1953 and is now ratified by all 45[1] members of the Council of Europe. Members of the European Commission of Human Rights, elected by the Committee of Ministers, serve as independent officers and not as delegates of their representing State. The European Court of Human Rights has become of vital interest to all Europeans in the safeguarding of their rights from arbitrary, capricious or unlawful actions of government. The principal documentation of these bodies has been examined in the previous chapter in considering human

1 Current membership of the Council of Europe is: Albania, Andorra, Armenia, Austria, Azerbaijan, Belgium, Bosnia & Herzegovina, Bulgaria, Croatia, Cyprus, Czech Republic, Denmark, Estonia, Finland, France, Georgia, Germany, Greece, Hungary, Iceland, Ireland, Italy, Latvia, Liechtenstein, Lithuania, Luxembourg, Malta, Moldova, Netherlands, Norway, Poland, Portugal, Romania, Russian Federation, San Marino, Serbia and Montenegro, Slovakia, Slovenia, Spain, Sweden, Switzerland, "The former Yugoslav Republic of Macedonia", Turkey, Ukraine and the United Kingdom. Monaco is a state candidate for membership.

rights materials. It is in this area of the creation of minimum standards in human rights that the Council of Europe is of most interest to Australia.

Electronic: The Council of Europe has recently finalised its home page: <*www.coe.int*>.

By accessing this facility on the net, the researcher can see at a glance the various institutions of the Council of Europe. However, the similarity of names between these and the institutions of the European Union will always lead to confusion. One excellent place to start researching, with commentary and links as well as a comparative table setting out these institutions, is Sophie Lobey, *History, role and activities of the Council of Europe: Facts, figures and information sources*, published by Globalex at: <*www.nyulawglobal.org/Globalex/Council_of_Europe.htm*>.

(b) The European Union

The Maastricht Treaty, formally known as the *Treaty on European Union* (TEU), came into force on 1 November 1993, following ratification of the Treaty by the 12 Member States[2] of the European Communities. There is an element of fulfilment of destiny about this latest move. The origins of the European Union are found with three Communities: the European Coal and Steel Community (established by Treaty in 1951-52); the European Economic Community (established by Treaty in 1957, the title of which was changed by *Maastricht* to "European Community") and the European Atomic Energy Community (established by Treaty in 1957). Initially each supported by separate institutions, in the mid-1960s there was a unification of the Commission and Council, leading to the use of the name "European Community" (EC). With the *Single Europe* legislation of 1986 formally (although not completely) coming into force on 1 January 1993, there was an effective abolition of border controls between the Member States. The aim is to promote economic and social progress including a single currency. On 1 January 1999, the Euro became the official currency of 11 Member States of the European Union although Euro notes and coins will not appear until 1 January 2002. This is known as the Community "pillar" of the European Union. The second pillar: "Provisions on a Common Foreign and Security Policy" and the third pillar: "Provisions on Cooperation in the fields of Justice and Home

2 Austria (1.195), Belgium*, Denmark (1.1.73), Finland (1.1.95), France*, Germany*, Greece (1.1.81), Ireland (1.1.73), Italy*, Luxembourg*, Netherlands*, Portugal (1.1.86), Spain (1.1.86), Sweden (1.1.95) and the United Kingdom (1.1.73). Both Switzerland (1993) and Norway (1994) have failed to gain national approval in plebiscites.
(* indicates original party)

Affairs" – were inserted by Arts J and K *Maastricht* into the foundation Treaties. These now provide the structure of the "new" European Union.[3]

That "new" Europe has recently had to take two steps in creating the political and institutional conditions to enable the European Union to meet the challenges of the future. The first was expansion. The **Treaty of Amsterdam**, signed in October 1997 and coming into force on 1 May 1999, formally allowed the expansion of the EU from 15 Member States. Much of the detail necessary was contained in *Agenda 2000*, a strategic document prepared by the Commission. (This document, together with *Strategy Paper 2001*, including national reports on the 13 front-runners, is at <www. europa.*eu.int*>.)

Treaty of Nice. Following the opening of negotiations for expansion with 12 nations, the EU at the Nice European Council in 2000 reached agreement on extensive reforms for its institutions. As a revision of the basic EU instruments, the resultant Treaty once signed (February 2001) needed both approval of the EU Parliament and ratification of all 15 current Member States. After an initial rejection in mid-2002, it was finally approved by the Irish in October 2002.

At the Gothenburg European Council a week later, the summit declared the enlargement process as "irreversible" (*Declaration of Enlargement*) and agreed to a clear timetable for that enlargement. The Treaty of Accession was signed in Athens on 16 April 2003 and on 1 May 2004 Poland, Slovakia, the Czech Republic, Estonia, Latvia, Lithuania, Hungary, Slovenia, Malta and Cyprus joined the EU. The accession of Romania and Bulgaria occurred on 1 January 2007 and negotiations are presently underway to admit Croatia, Turkey and the Former Yugoslav Republic of Macedonia.

The second recent major change has been the drafting of a Constitutional Treaty for Europe. Convened in February 2002 under the chairmanship of former French President Valéry Giscard D'Estaing, the completed draft merges the current EU and EC Treaties. Completed and adopted by consensus in Rome in July 2003, was finally adopted by the political leaders of all Member States in June 2004. Things went terribly wrong, however, when the electorates of the Netherlands and France rejected the draft Constitution in 2005. In an effort to re-establish the momentum to streamline many of the EU procedures but stopping short of a Constitutional underpinning, a new Treaty was signed in Lisbon in December 2007. Once again while it was hoped that all Member States

3 The three-pillar structure was to be accepted over a unitary model. This was supported by those who would support intergovernmental action in order to avoid erosion of national sovereignty.

would ratify by the end of 2008 for introduction on 1 January 2009 – before the European elections scheduled for June 2009. But the rejection of the Lisbon Treaty by the Irish in June 2008 will mean further delay.

The European Union and *Acquis Communautaire*

The creation of the Union was not seen as a revolutionary move, and the aim was to utilise the previous structure, practices and ideals of the EC. To this end Art C of *Maastricht* provided:

> The Union shall be served by a single institutional framework which shall ensure the consistency and the continuity of the activities carried out in order to attain its objectives while respecting and building upon the "acquis communautaire".

In order to bring about the necessary agreement at the time of the negotiations of the draft treaty at Maastricht, there was need for compromise in the extension of both social and economic polices of the new Union. Such compromises can now be seen in a number of Protocols which have been annexed to the Treaty of European Union. Currently there are nine covering such things as the exclusion of Denmark from the provisions of the Treaty relating to immigration and other matters (Protocol 5) and the exemption of Ireland from any provisions of the Treaties affecting Ireland's abortion laws (Protocol 6).

While Australia is beginning to look to Europe for ideas in legal development, see, for example, the adoption of the European laws of product liability, the importance to Australia of the European Union is principally as a trading partner. Indeed, the European Union is Australia's largest trading partner, and second, only to Japan, in Australian exports.

Awareness of this importance is now trickling down to the legal profession. With a single block of trade regulations to understand, the need to be able to find and interpret their law with confidence becomes essential.

This research will be greatly assisted by the fact that there should be few language barriers. With the United Kingdom part of the EU, the laws are in English, and we should be sufficiently competent to find the various provisions. There are some problems. Our research will not be helped by the civil law influence in the construction and interpretation of EU materials, but aids to assist in those processes do exist.

The first step is to understand the make up of the institutions in the European Union. However, some explanation of the recent change in name is needed. With the *European Union* being the preferred name, it does not mean that *European Community* ceases to exist. The latter will always be the term used to describe the formal relationship associated with the various foundation Treaties. The term *European Union* is wider and includes those original responsibilities, together with new areas adopted by the *Maastricht Treaty*. These are principally a common foreign and security policy and cooperation in the field of justice and home affairs. Thus whereas the diplomatic arm in Australasia use to be known as the "Delegation of the Commission of the European Community to Australia and New Zealand", the new title is the *European Union: Delegation of the European Commission to Australia and New Zealand*. The new title will also be adopted when referring to the territory previously referred to as EC, in such terms as the "EU Member States" or "EU market". It might be noted that the *Commission of the European Communities* and the *Court of Justice of the European Communities* have maintained their original names, insofar as both have obligations under the three original Community Treaties.

2. EU institutions

The principal institutions of the European Union are:

- European Commission
- The European Council
- Council of the European Union
- European Parliament
- Economic and Social Committee
- The Court of Justice of the European Communities
- Court of Auditors

In examining those relevant to us, researchers versed in the separation of powers model of government and decision-making should be wary of finding a pattern of statutes and regulations that they might have come to expect. There is a considerable degree of overlap and consultation between many of these organs of government, and their functions can prove misleading if this is not kept in mind.

(a) European Commission

While each of the three Communities originally had its own Commission (in one form or another) and Council, by a Treaty, signed in Brussels on 8 April 1965 to become effective mid-1967 (the Merger Treaty), these functions have now been transferred to a single Commission and single Council.

Functions

The Commission's functions are fourfold:

1. to ensure the application of the provisions of the Treaties and of the provisions enacted by the institutions of the Communities in pursuance thereof;
2. to formulate recommendations or opinions in matters which are the subject of the Treaties, where the latter expressly so provides or where the Commission considers it necessary;
3. to dispose, under the conditions laid down in the Treaties, of a power of decision of its own and to participate in the preparation of Acts of the Council of Ministers and of the European Parliament; and
4. to exercise the competence conferred on it by the Council of Ministers for the implementation of the rules laid down by the latter.

To put it simply, the Commission is the executive authority of the European Communities, the role of which is definitely supranational rather than international. It carries out all those tasks one would expect from the executive organ: initiating and supervising legislation, establishing budgets, imposing penalties on those who break competition rules, instigating the infringement proceedings where a member state appears to be in breach of Community law, and liaising with the Council of Ministers.

Membership

The membership of the European Commission is in a state of flux during the expansion period. While the Treaty originally provided for 20 Commissioners – and for many years the larger nations had two Commissioners – from 1 January 2005 they have all had one, and this will continue until a time when the Council, acting unanimously sets a number, and if there are more Member States than planned Commissioners, it shall be by rotation. Under both the 2004 Draft Constitution and the 2007 Lisbon Treaty it was agreed that the College (of Commissioners) set to assume office in 2009 would consist of one Commissioner from every member state and by end of 2014 the size of the College would be equivalent to two-thirds the number of members states with every country taking equal turns. With the Irish rejection of the Lisbon Treaty begin blamed on this point, there is some evidence that this provision may be jettisoned and all Member States continue to have the right to one Commissioner.

Under recent changes to the Treaty, the governments of the member states nominate by qualified majority the person who is to be President of the College of Commissioners, subject to the approval of the European Parliament. Only after this person is appointed is the governments of the member states – in *common accord* with the nominee for President – nominate the persons they wish to appoint as Commissioners. At this time the body as a whole is subject to a vote of approval by the European Parliament but not any individual appointee. The Parliament does appear to have the power to negotiate the redistribution of portfolios to ensure a person it disapproves does not have responsibility for a high-profile portfolio.

Once appointed for five years the members of the Commission shall "in the general interest of the Community, be completely independent in the performance of their duties." Each of the Commissioners has individual responsibility for a defined aspect of the work of the Commission, presently divided into Directorates-General and Services and as combined staff of over 32,000 persons.

Current Information

The *Directory of the Commission of the European Communities* is an irregular publication of the Office of Official Publications of the European Communities (OOPEC) which provides the names, addresses, contact names, policy and departmental responsibilities for the Commissioners and Eurocrats of the Commission. Much of this information, replaced annually, can also be found in the *Europa World Year Book* (Europa Publications).

Bulletin of the European Union: Published monthly, the *Bulletin* has an excellent coverage of the current activities of the Commission. It has a structured format with each issue being divided into three parts: *Special features; Activities in [that] month, year;* and *Documentation*. Of special interest is the second part, which is further divided into 15 special areas of EC activities, external relations, financing Community activities and political and institutional matters. The final division also is useful for finding information of other Community institutions, including meetings of the Council of Ministers and their main items of business.

Internet: There is now a homepage, entitled ***Europa***, run by the European Commission as a common endeavour for all of the EU's institutions. From it the researcher can obtain historic and statistical information relating to the EU, recent press releases, together with both White and

Green papers setting out proposed Commission legislative initiatives. ***Europa*** is located at *<http://europa.eu.int>*.

(b) The European Council

The heads of state or of government of the member states, together with foreign ministers, meet usually four times a year to discuss matters relating to the long-term development of the EU which are handled by the "political co-operation" system. This arrangement allows for foreign ministers to meet quarterly to co-ordinate foreign policy.

The Council was not originally part of the EC Treaty but came into existence after a communique of heads of government meeting in Paris in 1974. Its existence is not mentioned in the Treaty of Rome but can be found now in the *Single European Act* of 1986 and the Treaty of European Union (*Maastricht*).

Notwithstanding this apparent lack of 'status', the Council gives the EU the necessary impetus for the Union development and defines general political guidelines, particularly in the filed of Common Foreign and Security Policy. Under both the draft Constitution and the Treaty of Lisbon, the European Council would become a fully-fledged 'institution' in its own right with a direct role in the selection of the Presidency of the Commission.

Functions

Indeed the European Council received a considerable fillip with Maastricht. Pursuant to Art D, provision was made for the European Council to provide the Union "with the necessary impetus for its development and shall define the general political guidelines thereof". This would appear to relate to all three pillars, and places the European Council in a strong position vis-à-vis the other institutions.

Current Information

Although not formally published, information on these "summit meetings" can best be found in such services as *Keesing's Contemporary Archives*. The European Council submits a report to the European Parliament after each European Council meeting, together with an annual report on Union achievements.

(c) Council of the European Union ("Council of Ministers")

This is the principal decision-making and legislative organ of the Communities, and membership here does represent the interests of the member states. The Member is usually the Foreign Minister but will be replaced by the appropriate Minister according to the subject of the Council's agenda. This ensures that a principal function of the Council of Ministers, "to ensure co-ordination of the general economic policies of the Member States", is fulfilled. About 80 Council sessions are held each year, although the *Committee of Permanent Representatives* (COREPER) made up of senior officials from each State, tends to be in permanent session.

Functions

The principal function is to adopt the Communities legislation proposed by the Commission, to confer on the Commission powers for the implementation of the rules laid down by the EU Council while reserving the right to implement directly the rules themselves, to adopt the budgets, and conclude international agreements on behalf of the EC.

Voting

The Treaty of Rome provides for three types of voting depending upon the subject matter: simple majority, qualified majority (QM) and unanimity. There are few areas now where a simple majority is recognized and by far the most common for determining Council decisions is by qualified majority. Here a weighting factor has been introduced.[4] In a few remaining areas – common foreign and security policy, taxation, asylum and immigration policy – Council decision decisions still require unanimous voting.

Current Information

Unlike the Commission, there is no great dissemination of information from the Council of Ministers. There is a *Guide to the Council of the European Union,* issued twice a year, which gives general information on the Ministers and on the General Secretariat, but the official *General Report* tends to be slow in publication. The *Bulletin of the European Union* does supply further information. For access to the latest press releases concerning Council affairs and decisions, see <*http://ec.europa.eu/news/archives_en.htm*>.

---

4 [From 1 January 2007] Germany, France, Italy and the United Kingdom 29; Spain and Poland 27; Romania 14; Netherlands 13; Belgium, Czech Republic, Greece, Hungary and Portugal 12; Austria, Bulgaria and Sweden 10; Denmark, Ireland, Lithuania, Slovakia and Finland 7; Estonia, Cyprus, Latvia, Luxembourg and Slovenia 4, and Malta 3.

(d) European Parliament

While originally styled "European Parliamentary Assembly",[5] in 1962 it renamed itself "European Parliament"[6] although this was not formally recognised by some of the other EC institutions until the *Single Europe Act 1986*.[7] Until 1979 membership was determined by national Parliaments, but since then there has been direct election with voting by adult suffrage. Membership is now 785 and members are elected for a five-year term, with elections scheduled for 2009. Members tend to sit in the European Parliament in political groups rather than national groups.

The structure of the European Parliament indicates somewhat the complexity of its function: the Secretariat of the Parliament is based in Luxembourg, while plenary sessions take place in Strasbourg with most Committee meetings taking place in Brussels. It is in Brussels that the Parliament should one day centralise.

Functions

The powers until recently have tended to be consultative rather than legislative, with the Council of Ministers seeking advice about Commission proposals. Questions asked, in much the same way as the traditional Westminster-style, are important in their work. It is the standing committees that exercise a great deal of power through specialised scrutiny. However, the Parliament does have teeth – if required by two-thirds, the Commission must resign. This has never been exercised but, in both 1979 and 1984, the Parliament did reject the budgets prepared by the Commissions. The *Single Europe Act 1986* revolutionised the role of the Parliament, at least in certain areas set out in Art 6. Thus there is, in those areas, a co-operative procedure adopted by the Council of Ministers whereby it shall adopt a common position on draft legislation, based on proposals coming from the Commission, and a qualified majority opinion coming from the Parliament.

Current Information

Official Handbook of the European Parliament, now in paperback, provides short biographies of the Members of the European Parliament (MEPs), national electoral laws, rules of procedure, committees and political group membership. This last piece of information is sometimes needed quickly after a European Parliament election and can be difficult to piece

5 Resolution of 20 March 1958 (OJ 1958 p 6).

6 Resolution of 30 March 1962 (OJ 1962 p 1045).

7 Article 3(1).

together. Such publications as *Keesing's Contemporary Archives* will give the national results according to their political groupings but they do not always line-up with other national groupings. Until the Parliament is convened and the Members start voting it is difficult to "count the numbers". Once identified, this information is also contained in the official *List of Members*, obtainable from the Office for Official Publications of the European Communities. There is now a home page of the European Parliament (EuroParl at <*http: //www.europarl.eu.int*>) which provides a breakdown of the European Parliament by political party and by country. This was available within a short period after the June 1999 election. See also the current *Europa World Year Book* (Europa Publications).

Record of Debates

The *Official Journal of the European Communities: Annex: Debates of the European Parliament* is the source of the authoritative record of debates of a plenary session.

(e) Court of Justice of the European Communities

Sitting at Luxembourg, the Court consists 27 judges and eight Advocates General, all of whom have been nominated by the governments of the member states for renewable six-year terms. Since 1 September 1989, the Court of First Instance (CFI) of the European Communities has been the principal venue for actions brought by individuals and companies against decisions of EU institutions and agencies. The CFI consists of 27 judges, from each Member State, and no Advocates General. There is a right of appeal to the Court of Justice but only on points of law.

Functions

These are to ensure the observance of law in the interpretation and application of the principal Treaties and the implementation of regulations issued by the Council and Commission. Such functions make its powers extremely wide-ranging.

Procedure

The Court process is that of a European Court with procedures being basically inquisitorial rather than adversarial. Written submissions tend to be viewed as far more important than the oral argument. "In interpreting legal instruments the Court may consider preparatory materials and not merely the bare text. Its judgments are frequently terse, replete with statements of general legal principle and no dissenting opinion is delivered or announced": de Smith and Brazier, *Constitutional and Administrative Law* (1990). A recent text on the Court and its function is LN Brown & T Kennedy *The Court of Justice of the European Communities*, 4th ed, Sweet & Maxwell, 1994. The appendices include statistics and official publications of the Court.

3. Community's legal system

There are at least three, if not four, sources of law:

(a) The primary source is derived from the Treaties establishing the various Communities, with all amendments, together with the Acts of Accession of Denmark, Ireland and the United Kingdom (1973); Greece (1980); Portugal and Spain (1986); Austria, Finland and Sweden (1995); Poland, Slovakia, the Czech Republic, Estonia, Latvia, Lithuania, Hungary, Slovenia, Malta and Cyprus (2004) and Bulgaria and Romania (2007).

(b) The secondary sources are those legislative instruments like regulations, directives, decisions and recommendations issued by the Community.

(c) The wide range of international agreements concluded between the Community and non-member states or international organisations. These may not be inherently different but are treated to reinforce the international persona of the European Union.

(d) The fourth are possibly the decisions of the European Court of Justice. "Although the Court's role in interpreting and applying Community law differs in many respects from the pattern of precedent and authority that shapes much of the common law case law into a source, its jurisdiction is in effect a potent force in Community law." "European Communities" in E Moys, *Manual of Law Librarianship: The Use and Organization of Legal Literature*, 2nd ed, 1987.

4. Community documentation

(a) Primary

While there are versions of the original Communities Treaties published in all official languages, it is far easier to consult one of the many textbooks which set out this important source documentation. Probably the most comprehensive is:

Sweet & Maxwell's *Encyclopedia of European Community Law* (looseleaf) multi-volume, Volume "B".

Always remember the need in many countries for domestic or national legislation to be enacted to implement Treaties. Thus, when the United Kingdom enacted the *European Communities Act 1972* to joint the "Common Market", the Treaties were set out in that UK Act.

(b) Secondary

The greatest volume of Community law is to be found here as are the Acts made by the Council and Commission under powers conferred by the Treaties. They can be divided into:

Obligatory, and Non-obligatory, Acts

Obligatory Acts – 3 types: (names tend to reflect to whom they are directed)

regulations – are binding in their entirety and are directed to all member states who must enact legislation to implement them

directives – are binding on named member states who must enact legislation or in some other way implement them

decisions – are binding in their entirety and may be addressed to individuals, member states or corporations

Non-obligatory Acts – are provided for under the EC and Euratom Treaties as *recommendations* and as *opinions*. They can be viewed as "persuasive and constructive in the formulation and execution of the policies of the Community. Though they cannot be formally cited as sources of Community law they ought to be regarded, in the light of their potential, as auxiliary elements of the law-making process of the Community." D Lasok & JW Bridges, *An Introduction to the Law and Institutions of the European Communities*, 3rd, Butterworths 1982.

Tables of Legislation: In the major monographs or encyclopedias of EU law, the obligatory and non-obligatory legislation will be separated and there will be at least two tables of legislation contained in the work. There may well be other tables as well. The treaties, as primary legislation, tend to form their own table, while agreements, conventions, resolutions, protocols and declarations, known as "supplementary legislation," are usually grouped under "Other EC Legislation." That means there are usually *four* tables of legislation.

Sources of Secondary Legislation

Official: The *Official Journal*, as the official organ of the European Communities, contains all primary and secondary legislation. It is issued almost daily, is available in paper and microform, and the legislation contained therein is available on CD-ROM and online.

The *Journal* is published in two main series:

"L" Series: the *Legislation* series and containing the text of all Acts under the headings of "Obligatory" and "Non-obligatory"; and

"C" Series: the *Information and Notices* series and containing, inter alia, procedural business of the European Parliament, parliamentary questions and answers, details of new actions, recent judgments and requests for preliminary rulings in the Court, and a variety of information and public communiques developing from Council and Commission business.

"*Annex*" Series: since 1968, contains the debates of the European Parliament, which since issue no. 157, 1972-3, have been available in English.

"*Supplement*" Series: since 1978, contains commercial information relating to public tenders, contracts and project approvals arising mainly from the European Development Fund.

Subject Index to the Official Journal

It is necessary to be able to find one's way through the mass of information available in the *Journal*. This is done with the use of the index. Initially appearing in monthly parts, it is cumulated annually. Information within it is organised in two ways: either in the alphabetical index ("analytical index") or the "methodological index". The latter has all documents set out according to their number. The marginal use of the alphabetical index was well known: "Prior to 1984 the alphabetical table was in fact a classified index arranged by a selection of terms that required a good knowledge of the subject structure of EU business and the idiosyncrasies of EU terminology; as such it was an unspecific means of retrieval for many items. From 1984 the alphabetical index has been based upon keyword analysis of each document by use of the vocabulary in the EUROVAC thesaurus. Each document can now have up to five keywords entries, which has made the alphabetical index a more useful and usable index" Moys, pp 408-9. John Jeffries, because of his expertise in this area, should have the final few words on the index: "Those who are sufficiently desperate might try to use the index ... [although] the chances of finding it ... are remote ... All that can be said about the rotated keyword index introduced in 1984 is that it is somewhat more effective that what went before, but then what went before was terrible" *Legal Research and the Law of the European Communities*, Legal Information Resources, 1990, p 13.

Because of the initial problems, and the fact that there is no cumulation of the annual indexes, **privately produced indexes** of information about material in the Journal have been published and are now popular. These include the index and tables to vols 51 and 52 ("European Communities") of *Halsbury's Laws of England*, 4th ed supplemented by D Vaughan, *Laws of the European Communities Service*, the index and tables to Sweet & Maxwell's *Encyclopedia of European Community Law*, and *Guide to the EEC-Legislation*, produced by North-Holland in conjunction with the TM Asser Institute. This was first published in 1979 and has been supplemented since.

See also the online databases referred to below which allow access to the legislation contained in the *Official Journal*.

Secondary Legislation in Force

Official

The up-dating process of European Communities secondary legislation is a most complex one. The officially produced *Directory of Community Legislation in Force* is based on the files of CELEX.

The *Directory* is updated twice a year and covers:

- binding instruments of secondary legislation arising out of the Treaties establishing the three Communities (regulations, decisions, directives, etc ...)
- other legislation (internal agreements, etc ...)
- agreements between the Communities and non-member countries.

Each entry in the *Directory* gives the number and title of the instrument, together with a reference to the *Official Journal* in which it can be found. Any amending instruments are also indicated, with the appropriate references in each case.

The legislation is classified by subject matter. Instruments classifiable in more than one subject area appear under each of the headings concerned.

The *Directory* proper (Vol I) is accompanied by two indexes (Vol II), one chronological by document number and the other alphabetical by keyword (from advertisement in the *Bulletin of the European Union*).

Private

Encyclopedia of European Community Law (Sweet & Maxwell), 1973+

The *Encyclopedia of European Community Law* is in the process of being republished, and renamed the *Encyclopedia of European Union Law*. It will include constitutional texts, treaties and secondary legislation and will be updated by looseleaf insertions. It should remain an important aid in locating EU material.

European Communities Legislation: Current Status 1952-1991, 2 vols plus index vol and three supplements per year, Butterworths, 1992.

This is a service whereby the subscriber is able to check the current status of any secondary legislation enacted since its formation in 1952. Access to the information is either the chronological table or subject index. The text of the secondary legislation is not provided as part of the service.

Subject Collections of Primary and Secondary Law

Because of the problem of finding the legislation of the European Communities, there are now several publications where it has been brought together by subject. One such publisher is Butterworths. Through the *Butterworths European Information Service*, two series are currently being published. One is the *Compendium series*: here the core legislative, judicial and other official Communities materials relating to a subject are brought together with no commentary. The *Current EC Legal Developments Series* (CECLD) has both commentary and an appendix which contains secondary and proposed legislation. There are many titles in the series, which is very much geared to the legal practice.

Citation of Primary and Secondary Legislation

A number of examples of citation follow. They are guides only for it is acknowledged that there still wide variations in the way that outsiders cite this material. For a more complete collection of citation rules for European Community law, see "A Citation Manual for European Community Materials" (1994) 18 *Fordham International Law Journal* 694.

To this should be added *Note on the citation of the Treaties in the Publications of the Court of Justice and the Court of First Instance*, located on the homepage of the Courts at <*http://curia.europa.eu/en/content/juris/index_infos.htm* >.

This note was made necessary after the Treaty on European Union (EU) and the Treaty establishing the European Community (EC) were extensively renumbered by the Treaty of Amsterdam. With effect from 1 May 1999, the courts introduced a new method of citation of the articles of the EU, EC, ECSC and Euratom Treaties. These new citation rules are to avoid confusion as to *which* article (either before or after the amendments) is being referred to.

First, the courts have indicated abbreviations for the foundation Treaties. Thus:

- EU for the Treaty on European Union
- EC for the EC Treaty
- CS for the ECSC Treaty (expired on 23 July 2002)
- EA for the Euratom (or EAEC) Treaty.

Secondly, the courts have indicated a different order for references either before or after the changes, disregarding now the CS treaty.

Example 1

Thus "Article 234 EC" will denote the article of the Treaty after 1 May 1999, but "Article 85 *of the EC Treaty*" will refer to that Article before 1 May 1999. [Italicised for emphasis].

In addition, if reference is made to an Article before 1 May, the Courts may note the altered Article as well. Thus

"Article 85 of the EC Treaty (now Article 81 EC)" where it was not amended by the Treaty of Amsterdam; or

"Article 51 of the EC Treaty (now, after amendment, Article 42 EC)" where the article had been amended by the Treaty of Amsterdam; and

"Article 53 of the EC Treaty (repealed by the Treaty of Amsterdam)" where it had been repealed by the Treaty of Amsterdam.

Comprehensive lists setting out the new method of citation of the articles of the EC Treaty and the Treaty on European Union as they stood before 1 May 1999 are published as Sections I and II of the *European Court Reports* for May 1999. They are also on the Courts home page at *<http://curia. europa.eu>*.

Example 2

Statement: One of the institutions of the European Communities is the Court of Justice which has a duty to observe the law in the founding treaties.

Authority: Art 164 of the EC Treaty (now Art 220 EC); Art 136 EA

[Here there is no further citation to where the Treaty can be found. As a primary source, these Treaties can be located in most major works on the subject, including Sweet & Maxwell's Encyclopedia or it may be that only one will be included: the EEC Treaty in the Vaugan Service.]

Example 3

Statement: There is also Court of First Instance.

Authority: The *Single Europe Act*, OJ L169/1 (1987), inserted a new Art 168a (now Art 225 EC) into the EC Treaty, and Art 140a into the Euratom Treaty, empowering the Council to establish such a court by a later decision. The Council subsequently adopted a decision on 24 October 1988 (Council Decision 88/591/, EC, Euratom OJ L319/1 (1988) *corrected version* in OJ C251/1 (1989). That jurisdiction has been subsequently extended: Council Decision 93/350/, EC, Euratom OJ L144/21 Art 1, amending the previous Decision. It took effect on 1 August 1993.

[Legislation appears in the Official Journal and a citation in this form is usually given. Major Acts, like the *Single Europe Act*, or the *Treaty on European Union (Maastricht)*, will also be found in Sweet & Maxwell's *Encyclopedia*. The citation of the council decision is in the traditional form of putting the institutional origin of the Act (here Council), the form (here Decision), the year and Act number (1988/591), the institutional treaty basis (here the three treaties), and the year the Act was passed would go then unless included previously (as above in text). ***Note*** that since 1968, there is a variation between regulations on the one hand, and decisions and directives on the other. With regulations the reg number precedes the date, but it is otherwise with decisions and directives.]

Example 4

Statement: There have been recent changes to the jurisdiction of the Court of Justice pursuant to the Community Patent Agreement.

Authority: Since the signing of the Community Patent Agreement (Council Decision) 89/695/EC OJ L401/1 (1989), [1990] 2 CMLR 194), pursuant to art 2(2), the ECJ is competent to give preliminary rulings in accordance with art 177 of the EC Treaty whenever there is a risk of an interpretation of the agreement being inconsistent with the Treaty.

[The Agreement has an *Official Journal* citation but also can be found in the *Common Markets Law Reports*. This is not unusual, for while principally devoted to cases, it does contain material relating to courts and court procedure. This particular Agreement affects jurisdiction, and includes a Patent Litigation Protocol attached to the Agreement.]

Explanation of Official Journal Citations

No L 98/36 Official Journal of the European Communities 15. 4. 88

COMMISSION REGULATION (EEC) No 983/88
of 14 April 1988
laying down special provisions on the marketing of olive oil containing undesirable substances

Example

Commission Regulation 983/88/EC OJ L98/36 (1988)

These two citations are to the same Regulation but can be cited in various ways. However, they will refer the researcher to the same material:

Reg	=	Regulation
EC	=	one of the three Treaties under which it could have been made
983/88	=	Act No 983 for 1988
OJ	=	*Official Journal*
L	=	L (or *Legislation*) Series
98	=	issue number
36	=	page number

These two parts, the Act reference and where it can be found, can be separated. Thus:

> Commission Regulation 983/88/EC lays down special provisions for the marketing of olive oil containing undesirable substances (OJ L98 15.4.88 p 36)

Proposed Legislation

Example

Proposal for a Council Directive laying down health rules for the production and placing on the market of fresh meat [COM(89) 763 final] OJ C204/3 (August 1990)

COM = COM Document is the generic name given to a working document which contains draft legislation with explanatory memorandum. Notification of existence of the more important COM Documents may appear in the *Bulletin of the European Union* with the document itself. While not a public document at first, it is usually distributed to all depository libraries after it is placed on the agenda of the Commission. The word "final" then appears after the citation. After the Commission formally proposes the legislation it will appear in the *Official Journal*.

It may appear as a Supplement to the Bulletin of the European Union.

COM Documents can also relate to broad policy material and report on the implementation of policy as well.

Finding COM Documents. It was previously noted that the Bulletin of the European Communities does provide some assistance for finding the working documents of the EU, though it cannot be relied upon.

By far the most efficient is the annual *Catalogue of Documents*. Published with this title since 1985, the *Catalogue* has indexed the COM Documents, the Committee Reports of the European Parliament and the Opinions and Reports of the Economic and Social Committee[8] (ECOSOC

8 The Economic and Social Committee represents the principal lobby groups – labour, capital, environment, etc, chosen by the member governments. Since 1986 there have been 189 members. The function of the Committee is to advise the Council and Commission on Community proposals and any other matter it thinks relevant. The work of the Committee is organised by the Bureau of the ESC, and work is devolved to one of 9 groups. These groups report to a plenary session which meets in Brussels for two days about 10 times a year.

or ESC). Because of their nature and the desire to receive public comment of the matter under discussion, these are usually freely available.

For further information on citation, see: "Identification of secondary legislation", introduction to *Secondary Legislation of the European Communities: subject edition*, Statutory Publications Office, and generally, see Ian Thomson, *The Documentation of the European Communities: A Guide*, Mansell, 1989.

(c) Third Source: External Treaties

Collection of Agreements Concluded by the European Communities (1977-9), 5 vols. Annual supplementation.

Recent treaties can be found in the *Official Journal*, "L", because Council regulations are required to bring treaties into force, either in part I or II.

Private sources which include references to these treaties are:

Sweet & Maxwell's *Encyclopedia of European Community Law*

TM Asser, *Guide to the EEC-Legislation*

D Vaughan, *Law of the European Communities Service*, Butterworths

Electronic: Check the home page of the institutions as well. Thus, the home page of the courts has extracts from the three Treaties establishing the Court of Justice and Court of First Instance, with all relevant articles and related documents.

(d) Court of Justice of the European Communities

Official Series

There is an increasing amount of case law from the Court. Between 1953 and 1973 there were 1076 cases. Now the amount of cases is about 300 per year. The judgments are reported in the *Official Journal* but the full law reports are in:

Court of Justice of the European Communities, *Reports of Cases before the Court* (1954+)

These are commonly referred to as the *European Court Reports* and cited as "ECR" and include the Opinions of the Advocates General.

Since 1997, the full text of the decisions of the Court of Justice and Court of First Instance has been freely available on the internet. The Court stresses that it is for "informational" purposes, not the authentic text and thus subject to change. It appears on the site (<*www.curia.eu.int*>) under the heading "Case-Law" at 3 pm on the day the judgment is delivered.

Private Series

Common Market Law Reports, 1962+ (European Law Centre) [CMLR]

Common Market Reporter (CCH)

LEXIS

Example

Report Citation

The citation of these reports follows the European practice of using case numbers as well as names.

Commission v Council, Case 81/72 (Staff Salaries case), [1973] ECR 575; [1973] CMLR 639

BASF v Commission, Case T-79, 84/89, [1992] ECR II-315; [1992] 4 CMLR 357

[It is normal only to use "Commission" rather than "EC Commission", and the European practice of case numbers at the beginning is relegated to a position after the party names (but not always followed in European publications).]

Digest of European Cases

Digest of Case-law relating to Community Law

Published by the Court, the *Digest* presents not only cases decided by it but also selected judgments by national courts. The *Digest* currently comprises two series:

- *A Series*: Case law of the Court of Justice and Court of First Instance, excluding cases brought by officials and employees of the European Communities and cases relating to the Convention of 27 September 1968 on Jurisdiction and the Enforcement of Judgments in Civil and Commercial Matters (since 1977, with a consolidated version 1977-1990. To be published as supplements every 5 years);
- *D Series*: Case law of the Court of Justice and of national courts relating to the Convention of 27 September 1968 on Jurisdiction and the

Enforcement of Judgments in Civil and Commercial Matters in 1981 (it presently only covers case law to 1990).

Compendium of case law relating to the European Communities, 1953-1976, by HJ Everson and H Sperl

Guide to EC Court Decisions, covering the period 1954 – 1982, with further supplementation

The Digest (formerly the *English and Empire Digest*). Volume 21 (Green Band-Reissue) and annual supplementation

European Law Digest (monthly)

One of the most comprehensive collections of digests. It has been published since 1973 and the table in the last issue per year is used to locate the relevant case citations. Each issue is indexed according to major title headings. It is necessary to use each individual volume, however.

European Documentation Centres (EDCs) and EU Depository Libraries (DEPs)

There has been created within Europe and around the world a graded series of centres and libraries which receive EU materials. In Australia and New Zealand they are:

European Documentation Centre (EDCs)

La Trobe University, Bundoora (full)

University of Melbourne, Parkville (full)

University of Canterbury, Christchurch, NZ (full)

University of Queensland, (full)

Monash University, Clayton (specialised)

University of Auckland, NZ (specialised)

University of Sydney (specialised)

University of Tasmania, Hobart (specialised)

University of Western Australia, Nedlands (specialised)

University of Adelaide (specialised) – pending

EU Depository Libraries (DEPs)

Auckland Public Library, NZ (full)

State Library of New South Wales, Sydney (full)

State Library of Victoria (base)

National Library of Australia, Canberra (base)

Parliamentary Library, Wellington NZ (base)

There is also a library and information available from the European Union: Delegation of the European Commission to Australia and New Zealand, 18 Arkana Street, Yarralumla ACT 2600. Telephone: (02) 6271 2777; Facsimile: (02) 6273 4445; Homepage: <*www.delaus.ec.europa.eu*>.

5. Secondary source materials

(a) Researching Guides

Ian Thomson, *The Documentation of the European Communities: a Guide*, London, Mansell Pub, 1989

John Jeffries, A Guide to the Official Publications of the European Communities, 2nd ed, London, Mansell Pub, 1981

Eve Johansson, *Official Publications of Western Europe*, London, Mansell Pub, 1981, 1984-88 (2 vols).

DEsite – constructed and maintained by Tilburg University Library and Faculty of Law, this has an excellent coverage of historical and contemporary material relating to the EU, particularly for the researcher or student who is seeking a comprehensive guide to the institutions and powers of the EU. It can be found at <*http://drcwww.uvt.nl/dbi/instructie/eu/en/FS0.htm* >.

Marylin J Raisch, "European Union Law: an Integrated Guide to Electronic and Print Research" LLRX, at <*www.llrx.com/features/eulaw2.htm*>. This is the most complete and up-to-date researching guide presently available. Prepared by an expert researcher, it allows a user to find quickly all available electronic material via hypertexting. It mixes scholarship with practical guidance to obtain the relevant sources. And of particular use is the construction of a table, *EU Document Location Chart*, incorporating free and commercial services.

Duncan E Alford, "European Union Legal Materials: an infrequent user's guide" Globalex at <*www.nyulawglobal.org/Globalex/European_Union.htm*>. Another excellent guide also appearing in 97 *Law Library Journal* 49 (Winter 2005).

(b) Current Awareness Publications

Official

Bulletin of the European Union (10 issues pa)

The Bulletin reports on the activities of the Commission and the other Community institutions. It is in two parts with Supplements.

Part 1 deals with activities of the month under review under a number of general and recurrent headings.

Part 2 has the latest ECU rates against national currencies and other recent and relevant documentation.

The Supplements are a valuable source of full text material relating to recent Community conferences and policy declarations.

Private

Current Law

This current awareness publication which is produced for the British profession has, necessarily, a section that deals with EU material. It is now necessary for all members of the British profession to take Community law into account in all aspects of their professional life.

European Current Law

Commencing in January 1992, this monthly publication will give digests of published cases from all East, Central and West European countries and is a sister publication to that above. The emphasis will be on national court decisions emanating from Europe and these need not have a direct bearing upon the European Communities. It will have, however, an "abstract of important EEC regulations, directives and national statutes and decrees".

European Law Digest (1973-1991)

This publication ceased with vol 19 and was replaced by *European Current Law*. It is still useful for the citations of EC-related material emanating from a broad cross section of European national courts.

(c) Legal Journals specialising in Community Law

Journal of Common Market Studies (1962)

Common Market Law Review (1963-4+)

Legal Issues of European Integration (1974+)

European Law Review (1975-6+)

European Intellectual Property Review (1978)

Note: These, and many more, are indexed in *Index to Legal Periodicals* (or *WilsonDisk*), *Current Law Index* (or *LegalTrac*) or in the *Index to Foreign Legal Periodicals*. However, one specialist index is *European Legal Journals Index*, published by Legal Information Resources Ltd since 1993, which indexes over 300 legal journals and trade newsletter services published in English and is available on Westlaw. The specialist in-house publications from the fields of banking, insurance, etc, particularly when produced in the offices of lawyers and accountants, are of special importance because they tend to be published quickly, are accurate and contain valuable and practical information. See also the EU library catalogue ECLAS (<*http://europa.eu.int/eclas*>). There is also a catalogue of Internet resources, together with hypertext links, which indexes over 1500 journals world-wide for material on the European Union.

(d) Legal Encyclopaedias

The most comprehensive encyclopaedic coverage of the substantive and procedural law of the European Community is contained within vols 51 and 52 of *Halsbury's Laws of England*, 4th ed. This same material is published in a separate work under the editorship of D Vaughan with the title *Laws of the European Communities*. It is presently being gradually replaced by D Vaughan *Law of the European Communities Service* (Butterworths).

There is also a six-volume publication that is published by Matthew Bender: *The Laws of The European Economic Community: a Commentary on the EEC Treaty*, the original editors of which were Hans Smit and Peter Herzog. The current editor is Dennis Campbell, Director of the Center for International Studies, Salzburg, Austria.

This is one of the most detailed studies of the Treaty and provides the text, extensive commentary and relevant bibliographical reference. While not a true encyclopaedia in format, the content is wide ranging and it will serve both as an introduction and for further detailed study.

(e) European Union Databases

From 1995, the policy of the European Union has been to provide electronic information as widely as possible to the 400 million citizens of its Member States. The latest step in implementing that policy is provision of material – particularly legal information – on the internet. The previous need to gain access through official gateway agents is probably now unnecessary for most Australian researchers to access a wide range of EU electronic data besides its law. EUR-OP Office for

Publications is now responsible for marketing, managing and supporting the EU databases. It can be found at: *<http://publications.europa.eu/index_en.htm >*.

EUR-Lex

The primary internet researching site of European Union law is now EUR-Lex – located at *<http://eur-lex.europa.eu/en/index.htm>*.

The site provides direct and free access to, amongst other things, treaties, legislation, case-law and legislative proposals. Specifically, one can locate and search:

Official Journal of the European Union

"The site offers direct access to the latest issues of the L (Legislation) and C (Information and Notices) series of the *Official Journal,* together with the previous 10 days' issues. Entering the date and the publication reference, allows direct access to a particular issue of the *Official Journal.* Lastly, there is the possibility of consulting the issues of the *Official Journal* made available online since 1998.

The texts published in the *Official Journal,* including texts prior to 1998, can also be accessed using the search functions provided on the site."

Collections

Treaties: Set out here are the basic legal texts on which the European Union and the European Communities are founded: the founding Treaties (original versions and updates), the amending Treaties, the Accession Treaties for each subsequent enlargement, plus other essential documents.

International Agreement: these include agreements concluded by the European Communities with non-member countries or international organizations; agreements concluded jointly by member states and the European Communities in shared areas of responsibility and decisions of joint committees set up in pursuance to an international agreement. These can be searched by classification heading or general subject matter.

Legislation in Force: Contained within a broad classification (20 titles) according to the Directory of Community legislation in force, one can locate agreements, directives, regulations and decisions. Where possible there are also consolidated texts which, although having no legal authority, do provide a valuable aid in researching.

Preparatory Acts (legislation in preparation): An explanation of the scope of this collection comes from the page:

> "Preparatory documents" means all documents corresponding to the various stages of the legislative or budgetary process. They include Commission legislative proposals, Council common positions, legislative and budgetary resolutions and initiatives of the European Parliament, and opinions of the European Economic and Social Committee and of the Committee of the Regions, etc.
>
> These documents will be made available gradually over the next few months. The current version already provides access to the legislative proposals and other Commission communications to the Council and other institutions (COM documents).
>
> EUROPA Preparatory Acts

Case-Law: Includes judgments from the Court of Justice, Court of First Instances and the Civil Service Tribunal. With a table of recent decisions, previous decisions can be searched by year and case number. It should be remembered at this point that the Court of Justice – on its own webpage CURIA – <http://curia.europa.eu/en> also allows searching by subject matter but only in French. There are other commercial services that allow subject searching in English, including LexisNexis, Westlaw, Justis Celex and Lawtel EU.

Parliamentary Questions: questions asked by MEPs to the Commission and Council are available here once the answer from the directed institution is published in the *Official Journal*.

PreLex (<http://ec.europa.eu/prelex/apcnet.cfm?CL=en>)

> PreLex is the database on interinstitutional procedures. It monitors the major stages of the decision-making process between the Commission and the other institutions and provides information on:
>
> - stage of the procedure;
> - decisions of the institutions;
> - names of the people and departments responsible;
> - document references.
>
> It follows all proposals (legislative and budgetary, and the conclusion of international agreements) and the work of the various institutions involved (European Parliament, Council, Economic and Social Committee, Committee of the Regions, etc.) from the transmission of a proposal to its adoption or final rejection. ("What PreLex Offers" – FAQ)

The Legislative Observatory
(<www.europarl.europa.eu/oeil/index.jsp>)

> The Legislative Observatory is a database analysing the institutions' activities as part of the decision-making process of the European Union. In practical terms, it is a tool providing information, follow-up, forecasting and research on legislative procedures. In particular, it offers a means of monitoring and evaluating the work of the European Parliament, the Commission's annual programme and the proposals of each new Council Presidency. ("What the Legislative Observatory offers" – FAQ)

Chapter 10

Non-Commercial Internet Addresses for Legal Research

The collection of URLs associated with law has had an interesting history. From the early days when certain addresses contained key words – like law, legal, solicitor, etc – and sometimes were valuable commercial assets, we have now reached the stage when by using Google most people can quickly find what they want rather than consulting lists.

But the authors still feel that there is an advantage to have lists of some of the more important sources if only to give the novice a starting point. This list is provided for the benefit of those who may not be totally sure of what they want and where is may be found.

As always with URLs, a great deal of effort has gone into making sure they work for you.

AUSTRALIA

Legislation, federal

Commonwealth Law (ComLaw)

www.comlaw.gov.au

Delegated legislation, federal

Commonwealth Law (ComLaw)

www.comlaw.gov.au

Law reports, Federal Courts

Australasian Legal Information Institute (AustLII)

www.austlii.edu.au/au/cth

AUSTRALIAN STATES

New South Wales

Legislation and delegated legislation

Australasian Legal Information Institute (AustLII)

www.austlii.edu.au

(Official) New South Wales Legislation

www.legislation.nsw.gov.au

Law reports

Australasian Legal Information Institute (AustLII)
www.austlii.edu.au

Queensland

Legislation and delegated legislation

Queensland Office of Parliamentary Counsel
www.legislation.qld.gov.au

Law reports

Australasian Legal Information Institute (AustLII)
www.austlii.edu.au

(Official) Queensland Courts
www.courts.qld.gov.au

South Australia

Legislation and delegated legislation

(Official) South Australian Legislation
www.legislation.sa.gov.au

Australasian Legal Information Institute (AustLII)
www.austlii.edu.au

Law reports

Australasian Legal Information Institute (AustLII)
www.austlii.edu.au

Tasmania

Legislation and delegated legislation

Official Tasmanian legislation
www.thelaw.tas.gov.au

Law reports

Australasian Legal Information Institute (AustLII)
www.austlii.edu.au/primary

(Official) Courts and Tribunals Tasmania
www.courts.tas.gov.au

Victoria

Legislation and delegated legislation

(Official) Victorian Legislation and Parliamentary Documents
www.dms.dpc.vic.gov.au

Australasian Legal Information Institute (AustLII)
www.austlii.edu.au

Western Australia

Legislation and delegated legislation

(Official) State Law Publisher

www.slp.wa.gov.au

Law reports

Australasian Legal Information Institute (AustLII)

www.austlii.edu.au

AUSTRALIAN TERRITORIES

Australian Capital Territory

Legislation and delegated legislation

(Official) ACT Legislation Register

www.legislation.act.gov.au

Law reports

Australasian Legal Information Institute (AustLII)

www.austlii.edu.au

Northern Territory

Consolidated legislation and delegated legislation

(Official) Current Northern Territory Legislation Database

www.nt.gov.au/dcm/legislation/current

Sessional Acts

(Official) Register of Legislation

www.nt.gov.au/dcm/legislation/register

LAW REFORM AGENCIES

For a comprehensive coverage of law reform agencies around the world, see

Law Reform Links (Lawlink New South Wales)

www.lawlink.nsw.gov.au/lawlink/lrc/ll_lrc.nsf/pages/LRC_links

Australian Law Reform Commission

www.alrc.gov.au

NSW Law Reform Commission

www.lawlink.nsw.gov.au/lrc

Queensland Law Reform Commission

www.qlrc.qld.gov.au

Victorian Law Reform Commission

www.lawreform.vic.gov.au

Law Reform Committee of Victoria
www.parliament.vic.gov.au/LAWREFORM/

Western Australian Law Reform Commission
www.lrc.justice.wa.gov.au

Tasmanian Law Reform Institute
www.law.utas.edu.au/reform

Northern Terrritory Law Reform Committee
www.nt.gov.au/justice/policycoord/lawmake/lawref.shtml#curr

For the ***Law Reform Database*** see the British Columbia Law Institute *www.bcli.org*

CANADA, Federal

Key References

Ted Tjaden, "Researching Canadian Law"
www.nyulawglobal.org/globalex/Canada1.htm

Ted Tjaden, "Doing Legal Research in Canada
www.llrx.com/features/ca_top.htm

LexUM, University of Montreal
www.droit.umontreal.ca

Canadian Legal Information Institute (CanLII)
www.canlii.org

Legislation

Canadian Department of Justice: Consolidated Statutes
http://canada.justice.gc.ca

Annual Statutes of Canada
http://canada.justice.gc.ca

Delegated legislation

Consolidated Regulations of Canada
http://canada.justice.gc.ca

Law reports

Supreme Court of Canada, decisions
www.lexum.umontreal.ca

CANADA, Provincial

Legislation and Delegated legislation

Ted Tjaden, "Doing Legal Research in Canada" Canadian Legislation (LLRX)
www.llrx.com/features/ca_top.htm

Law reports

Ted Tjaden, "Doing Legal Research in Canada" Canadian Case Reports (LLRX)
www.llrx.com/features/ca_top.htm

Canadian Law Information Institute (CanLII)
www.canlii.org/

Quebec

Key references

Ted Tjaden, "Doing Legal Research in Canada" (LLRX)
www.nyulawglobal.org/globalex/Canada1.htm#_Legal_Research_in_Quebec

LexUM, University of Montreal
www.lexum.umontreal.ca

Legislation

Civil Code of Quebec
www.justice.gouv.qc.ca/English/sujets/glossaire/code-civil-a.htm

Consolidated Legislation and Regulations of Quebec (CanLII)
http://canlii.org/qc/laws/index.html

NEW ZEALAND

Key references

Margaret Greville, "An Introduction to New Zealand Law & Sources of Legal Information", August 2005
www.nyulawglobal.org/globalex/new_zealand.htm

Waikato University Law Library
www2.waikato.ac.nz/lawlib

Legislation

New Zealand Legislation
www.legislation.govt.nz

UNITED KINGDOM AND IRELAND

Devolution, UK, Scotland, Northern Ireland and Wales

Stephen Young, "Devolution in the United Kingdom: a revolution in Online Legal Research" (LLRX)
www.llrx.com/features/devolution.htm

Legislation

Unconsolidated United Kingdom Statutes from 1988; Irish Statutes 1922+; Scottish Statutes; Northern Ireland Statutes
www.baillii.org/databases/html#uk

Delegated Legislation

United Kingdom Statutory Instruments from 2002; Irish Statutory Instruments 1922-1998; Welsh Statutory Instruments 1999+; Scottish Statutory Instruments
www.baillii.org/uk/legis/num_reg/

Law reports

United Kingdom and Commonwealth; England and Wales; Ireland, Scotland and Northern Ireland
www.baillii.org/databases/html#uk

UNITED STATES

Key references

"Guide to Law Online", Library of Congress
www.loc.gov/law/help/guide.html

Legal Information Institute (LII), Cornell
www.law.cornell.edu

Constitutional material

The Constitution of the USA: analysis and interpretation
www.gpoaccess.gov/constitution/index.html

UNITED STATES, Federal

Legislation

Acts and major Bills, US Federal
http://thomas.loc.gov

US Code
www4.law.cornell.edu/uscode/

Delegated legislation

Code of Federal Regulations
www.gposaccess.gov/cfr/index.html and *http://cfr.law.cornell.edu/cfr/*

Law reports

Supreme Court of the United States
www.supremecourtus.gov/

Supreme Court Briefs
http://supreme.lp.findlaw.com/supreme_court/briefs

Supreme Court [Judgment] Collection, by topic, author and party
http://supct.law.cornell.edu/supct/

UNITED STATES, States

Legislation

US State legislation – by jurisdiction
www.law.cornell.edu/states/listing.html

Uniform Commercial Code
www.law.cornell.edu/ucc/ucc.table.html

Law reports

State Courts – by jurisdiction
www.law.cornell.edu/opinions.html#state

COUNCIL OF EUROPE

Council of Europe
www.coe.int/

EUROPEAN UNION

Commission

Europa
http://europa.eu

Parliament

EuroParl
www.europarl.europa.eu

Court of Justice of the European Communities

Curia
http://curia.europa.eu

Legal Database

EUR-Lex – the access to European Union Law
http://eur-lex.europa.eu

EU Bookshop

http://bookshop.europa.eu

General Guides

Duncan E Alford, "European Union Legal Materials: and infrequent User's Guide", September 2005
www.nyulawglobal.org/globalex/European_Union.htm

Marylin J Raisch, "European Union Law: an integrated guide to electronic and print research", May 2007
www.llrx.com/features/eulaw2.htm

INTERNATIONAL LAW

International Court of Justice
www.icj-cij.org

"Germain's International Court of Justice Research Guide"
http://library.lawschool.cornell.edu/WhatWeDo/ResearchGuides/ICJ.cfm

Treaties

Australian Treaties Library (DFAT)
www.austlii.edu.au/au/other/dfat/

United Nations Treaty Collection
http://untreaty.un.org/English/treaty.asp

Mark Engsberg, "An Introduction to Sources for Treaty Research" March 2006
www.nyulawglobal.org/globalex/Treaty_Research.htm

Jill McC Watson, "Treaties" – ASIL Guide to Electronic Resources for International Law
www.asil.org/treaty1.cfm

Environment

Anne Burnett, "International Environmental Law" – *ASIL Guide to Electronic Resources for International Law*
www.asil.org/env1.cfm

GLOBELAW – International Environmental and Transnational Law
www.globelaw.com/

Human Rights

Marci Hoffman, "Human Rights" – *ASIL Guide to Electronic Resources for International Law*
www.asil.org/humrts1.cfm

ILS Web Sites: Human Rights (Harvard Law School Library Guide)
www.law.harvard.edu/library/services/research/guides/international/web_resources/human_rights.php

International Criminal Law

International Criminal Court
www.icc-cpi.int/

Rome Statute of the International Criminal Court
http://untreaty.un.org/cod/icc/index.html

Gail A Partin, "International Criminal Law" – *ASIL Guide to Elecronic Resources for International Law*
www.asil.org/crim1.cfm

Index